Teresa Burrell

The Advocate's Betrayal

BOOKS
LONG BEACH

ZOVA BOOKS

First ZOVA Books edition 2010.

Text set in Adobe Caslon Pro

Cover design © Matthew J. Pizzo

To every child who has endured the physical or emotional pain from abuse or neglect.

To my family who shared the pains of childhood with me while giving me many precious moments to carry forward; and to my family and friends who continue to give me comfort and inspiration as an adult.

To the staff at ZOVA Books who constantly hold my hand.

And in loving memory of my sister, Elaine Johnson Lecy, who will forever remain in our hearts as one of the most unique and fun-loving women to ever walk the face of this earth.

Prologue

Pain, from a sharp knife plunged into his chest, yanked John out of a deep sleep. He forced his eyelids open. The only thing worse than the pain was the shock when he saw who was standing over him. It wasn't until the blood dripped on his face that he realized it was not a dream.

"No, no, not you...." John reached out, hitting his hand against the wall. He tried to speak again, but could only mumble. "*Our Father, who art in heaven...*"

The killer mockingly said, "Are you praying, old man? Here, use this....," tossing John's rosary at his open hand near the floor. It caught on his fingertips and dangled there. John felt his air diminishing as his lungs filled up with blood. He fumbled his fingers until his thumb and index finger clasped the first large bead, the words no longer audible. "*...hallowed be Thy name...*"

His attacker stepped back, gazing at him lying there, holding the knife dripping with blood, his blood. John reached for his chest, but his arm wouldn't move. "*...Thy kingdom come...*" The naked walls of the trailer felt like a box. They were so close on every side. It was stifling. This was his box, his cage, his coffin. The only illumination came from the front room. He listened as the footsteps echoed back and forth at the end of his queen-size bed that filled the room, leaving less than a foot on each side. And then he heard the rubber soles of the shoes exit the bedroom.

He heard water run. His backside felt wet. Was it water? No, the water came from the kitchenette; blood pooled around his body. John heard his assailant washing away his blood in his kitchen—his murderer washing away the evidence. "...*Thy will be done, on earth as it is in heaven...*"

Footsteps returned to John's bedroom, and with them returned his fear. Was the attacker returning to finish the job? John couldn't protect himself; he couldn't even move. Then the fear subsided. It was too late. The damage already done. "...*Give us this day, our daily bread, and forgive us our trespasses...*"

The floor creaked all the way to the front door. Click—door unlocked, opened. The lights went out in the front room, completely dark, or was it the light in his mind that ceased? The pain in his chest intensified. His body felt lethargic. The front door closed. John listened carefully—no lock. The trailer shifted when the last step was vacated. He was alone, left to die alone.

John tried to move, to struggle, to fight, but his body wouldn't budge. He saw his life—the despicable parts when he was a kid, the pain he inflicted on others—but mostly he thought of the man he had become. The man who tried his whole life to fix what he had done as a child, that's who he really was. It pained him to have to think he would suffer eternal damnation for the crimes he committed so long ago. Was this his punishment—betrayal, death, eternal damnation? "...*as we forgive those...*"

1

When the phone rang at four o'clock in the morning Sabre knew it could only mean trouble, but she was used to trouble. "Who screwed up now?" she mumbled, forgetting for a second Luke lying in bed next to her.

"Umm...," Luke groaned.

Sabre savored the smell of clean sweat and faint cologne, reliving the touch of his mouth on the nape of her neck and his hard body holding her, making love to her for the first time. It had been a long time coming. She struggled to find the phone on the nightstand, knocking over a glass of wine. "Damn it," she mumbled. When she put the phone to her ear, she heard her friend Betty breathing heavily and stammering over her words as she tried to speak. Sabre's heart quivered in her chest.

"He's d..dead. John's dead," Betty cried.

"Betty, where are you?" Sabre's heart beat faster. She felt a sick feeling in the pit of her stomach.

"At home. Th...there's so much blood."

"What happened?"

"I don't know."

"Are you hurt?"

"No."

"I'll be right there." Sabre's arm felt weak. She dropped the phone to her chest and lay there for a second, her body still and in shock. Luke reached his arm around her waist and pulled her shapely naked body close to him, nibbling on her earlobe. Sabre yanked away, throwing his arm off her and slamming the phone into the cradle. "Not now," she said curtly, but with no anger in her voice. She stood up and flipped on the light.

"What is it?" Luke asked, scratching his head as he sat up.

"John's dead." She snapped, sounding more like a question than a statement, propelling Luke from the bed. "I'm going to help Betty." She stepped into her jeans, wrestling with her sweatshirt as she pulled it over her head, twisted her shoulder-length, brown hair up on top of her head, and stuck a clip in it.

Luke had his shirt on before she finished speaking, looking around for his pants and shoes. "I'm going with you." He reached for her arm, squeezing it lightly. "I'm so sorry, Sabre."

Tears filled her dark brown eyes. John and Betty were her friends, and although Sabre was about thirty years their junior, they had grown very close. They were extended family, more like an aunt and uncle to her. They had been there for her during her turmoil last year, and now John was dead and Betty needed her.

The summer morning air felt cool on Sabre's tear-filled face as she ran to the car. "Put your keys away. I'm driving," Luke said. Sabre's hand shook as she opened the door to Luke's silver metallic BMW Z4 Roadster.

Luke drove east on I-8 at speeds above eighty. Sabre didn't complain about the speed as she would have under normal circumstances. She didn't even notice. She watched as the buildings passed her window, most of them barely visible without their lights on. Only a few cars on the freeway, but too many she thought. *Where were they going? How many were going to help a friend whose husband had just died? Why John?* It felt like losing her father all over again, and a piece of her brother, Ron, as well. Ron had introduced her to John and Betty just a few months before his disappearance. The couple had been such a great help to her, consoling her and always trying to keep her hopes up. John reminded her so much of her father—the same lighthearted strength that is so hard to find in a man, and a deep, resonant voice that always brought her comfort. She'd never hear that voice call her "Sparky" again. He tagged her with that nickname the first day they met, and he never called her anything else. Sabre remembered that day. The couple was always holding hands, only letting go when Betty went to get John a cup of coffee – before he ever asked – or when John went to check the gas in Betty's car. They took care of each other.

Luke and Sabre drove for about two minutes without speaking.

Luke broke the silence. "What happened? Do you know?"

"No, she didn't say, just that he was dead…and there was blood." Sabre shook her head. "What will Betty do without him? She loved him so much. She used to say, 'I'd like you to find someone just like my John, but there's no one quite like him.' That's why she tried so hard to get us together, you know."

"I know." Luke squeezed her hand. "I'm glad she did."

Within fifteen minutes of the call, they had driven into the motor home park and pulled up in front of space number twelve, a thirty-five foot, twenty-year-old trailer, the only home in the park with lights on. As they stepped out of the car, the lights went on next door. No light illuminated Betty's porch. Luke took Sabre's hand as they went up the short, dark walkway. She couldn't see much, but she could smell the gardenias along the path. Just as they reached the door, the porch light went on and Sabre heard the click of the door unlocking. She felt an ache in her stomach when she saw Betty's puffy eyes with black liner smeared down her face, her usual perfectly spiked, fire-red hair flat on one side and the rest sticking out in clumps, and the deep lines of confusion on her forehead. What had once been white kittens on the side of her pale blue pajama top were now soaked red with blood. When Sabre hugged her friend's plump body, it felt listless and tears dampened Betty's cheeks.

"Where is he?" Luke asked.

"In there." Betty pointed to the bedroom.

Luke walked to the back of the trailer, his body tall and straight. Sabre could see the muscles strain on the back of his neck as she and Betty followed. Sabre noticed Betty held a rosary. As far as she knew, Betty wasn't Catholic. She stopped and put her arm around Betty's shoulder. "Were you praying?" she asked motioning toward the rosary.

Betty slipped it in her pocket and said, "It belonged to J…John. The only thing he had from his childhood."

They walked into the bedroom, Luke several steps ahead. "Oh…" Sabre covered her mouth to stifle her cry. John lay on his back, the blankets pulled up to his waist. His right arm hung over the edge of the bed, the left side of his chest covered in blood. Sabre suddenly longed for her strong, energetic friend, John. She wanted him to comfort her. This wasn't him. A lifeless, slaughtered body laid in his bed, no longer the man who gave her fatherly advice or comforted her when she needed to feel like a child.

Luke put his arm around Sabre. He reached down and touched John's arm. "He's cold," he said.

"Have you called the police?" Sabre asked.

"No."

"Why not?"

Betty started to sob, "I didn't kn..know what to do. So, I called you."

Sabre walked over to where Betty stood in the doorway, her voice low and undemanding. "Betty, what happened?"

"I...I don't know."

Sabre reached out and took Betty's hand. "Tell me, what did you do when you left us at Viejas?"

"I came straight home and went to bed."

"You just crawled into bed next to John?"

"I thought he was sleeping, so I kept very quiet." She gulped. "I didn't even turn on the light in the bedroom. I just put my pajamas on and slipped into bed beside him." Sabre nodded encouragement. "I went right to sleep because he wasn't snoring." Betty stopped to catch her breath and shook her head from side to side. "He always snores. Why didn't I know there was something wrong?" She sobbed. "I was so thankful he wasn't snoring, I didn't even check on him."

Sabre squeezed her hand a little tighter. "Betty, when did you know there was something wrong?"

"When I got up to go to the bathroom, I felt my wet, sticky pajamas. I turned on the light and saw it was bl...blood. Then I saw John." Betty's chest throbbed as she continued to sob. "He just lay there all covered with blood."

"Betty, we need to call the police."

"W…would you?" Betty took a step forward, then back, then stood there rocking, confused.

"Of course."

Sabre called 9-1-1, and within minutes three squad cars arrived, plus two detectives in an unmarked car and an ambulance followed by a coroner. The dawn broke as neighbors exited their mobile homes to catch a glimpse of the show, many of them watching from their porches, others edging closer and forming a crowd near Betty's and John's trailer. They stretched their necks to see. Some asked questions of the officers, others relayed what they saw and what they speculated, but all buzzed with curiosity as the police put up the yellow and black ribbon partitioning off the area.

One man wandered onto the green rock lawn. "Please step back," a short, young man in uniform said curtly. "Please stay behind the police line."

A police officer entered the motor home, glanced around, and started spouting orders like he was reading from a bad script. "I need everyone to step outside. This is a crime scene. Please don't touch anything."

"Sabre, what are you doing here?" Detective Gregory Nelson asked, as he walked up to the mobile home while pulling on his tie.

"These are friends of mine. Betty called me."

"I'll want to talk to you, but first I need to go inside. Please wait out here."

Betty stumbled to a folding chair outside near the door and sat down. With one elbow on the arm of the chair, she lay her head in her hand and wept. Sabre approached her and put a hand on her shoulder, but she didn't know what to say. Betty continued to cry. Sabre looked back and saw Luke standing with his hands in his pockets by the pink geranium bush, watching her from a distance.

When Detective Nelson came out, he asked Betty for her name and the name of the victim, about what she had seen, and when. He wiggled the knot on his tie. "Sabre, would you mind getting Betty some clothes? We'll need the pajamas."

"Greg, is she a suspect?"

"Not at this point, but we need the pajamas. They have blood on them, and they may be evidence." He turned to an officer standing at the door. "Please escort Ms. Brown inside. She needs to get a change of clothes for the victim's wife."

As Sabre entered the trailer she focused on two policemen walking around the living room with kits and brushes, dusting for fingerprints. She saw an officer pick up a knife from the sink, put it into a bag, and zip the bag closed. She watched as they opened drawers and cupboards, invading her friends' home. She walked past the kitchen table containing the ceramic rooster, two placemats, and a deck of cards. She scanned the room for answers but saw only a worn, dark green sofa with two pillows, an end table next to it with a stack of loose newspapers and a pair of reading glasses, and Betty's sketch book. A small desk across from the sofa housed a laptop computer. Only one picture adorned the wall, a drawing Betty had done of an old cabin in the woods, and except for the shelf with a small collection of salt and pepper shakers, the room contained very few mementos, an observation Sabre hadn't made until now.

When they approached the bedroom, Sabre could see an officer taking photos. It hit her that something was missing. She looked around and saw only a few picture frames with photos, and none of them photos of Betty or John. She wondered how she had missed that before, and if it mattered.

Sabre continued to observe the officers as she gathered up Betty's things. She looked around, processing every detail of each officer's task. She watched as they bagged evidence—the pink rug with the blood stain, the book of matches from a Las Vegas casino, and the Viagra bottle by the side of the bed. It didn't seem real. Never in her twenty-nine years of life, including her six years of practicing law, had Sabre seen anything so gruesome. She had dealt with many crime scenes in court, but she'd never seen an actual murdered body or the officers at work gathering the information on a crime. This was a corpse, not her friend whom she had known for five plus years and to whom she had grown very close. Emotions confused her—sadness for her friend John, concern for Betty, and fascination at the process she observed.

When she brought the clothes out to Betty, Detective Nelson approached her. "Sabre, will you and your friend....Lucas, is it?"

"Yes sir, Lucas, Luke Rahm," Luke said.

"Will you two please meet me down at the station? I'd like to speak to each of you. I'll take Betty with me."

Up until this point, Sabre had been there as Betty's friend, but Betty was a suspect, regardless of what Nelson said. Sabre realized she should be treating her like a client and advising her accordingly. She took a deep breath and cleared her head. She needed to think like an attorney. She didn't have the luxury of being just a friend.

Sabre touched Betty gently on the shoulder. "Betty, you ride with Detective Nelson to the police station. I'll be right behind you. Here are your clothes. And listen carefully to what I'm about to say. You do not talk to him," she said, pointing at Nelson, "or to anyone else until I get there. Don't say a word. Understand?"

"Do I have to go?"

"I'm afraid so. If you don't, it'll only be worse."

"Sabre, I'm scared. I don't want to go," she pleaded. Sabre felt physical pain for her friend. Betty had been there for her so many times. She had held her when she cried for her missing brother. She had become family to her, an aunt she could confide in when she couldn't talk to her mother. Simple yet worldly, Betty didn't talk much about her past, but Sabre knew she had experienced some pretty rough times.

Sabre put one hand on each of Betty's shoulders, looked her directly in the eye, and said, "I'm sorry, but they'll take you one way or the other. Just go with Nelson, and please don't say anything. Just tell them you're waiting for me. Understand?"

"Okay," Betty said, her chin buried in her chest as she walked to the car.

Sabre turned to Detective Nelson, "Greg, don't question her without me. I'm her friend, but I'm also her attorney," Sabre said sternly.

"We're not arresting her," he said.

"I know, but I'm shaken up about all this and about losing John, and I haven't been thinking clearly either. Just give me a little time to get my act together here, too. A crime appears to have been committed. Betty and John are my friends and I don't want anything to go wrong."

"Your call. I'll see you there in a few."

Luke and Sabre maintained silence on the way to the station. With his left hand on the wheel, Luke reached with his right and put it on Sabre's knee. She took a deep breath and sighed. She looked at Luke, his face solemn. She hadn't really thought about the effect this had on him, but John and Betty were his friends, too. She squeezed his hand.

Sabre's mind drifted back two months to when she first met Luke at a barbecue at Betty's. Betty claimed she hadn't been trying to set them up, but Sabre knew differently. When she arrived at their house, Betty sent Luke out to her car to help her bring in the ice. Sabre was smitten the moment she looked into his dark, bedroom eyes. He apparently felt the same because, after a few hours together that afternoon, he asked for her phone number. He called the next day, and within a few weeks they were exclusive.

A feeling of warmth came over her as she remembered that afternoon. John leaned over the barbeque to flip a burger. Betty brought him a beer. They both looked at Sabre and Luke, chuckled a little, and when Betty walked away, John tapped her lightly on the butt. Betty lunged forward a little.

"Oof," she said.

Sabre and Luke had driven on surface streets about five miles from the police station when Luke asked, "Are you okay?"

"Yeah, just trying to process everything." She shifted in her seat. "Not such a great way to end the evening, our first time making love and all."

"I know, baby, but I'm glad I was there with you." He pulled her hand up to his lips and kissed it, holding it there for several seconds.

"Me, too." She sighed. "I just feel so bad about John, and I'm so worried about Betty."

"You don't think she had anything to do with this, do you?"

Sabre responded with indignation that he would even ask. "Of course not. She wouldn't hurt anyone, certainly not John. You know how much she loved him." She looked at Luke, eyebrow raised. "Why, do you?"

"No…no, I don't think so, either," Luke said as he looked out the window, his voice trailing off.

"Besides, he must've been killed while Betty was with us. We're her witnesses. We can vouch for her."

"True." Luke cleared his throat. "At least you can. I wasn't with her the whole time. I was playing blackjack for a couple of hours while you two were off doing whatever it was you were doing. You were together, right?"

"Not the whole time. We went to play bingo, but then Betty decided she wanted to play the slots, so I stayed and she went to play the machines." Sabre shifted in her seat and took a deep breath. "But she was there. I know she was there. I saw her about ten-thirty on the slots, and she told me she'd be leaving shortly."

Silence filled the car the rest of the way to the police station.

2

"Thank you for coming in, Sabre."

"We shouldn't even be here, Greg. She doesn't know what happened." Sabre tilted her head to one side and looked Nelson directly in the eye. "You think she killed him, don't you?"

Detective Nelson loosened his tie. "I have no idea who killed him, but you know the drill, Sabre." His voice softened. "I just need to ask her some questions." He took Sabre by the arm. "Come on, let's go talk to your client," he said, as he led her to the interview room. The tiled floor resounded with the click of her heels as Sabre walked through the nearly empty corridor. When they reached the door, Detective Nelson opened it and held it for Sabre to pass. "Go on in. I'll be there in just a second."

Betty sat in the sparse interview room in the brown pants and the jailhouse orange, long-sleeve shirt Sabre had picked out for her. Sabre suddenly regretted her fashion choice for Betty. The bloody pajamas had been placed in the custody of the San Diego County Sheriff's Department. The room contained only a table and two chairs, the dirty cream-colored walls needed paint, and the tile screamed "early fifties." It resembled every other interview room in the county justice system—no windows and poor lighting.

"How are you holding up, Betty?" Sabre asked when they came in.

"Ok," she said.

"Did they try to question you before I got here?"

"No, the officer just asked if I wanted something to drink. Nothing else."

"Good."

"What do they want from me?" Betty spit out the words as she stood up and ran her hand through her hair. "Oof," she said bringing her hand down quickly.

"Right now they're just trying to get information. Just tell the detective what you told me and hopefully we can get out of here. If I don't like the questioning, I'll stop it."

"Do they think I had something to do with this?" Before Sabre could answer, Betty said, "I didn't, you know." She sounded so vulnerable and childlike.

"I know you didn't." Sabre was taken aback by Betty's statement. "They need to start somewhere, and you were the last one with John as far as they know."

Detective Nelson came in carrying another chair and seemed to take control of the room. He sat down and took Betty's statement. "Why did you call Sabre and not the police?" Nelson asked.

"John was dead. I was upset." Betty shrugged her shoulders. "I don't know. She's the first person I thought of."

"Why didn't you just call the police?"

"I don't know."

"Did you and your husband have a fight tonight?"

"No, we seldom fight," Betty said assertively.

"Why didn't he go to the casino with you?"

"He doesn't gamble."

"Does he ever go to the casino with you?"

"He's been once or twice, but he gets bored, so when I go it's usually with friends. I don't go very often, either, a couple of times a year maybe."

"Do you know anyone who might want your husband dead?"

"No." Betty shook her head.

"Has he fought with anyone recently? Neighbors? Fellow workers?"

"No, not that I'm aware of." Betty's brow wrinkled. "He never fought with anyone. Everyone loved him. Sabre and Luke loved him. I loved him. Everyone loved him."

"I'm sure they did, but why didn't you call the police when you found him?" Nelson asked again.

"I don't know."

"What time did you last see John?"

"Around six-thirty. We usually eat dinner around that time, but

I fixed John's dinner a little early because of my plans to eat with Sabre and Luke. John ate about six and I cleaned up the kitchen and left. I left in such a hurry, I didn't even kiss him goodbye." Betty began to cry.

Nelson stopped his questioning for a moment and then asked, "Did he seem upset about anything before you left?"

"N..No."

"Did you talk to him after that?"

"No," Betty sucked the air in through her nose, stifling her cry. Sabre brought her a Kleenex, glancing at Nelson out of the corner of her eye.

"What time did you get home?" Nelson asked.

"About eleven P.M."

"But you didn't notice there was a problem until this morning?"

"No, I thought he was asleep."

"When you saw the blood, why didn't you call the police?"

"Greg, she said she didn't know," Sabre interrupted.

"She was in shock when I got there." Nelson looked at his notes and Sabre continued. "She's answered all your questions. Most of them more than once. May we go home now?"

"Yeah, we're done for now."

Sabre, Luke, and Betty left the police station heading west on I-8, the morning commuter traffic in full force. Sabre, afraid she would be late for court, called her friend Bob and asked him to cover until she arrived.

"I'm taking you to my house, Betty. You can get some rest there. Luke will stay with you. He has his computer so he can work from there today." Sabre turned to Luke so Betty couldn't see her and mouthed, "Thank you."

Luke winked back at her.

"Sure," Betty responded, wringing her hands together. "Whatever you think."

Sabre arrived at court about ten-thirty. The parking lot was full, so she had to park in the dirt and walk past Juvenile Hall. With an arm full of files, dressed in her black power suit and her Gucci high-heeled pumps, Sabre rushed to the courthouse. Inside at the metal detector, the bailiff waved her through. She walked across the crowded hallway and set her files on her usual shelf, one that protruded from the wall near the information desk.

Bob tapped her on the shoulder. "Hey, Ms. Sabre Orin Brown. How's my little Sobs this morning?" Sobs was Bob's nickname for Sabre. Sometimes he called her his little S.O.B. He loved to tease her about her initials.

Sabre managed a smile. She looked at her friend and thought how much he reminded her of the actor, Bill Pullman, but with prematurely-gray hair. He wasn't movie star gorgeous, but was still devilishly cute, and he delivered his lines with great finesse. "I'm hanging in there."

"Well, I'm glad you're here. It's been a crazy morning."

"Yeah, tell me about it." Sabre didn't look up at her friend but she felt better just having him near. Sabre and Bob met when they both started working juvenile about six years ago. They had their first jurisdictional trial together, which they won, and soon after discovered that winning was no easy task. Their work at juvenile court and their deep compassion for the children bonded them. They were best friends, but they never gave Bob's wife, Marilee, anything to worry about.

"Hey, are you okay? What's going on? And why are you late?"

"You know my friend Betty, the little red-headed spitfire?"

"Yeah, I've seen her a few times. Why?"

"Her husband, John, is dead. He was murdered last night."

"Murdered?" Bob said loudly, as he placed his hand on Sabre's shoulder. "How?"

"Someone stabbed him in his bed. When Betty came home from the casino, John was apparently already dead. Betty didn't know it until she rose to go to the bathroom and found blood on her pajamas. Luke and I went over there as soon as she called. We've been at the police station most of the night."

"Do they know who did it?"

"Not yet. Remember Detective Greg Nelson from the Murdock

case?"

"Yes."

"He's one of the investigating officers, and I'm glad, because he treated her better than someone else may have."

"Are they accusing her of the murder?"

"No, at least not yet, but they don't have any other suspects."

"Attorneys Brown and Clark, please report to Department Four." Mike, the bailiff, announced their surnames over the intercom.

"I guess we better go," Bob said. "I did a couple of your reviews in Department One, but I haven't done anything yet in Four."

Bob and Sabre hustled into Department Four. Mike, her favorite bailiff, was assigned to this department. Apart from being good looking and intelligent, he was also a dedicated father. He asked, "What shenanigans are you two wild and crazy ones up to this morning?"

"The usual," Bob answered. "Wreaking havoc in Kiddie Court."

Mike shook his head. "Like we'd expect anything else." He turned to Sabre. "Brown, you ready?"

"I'm ready on everything except Thomson. My client's in custody and I need to speak to her before the hearing," Sabre responded.

"Well, let's see what else we can get done here, and then I'll put Thomson in an interview room for you," Mike said.

They completed four cases before they started losing attorneys to other departments. Sabre walked toward the interview room to speak with her client in custody, and Bob went to another department to finish his calendar. On her way to the interview room, Sabre walked past a minor with green, spiked hair and holes in his earlobes the size of quarters reading a newspaper and a man in an expensive business suit and bare feet.

She also passed a bedraggled looking couple with seven children. Sabre had just spoken with the social worker on that case who, without telling the parents the reason, had the children brought into court to be taken into protective custody. Someone must have let it slip, because just as Sabre passed by, the parents started shouting and the children began running in different directions. One of them, a child of about seven years old, almost knocked her down trying to reach the door. Bailiffs rushed from the courtrooms and the back office, chasing children aging from two to sixteen. The six-year-old twin boys ran out the back door onto a patio expecting to find a way out, but were trapped and grabbed up by one of the officers. One girl ran down the hallway and ducked under a bench. Another ran up the stairs and into the bathroom, once again trapped. They found her crouched on a toilet seat crying. The bailiffs quickly blocked the front door, but not before the oldest boy ran away carrying his two-year-old baby brother.

Sabre was no longer shocked by the sights. Her six-year stint at juvenile court had long since hardened her reaction to the behaviors of the perpetrators or their victims. Occasionally she would have a weak moment, especially if a child was testifying or accounting an abusive event, but she couldn't let that be the practice or she wouldn't survive. Nevertheless, this affected her. The frightened looks on the faces of those poor children brought a sick feeling to the pit of her stomach. According to the social worker, the children needed to be removed; it was just unfortunate it happened this way.

Sabre continued through the crowd of attorneys who spent their lives at juvenile court diligently working to make a difference, sheriffs trying to keep order, interpreters speaking several different languages, and the abused and the accused. By the time she reached her courtroom she saw an officer walk in the front door with the sixteen-year-old escapee and his little brother.

3

Sabre completed her calendar and waited in the courtroom while Bob finished. She listened as the court clerk called Bob's last case. "In the matter of Kat and Kurt Kemp." Sabre saw a tall, blue-eyed, blond, hard-looking but not unattractive man with a shaved head sitting next to Bob. Next to him sat a slightly overweight, bleached blonde woman with big hair with no attorney present.

Judge Hekman shook her head as she looked at the report, then up at the mother and father. She sighed. "I see this is a detention hearing. Mr. Clark, you're available for appointment for Mr. Kemp?"

"Yes, Your Honor. I represented Mr. Kemp on a previous case," Bob said without flinching.

"Fine, then you're appointed to represent Mr. Kemp, and the Public Defender, you're appointed for the minors."

A short, round woman with salt and pepper hair spoke up. "I'm sorry, Your Honor, the Public Defender's Office has a conflict with this case."

The judge looked at her file and then to the back of the courtroom. "Ms. Brown, can you take this case?" Sabre stood up, but before she could answer Judge Hekman said, "Of course you can. This case is tailor-made for you. You're appointed to represent the minors."

Sabre walked forward, opened the gate, and stepped inside. As she approached Bob, she observed a ring of swastikas tattooed around his client's neck. The client scowled as Sabre walked up. He asked Bob, "Why does the judge want her on the case? What did she mean by that? 'Tailor-made?'"

"I'll explain later. Don't worry. Ms. Brown is as fair and open-minded as you're going to get. We could do a lot worse."

Bob handed Sabre his report. She tried not to show any

emotion as she read the allegations.

The judge turned to the mother, shaking her head in disapproval. "And Mrs. Kemp, do you have counsel?"

Before she could answer, county council spoke up. "Mr. Rodriquez was on the rotation this morning, but Mrs. Kemp refused to speak with him. He opted to pass on the case. There's no one here this morning to counsel her, although Mr. Clark explained the process to her. There is definitely a conflict between the mother and father that would warrant separate counsel."

"There's no conflict between us. What the hell is he talking about?" Mr. Kemp said to his attorney but loud enough for everyone to hear.

"Mr. Clark, does your client have something to say?"

Bob whispered to Mr. Kemp and then stood up. "Your Honor, I've explained to my client that his wife will need her own attorney because of the 'legal conflict' in this case. He wanted the court to know they are together on this petition but understands I can't represent both of them."

The judge continued. "Fine, an attorney will be appointed for the mother. This case is trailed until tomorrow morning."

Mr. Kemp leaned over and whispered to Bob. Bob spoke up, "Your Honor, my client would like to be heard on detention. He's asking the children be detained with him."

"I'm sure he is, Mr. Clark, but that's not happening. The children will remain in Polinsky." She turned to Sabre. "Can you go see them today?"

"Yes, Your Honor. I haven't had a chance to read the report, but if there…"

"I know what you want Ms. Brown. You want concurrence for any change, but there isn't going to be any change. Those kids are staying right where they are tonight. They're not going to family or anywhere until after the hearing tomorrow."

Bob stood up to speak. "Sit down, Mr. Clark. I know what your client wants, but he's not getting it. There'll be no visitation today. We'll talk about it tomorrow. I'm sure you can explain the reasons behind my decision to Mr. Kemp." She closed her file. "The detention hearing is trailed until tomorrow morning at eight-thirty." The judge stood up and walked out of the courtroom before any more objections could be made. Just before she reached the door, she turned. "Mr. Clark, I think you need to have a long talk with your client about courtroom protocol."

"I will, Your Honor."

Bob walked out of the courtroom and sat down to speak with his client. Sabre went outside to wait for Bob. It was his turn to pick the lunch venue, the choices limited since Bob would only eat at a few places.

As Bob walked out of the courthouse he reached inside his jacket pocket, but came up empty. "Looking for a death stick?" Sabre asked.

"Yeah, I guess so. I haven't smoked since I made that promise to you six months ago, but I still keep reaching for my cigarettes. It hasn't been easy."

"I know, but just think how much longer you'll be around to taunt me. So, where are we eating?"

"Want to Pho-nicate?"

"Sure, Pho's it is. You can drive."

They drove to Pho Pasteur, the Vietnamese Restaurant they had discovered when they started practicing at juvenile court. A favorite lunch spot, they frequented Pho's about three times a week. They walked into the restaurant, past a cluttered counter and a huge fish tank, and into the main dining area. Pictures of menu items decorated the walls with the item name in Vietnamese. The simple, square tables with pink, polyester tablecloths sat all along the walls. In the middle of the room two large, round tables filled the remaining space. A plastic flower in a glass vase adorned each table, dwarfed by a huge bottle of red hot sauce.

"Nice client, your Mr. Kemp," Sabre teased.

"Yeah, he's a real peach. Did you read the report?"

"Some of it. What a mess."

"Yeah, this is going to be interesting with Hekman on the bench."

"My client already hates her," Bob sniggered. "So, how are things with you and Luke?"

"They're good. We just had our two-month anniversary. That's a record for me lately. Mostly I'm done after the first date, but he's different. He's good to me. Luke's a lot of fun, and he's a pretty smart cookie. And best of all, he's not clingy. I can do my own thing and he doesn't seem to mind, so I don't have to be with him every minute. You know how I hate to feel caged."

"He seems like a good enough guy, except for the Republican part."

"Hey, I didn't say he was perfect."

"He just better be good to you, or I'll have to kick his ass."

Sabre chuckled at Bob's brotherly concern and at the thought of Bob "kicking his ass." That was unlikely. Bob didn't look like a fighter. He wasn't overweight, but he wasn't toned, either. Luke, in contrast, worked out every day and had a six pack that would put most athletes to shame.

"Well, there he is now." Sabre smiled as she answered her cell. "Hi, Luke. What's up?" Sabre listened for a moment and then said, "Oh no, I'll be right there. Just tell her not to talk." Sabre stood up as she hung up the phone.

"What is it?" Bob asked.

"The police are there...about Betty."

"Let's go." Bob jumped up, put his arm around Sabre's waist and escorted her out to the car.

By the time Bob and Sabre arrived, Betty was about to be handcuffed.

"Sabre, help me," Betty yelled.

Sabre approached the officer. "I'm this woman's attorney. What's going on?"

"She's under arrest for the murder of John Smith."

"I didn't kill John. I didn't kill him," Betty cried, jerking away from the officer and stepping toward Sabre. "Sabre, tell him I didn't kill John."

The policeman yanked her back, slapped the handcuffs on her, and pulled her toward the police car.

"Betty, listen to me. You need to calm down," Sabre said, moving as close to Betty as she felt legally comfortable.

"But I didn't do anything," Betty said, her voice a little quieter.

"I know. I'll get this sorted out."

The policeman helped Betty into the police car.

"Betty, don't say anything to anyone. I'll be right there to speak with you. Just tell them you want your attorney."

The policeman closed the door. Betty nodded at Sabre without looking up as they drove off.

4

Bob returned to court and Luke sped to the police station with Sabre. She wanted to see Betty before they booked her. When they arrived Luke took hold of Sabre's hand and squeezed it, letting go as they entered the building.

"Thanks for coming with me," Sabre said.

"I wouldn't be anywhere else," Luke said, kissing her lightly on the forehead. "I'll wait out here until you're finished. I have my computer in the car. If it takes too long, I'll do some work." He walked over and sat on a wooden bench in the lobby.

Sabre walked up to the desk, showed her bar card and identification, and asked to see Betty Smith. She took deep breaths, trying to calm herself, but she was still shaking when the officer opened the door and took her to the back room. She met Detective Nelson just as he brought Betty in. Betty stood between two officers, with her hands cuffed behind her back. Her raccoon eyes from the smeared, black mascara were red and puffy, and her hair was disheveled.

"I'm sorry, Sabre. I know she's your friend," Nelson said.

"May I please see her alone?" Sabre sighed.

"Come in here. I'll give you a few minutes."

"Thanks." Sabre took a deep breath and stood up straight. She had to be brave.

Nelson brought Betty into an office and removed her handcuffs. "You only have a minute. You may see her again this afternoon after she's booked."

"I appreciate it, Greg." The detective left the room and Sabre spoke to Betty. "Are you okay?"

"Just scared. What will they do with me?"

"They're going to put you in lockup, and in a few days they'll have an arraignment and bail hearing. I'll be there for you."

"I don't have any money for a lawyer or for bail."

"I'm going to help you, Betty."

"No, I can't expect you to. You've done so much already. They'll appoint me a public defender, won't they?"

"They will, but don't worry. I'm going to help you through this." Sabre put her hand onto Betty's shoulder.

"I didn't do it." She spoke softly but with conviction.

"I know," Sabre said, confident her friend spoke the truth. "I'm so sorry."

Betty turned and saw her reflection in the window. "God, I look just awful. Look at my face, and my hair."

Sabre reached up and pulled out some of the spikes on Betty's hair, filling the gaps that had formed. She took a Kleenex from the desk and wiped away the smeared mascara. "There, all fixed."

"Thanks." Betty's voice cracked.

Nelson opened the door. "Got to go, Sabre."

"Okay." She turned to Betty. "I'll be back here right after my trial this afternoon. You don't tell them anything, just name and address and basic information, nothing about the incident."

Betty's brow wrinkled and her eyes opened wide. "Right," she said as she walked out with Detective Nelson.

Sabre left Nelson's office and walked past an officer questioning a suspect dressed in dirty, ragged clothes. The man reeked of urine and body odor, the smell so strong it caught her breath. Trying not to breathe, she continued to the lobby of the precinct wondering how she could help Betty. *And what was I thinking, calling John's death "the incident?" How insensitive can I be?* she thought. The law reduced his death to something impersonal, and she embraced the system that carried it out.

Sabre had been through this procedure many times with juvenile clients, but never with a friend. She knew she had to keep focused and maintain a professional distance, but it wasn't easy. She gave a half smile when she saw Luke waiting for her in the lobby.

"You okay, babe?" he asked.

"Yeah, I guess. This is just hard. She looks so depressed and I feel so helpless."

Luke put his arm around her shoulder. "You are helping her. You're helping her a lot. How many people have a good friend with them through a process like this? She has someone by her side she can trust. That's invaluable."

"I know. It just doesn't seem like enough."

"Sabre, I need to tell you something," Luke said dropping his arm from around her and turning to face her. "I'm afraid I may have screwed up."

"Why? What did you do?"

"When Detective Nelson asked me if I could vouch for all of Betty's time at Viejas Casino the night of the murder, I told him I couldn't. I told him I was playing blackjack and she went with you to play bingo."

"Well, that's the truth. That's all you can do."

"He asked me if you were with Betty the whole time, and I told him I didn't know for sure because I wasn't with you."

Sabre threw her hands in the air, waving them back and forth.

"What does he think? Does he think she killed John and then went out to gamble with her friends?" Sabre paused. "Or does he think Betty left the casino and drove home, killed him, and then came back and played the slot machines?"

"I don't know, but I didn't know what to say. I hope I didn't cause problems for Betty. I wouldn't want to do anything to make her life worse right now."

Sabre's voice calmed. "No, you did fine. I'm not going to lie about what happened, and I certainly don't expect you to, either. I just think it's absurd they think she planned this whole thing." She hit her file folder against the chair, her voice raised. "Damn it. Premeditated murder? She's not capable of that." Sabre looked around and saw all the eyes in the room on her.

Luke put his arm around her and led her out of the building. Sabre took a breath and her voice leveled. "I'm just going to have to work even harder to pinpoint the time. And then I'll have to convince the jury she didn't have time to kill him while she was with us."

They walked across the blacktop of the parking lot, weaving in and out of cars with Luke's arm still around her shoulder. By the time they reached the car Sabre was crying. Luke pulled her head against his chest and they stood there, not speaking, for several minutes. When Sabre stopped sobbing he opened her door, but before he let her in, he drew her close to him and gave her a short but tender kiss on the lips.

As they drove off Sabre realized how happy she was to have Luke in her life. Things were going so much better for her in so many ways. She wished Betty were as lucky.

Sabre composed herself and called Bob to let him know she was on her way back. She didn't have time for lunch, but at least she wouldn't be late for court. He was waiting inside for her when Luke dropped her off at the courthouse.

"How'd it go?" he asked.

"She's really scared. It's awful. First, she loses her husband and now she's charged with his murder. And I don't know if I can help her."

"We'll do what we have to do," Bob assured her.

Sabre pushed her hair back, sliding her hand down the back of her head. "Do you think I should handle the case?"

"Would you rather she was represented by a public defender?"

"There are some really good lawyers in that department. We've worked with some of them, and they do this every day. Maybe she'd be better off with one of them."

"Yeah, but there are some bad ones, too, and you don't know who she'll draw. It's not high profile, so she isn't going to get the cream, maybe even some rookie."

"You mean like me?" Sabre said, tilting her head to the side and rolling her eyes

"You're no rookie, my Queen." Bob hugged her. "You're the best of the best. You've handled plenty of criminal cases. You've handled plenty of felonies for delinquents, and several of them were sent downtown to be tried as adults. And you just finished a manslaughter case with that kid."

"Yeah, that turned out well."

"He was guilty. You can't change that."

"I know in this element I'm good at what I do, but I'd be playing with the big boys downtown on a murder case. A murder. I've never handled a murder, and my friend's life is at stake."

"Well, if you're asking me if you're up to the task, I'd have to say 'yes,' and no one is going to put the effort into it that you would."

Sabre turned to him with a sheepish smile and asked what she had been thinking for some time. "Would you second chair with me? I know together we could do it."

"You know I will."

"It's pro bono, you know."

"I wouldn't expect anything else."

"Thanks, honey." Sabre grinned. "I'll go meet with her this afternoon. I'll get the police report and get you up to speed on the hearing dates and all. The hard part is going to be getting our cases covered in juvey when we're both gone."

"We'll manage." Bob put his arm around Sabre's shoulder. "We better go finish our trial." They walked into the courtroom, arms still around each other.

Fortunately for Sabre, she didn't have an active role in her afternoon trial. Her client lived out of state, he supported the recommendations of the Department of Social Services, and he had little interest in the outcome of the case other than the negative effect it would have on his ex-spouse, for which he seemed to be gleaning a perverse kind of pleasure. Sabre's mind focused more on Betty and John than the case before her.
Because she had handled this type of case so many times before, she could do this without any conscious thought. She responded when needed to, objected when warranted, and concurred with County Council's argument at the end.

She left court and went to see Betty at the substation, since they hadn't transported her to Las Colinas Detention Facility yet. Betty wasn't available to interview when Sabre arrived, so she took a seat in the lobby, removed a file from her bag, and read through the Kemp report while she waited. The words made her physically ill.

> *Three-year-old Kurt K. Kemp lifted the gun and pointed it at the picture of the black man taped to the wall. Mr. Kurtis K. Kemp prompted him, "What do you do now, Kurt?"*
>
> *"Kill the nigger, Daddy. Kill the nigger."*

Sabre was glad she hadn't eaten, certain she would've thrown up if she had any food in her stomach.

Betty sat in a damp, musty holding cell containing only a pay phone, two hard benches against the wall, and the cold, gray concrete floor. As she sat down, a pain shot through her leg from her backside all the way to her ankle. She stood up, wobbly and a little dizzy. She looked around. Everything seemed to be the same color, and it all felt so cold. She shivered and started to walk around the ten-by-ten foot room in an attempt to alleviate the pain from her sciatic nerve, which hadn't bothered her in weeks until now.

She waited there alone for about fifteen minutes, until they brought in another woman wearing a low-cut top, her breasts exposed almost to the nipples, and a skirt barely covering her crotch. Her bare midriff exposed a roll of fat hanging over her hip-hugger skirt. Her ratted, bleached hair matched her thick, poorly applied makeup. She reeked of cheap perfume and strong body odor, making Betty feel queasy. Within the hour, officers escorted three more women into the cell, all very thin from what Betty surmised was from drug use. One had open sores on her mouth and bruise marks on her throat. Each of them had missing teeth and disheveled hair.

The women spoke loudly and profanely at each other and at the guards. Their voices echoed off the cinder block walls. Betty's head ached and her stomach hurt. When they tried to engage her in conversation, she said as little as possible. She wondered how she came to be in such a place with these women with whom she had nothing in common. Or did she? She knew that in some ways she really wasn't that different. They basically all wanted the same things—to have food and shelter, to love and be loved, and to be safe and free—and she had broken the law, just like they had.

A female officer, not much taller than Betty, with long, manicured nails, approached the cell calling her name. Betty stood up and followed her to a desk where another officer fingerprinted her. A different officer, a male this time and young enough to be her grandson, returned her to the holding cell, where she waited for another hour before someone escorted her to a second room. Betty was handed a brown paper bag as she walked in. A dozen other women mulled around with their bags in hand. Three female officers spread themselves around the room. One of them, with a very deep, commanding voice yelled, "Quiet." There was a slight murmuring and then silence fell over the room. "You're here for a cavity search in case you're wondering. You need to strip, squat, and cough. Most of you know the drill."

Betty looked around as everyone started to remove their clothes. She stood there for a second, not moving, knowing she had no choice but to do what they said. Yet, she thought she could just as well have removed her clothes in the middle of a shopping mall. An officer walked up to her and quietly said, "You need to do this, ma'am." Betty slowly began to unbutton her blouse, gritting her teeth and fighting back the tears. She attempted to cover herself with her hands and shelter her breasts with her arms, but she continued to expose herself as she removed her garments and placed them in the brown paper bag. By the time they did the body search on her, everyone else was done and standing around watching. She shut her eyes and pretended to be alone, but it didn't work. She felt dizzy, her head hurt, her stomach twisted in knots. She heard the officer say, "Cough." She coughed, vomit spewing over several inmates as they scrambled to move out of the way. Betty tumbled over in her own puke.

The officer in charge shook her head. "Damn it. Get her to the shower."

Two officers helped Betty up. One picked up the brown paper bag with her clothes and shoved it at her. The officers led Betty to the shower. She shivered as the cold water sprayed out over her head. She reached for soap, but there was none. Less than a minute later, the officer shut the water off.

"That's it." The officer handed her a towel. It smelled musty as Betty put it to her face. "Make it quick," the officer scowled.

Betty dried off as quickly as she could and then started to wrap the towel around her when the officer took it out of her hands and led her back into the room where the search took place. The other inmates were all dressed. Betty was handed some garments to wear, with little regard for their size. She put them on without complaint although the bra was too small and it cut into her back; her pants hung so low she had to roll them up twice at the waist and roll a cuff at the bottom of the leg. Humiliated, Betty walked to another cell where she waited for the bus to take her to her new home, but before her transportation arrived, another officer came in and informed her of her attorney's presence.

The deputy sheriff brought Betty into the interview room and spoke to Sabre. "Don't be too long or she'll miss her bus to Las Colinas and have to take the late one." Then she handcuffed Betty to the bench and walked out.

Betty's hair lay flat against her head, still damp from the shower, and with a hint of gray growth at the roots creeping through. Her clean face, stripped of all makeup, made her look like a different person. All the spunk seemed to be drained out of her. Sabre's chest ached from the sight of her. Under normal circumstances, her friend would never be seen without perfectly spiked hair, open-toed high heel pumps, and well-applied makeup.

"Are you okay?" Sabre asked. "Of course, you're not okay. Why do I keep asking you that?"

Betty slowly lifted her head, the terror evident in her eyes. "They made me strip, squat, and cough while they all watched. It was so humiliating."

"I'm so sorry." Sabre shook her head from side to side. "I'm just so sorry you have to go through this."

Betty lowered her eyes. "I'll be okay. How much worse could it possibly get?"

Sabre didn't want to tell her it could possibly be a lifetime of this humiliation. "Betty, listen to me. If you want me to represent you, I will. And Bob said he'd help. We'll get this thing all sorted out. But you need to know that although I've done a lot of criminal work, most of my experience has been in juvenile court, and while the rules of evidence are the same, the system is quite different."

"How's that?"

"Well, for one thing, there are no jury trials in juvey, and you'll definitely need a jury trial. And there are other things, too. I don't know the judges, and they don't know me. Sometimes that can be an advantage, but sometimes not. I want you to decide what you want, but know that either way, I'm going to be here for you."

"Thanks." Betty looked up at Sabre like a whipped puppy. "I'd feel much better if you were my attorney, but you know I don't have any money to pay you. All I have is the trailer and it's not worth much, but I'll give you everything I have."

"I know that. Don't worry about it. I don't want your money, but I need to tell you up front that I've never handled a murder case. So if you'd be more comfortable with a public defender, it's your choice."

"No, I want you. I trust you. And you know I didn't kill John. They may not believe me. You do believe me." She paused and looked at Sabre. "Don't you?"

"Of course I do. I know you didn't do it. I've known you what, five years now? No, almost six. I know you couldn't kill anyone and especially not John. I know how much you loved him."

"God, I miss him so much. He'd know what to do right now. I don't know what to think or what to say. He always handled the big stuff." Betty put her hands over her face and cried.

"I'm so sorry. I know this is hard." Sabre's heartfelt words sounded empty even to her. "Listen, Betty, hopefully I'll have the police report tomorrow or the next day. Arraignment should be set for Tuesday. Once I have the report we can see what kind of case they have. Do you have any idea why they're charging you, other than that you were with him?"

"No," she sobbed, "but I didn't do it."

"I know. We'll get to the bottom of this." Sabre waited a moment while Betty composed herself. "Did John have any enemies?"

"No, everyone loved him."

Sabre, in an effort to reassure Betty, said, "I'm going to talk to a private investigator I know and get him started on the case."

"What will a PI do?"

"Try to find out who really killed John. He'll dig into his past and see…."

Betty sat up straighter. "Why would he do that? I told you John didn't have any enemies," Betty said with a hint of anger or fear in her voice. Sabre wasn't sure which.

"We just want to find out who did this," Sabre said softly as she touched Betty on the shoulder. "Is there anything else I should know, anything you may have forgotten to tell me?"

Betty looked up at Sabre and then she lowered her eyes. "No, I'm sorry. I wish I could help."

5

Sabre walked through the front door of Polinsky Children's Center, a facility consisting of ninety-two thousand square feet of buildings that stretched over ten acres. It had an Olympic-sized pool, sports fields, and a library. It was a far cry from the old facility that had housed abused and neglected children for so many years in San Diego. Still, although the new accommodations were clean and comfortable, the children who had been removed from their homes, more often than not, would have preferred to stay in the squalor and pain just to be with their families. Sabre looked around at the freshly painted walls and the white tiled floor and wondered, as she always did, what this case would bring.

Sabre handed her bar card and driver's license to the young receptionist with a purple streak in her hair. "I need to see Kat and Kurt Kemp," Sabre said. The receptionist rolled her eyes, picked up the phone, and asked someone to bring the children down to the lobby to see their attorney.

"Is there a problem?"

"No," she said abruptly. She added in a softer tone, "They'll be right down."

Sabre wondered what the receptionist meant as she waited in the lobby until an attendant appeared with two beautiful blond-haired, blue-eyed children. The three-year-old boy, Kurt, with his military short, almost white hair, and deep ocean-blue eyes marched in like a little soldier. Five-year-old Kat's sandy blonde hair hung almost to her waist in soft curls. Her eyes were much lighter, and she appeared delicate and very feminine. She reached for her brother's hand but he pulled away.

"You must be Kat," Sabre said to the little girl.

"Yes, my name is Kat K. Kemp."

"And this is your little brother, Kurt?"

"Yup," Kat said. Sabre walked the children to an interview room with a sofa, two stuffed chairs, a bookshelf with children's books, and a box of colorful toys. As they entered Kurt immediately headed for the toys.

Sabre led Kat to the sofa where they sat down. "My name is Sabre Brown and I'm your attorney. Do you know what an attorney is?"

"Nope." Kat shrugged her shoulders.

"An attorney is someone who helps you when you have a case in court. I'm here to help you and to appear for you in court so you don't have to. Did the social worker explain to you why you are here?"

"She said it's not safe at home right now, but I don't get it."

"She's right. There are some adult problems going on, and the judge has to decide when it is safe for you to go home. And I will appear in court for you and let the judge know what I think is best for you and what you want."

"I want to go home," Kat said, her eyes suddenly wet with tears.

"I know, sweetheart, but for now that's not possible. We will sort this out as soon as we can." Sabre's heart ached as it always did when children were removed from their families. "But right now I need to ask you some questions. Do you think you can help me understand what's going on?"

"I guess," Kat responded, while Kurt found a toy truck in the corner and amused himself.

"How old are you, Kat?"

"Five, but I'll be six next week."

"I'm going to talk to you about a really big word. The word is 'confidential.' Do you know what that is?"

Kat shook her head.

"Well, when something is confidential, it's like a secret. Do you know what a secret is?"

"Yup."

"Attorneys can't tell any secrets their clients tell them. Since I'm the attorney and you are my client, if you tell me a secret and you don't want me to tell anyone, then I can't tell." Kat squirmed in her seat. "Do you understand?"

"I guess."

"Do you have any secrets?"

"My mama and daddy have a secret siety?" Kat said proudly.

"How do you know that?"

"Because they talk about it and we go sometimes."

"You go, too?"

"Yeah, but we play with the other kids. We don't do the secret stuff." Kat stood up and went to the toy box. Sabre followed.

"What kind of secret stuff do they do?"

Kat shrugged her shoulders, and picked up a Barbie doll. "She's pretty."

"Kat, can you bring your Barbie and sit and talk with me just a little longer?" Kat walked back to the sofa with Sabre and sat down, fiddling with the doll's hair. Sabre asked, "Do you go to school?"

"I was in kindergarten, but now I'll be a first-grader."

"Do you like school?"

"Yup."

Sabre looked at the report for a second, pinpointing something she had read earlier. "It says here you had some fights last year in your classroom. Can you tell me about that?"

Kat shrugged her shoulders.

"Who did you fight with?"

"Jasmine, but it wasn't my fault."

"Who's Jasmine?"

"She was my friend, but she tried to hug me so I pushed her." Kat shook the doll at Sabre like a pointer.

"Why didn't you want her to hug you?"

"Cause she's dirty." Kat wrinkled her nose. "You know."

"No, I don't know. What do you mean?"

"Ahem…" Kat exhaled, "…I don't want to be a nigger. If she touched me I would get dirty like her."

Sabre's mouth opened in total astonishment. Just when she thought she had seen and heard it all, she gasped with horror at the injustice done to this little girl. She cleared her throat and went on. "Kat, who told you that?"

"My mom. She said I could play with Jasmine as long as I didn't touch her."

"And your dad, what did he say?"

"He was real mad 'cuz I even played with her. Then I got in more trouble for not beating her up when she touched me."

"Were you punished?"

"My dad spanked me and sent me to my room." She pulled the doll's hair up in a twist on her head.

"What did he spank you with?"

"His hand. He took his belt off, but mama stopped him."

"Has he ever hit you with a belt or anything besides his hand?"

"Just once, with a belt."

"What happened that made him hit you with the belt?"

"I can't remember." Kat shrugged.

"Has he ever hit Kurt with anything?"

"He spanks him. That's all." Kat stood up again, laying the doll on the sofa.

"Kat, what about your mama? Does she spank you or Kurt?"

"Not so much."

Sabre had to bite her tongue to keep from lecturing this little girl on the evils of bigotry, but it wasn't the time or place. She made a note in her file to obtain therapy for these children as soon as possible. She also made a note to ask for a CASA worker, a volunteer from the Court Appointed Special Advocates program. Sabre had worked with some wonderful child advocates from the Voices for Children, the San Diego CASA chapter. They were always dedicated individuals, and this case needed a dedicated volunteer more than most—someone to monitor the services and to help the children make sense of their brainwashing.

Sabre could see Kat was getting antsy and tried to engage her in something less threatening. She wanted to put her at ease again before she took her back. "Do you listen to music?" Sabre asked.

"Yes, mama always has music on."

"What kind of music?"

"Different stuff, but not any of the 'jungle bunny' stuff."

Sabre took a deep breath and tried again. "Do you go to church?"

"Yeah, we go to the white church."

"Is it pretty?"

"Yeah, sort of." Kat picked up an outfit for the doll and brought it back to the sofa.

"What does it look like, besides being white?"

"It's not white. It's kinda yellowish," Kat responded as though Sabre should understand.

"But you said it was whi…" Sabre paused. "What did you mean when you called it the 'white' church?"

"It only has white people. It's God's church."

Sabre put both hands to her head, ran them through her hair, and exhaled. Everything came back to hatred. This was worse than physical abuse, and emotional abuse was so much harder to prove. Besides, she knew she was dealing with constitutional issues that would make a good argument for the parents. As much as she believed these children needed the protection of the court, she knew she could easily lose this fight.

6

The sun had risen, but very little light shone through the windows in Sabre's bedroom. June gloom brought another overcast day to San Diego. Sabre sat up, reached into the nightstand, and removed the little, tattered, red notebook her brother had given her on her sixth birthday. She used it as her life plan. Everything major she ever accomplished started as an entry in her notebook. It was her tribute to her brother's memory; he had been gone for over five-and-a-half years now.

She read through her list. The first and only entry she ever crossed out read, "Marry Victor Spanoli." She had met Victor two days after her sixth birthday and remained his best friend until he moved away at the ripe old age of eight. She had long since given up on marrying Victor or anyone else for that matter, until now. Although it was way too early to consider marriage to Luke, he was the first man in a long time with whom she felt comfortable. They liked a lot of the same things, and when they didn't agree on something, he could compromise. More than anything, though, they just enjoyed each other's company. She loved John and Betty all the more for introducing them.

Sabre continued down the list of things in her notebook she had yet to accomplish. She made a new entry whenever she developed a new goal. It had been some time now since she had added anything. The last entry was made about six months earlier, right after she was abducted and almost killed by the maniac who burned her house down. It read, "Run a marathon." She had started to train a few months back, and although she was comfortable running about five miles, she still had a long way to go. It would take time. "I'll beef it up this month. Perhaps get to ten miles by the end of summer," she said aloud.

With nothing new to add to her notebook, she stepped out of bed, passing boxes half-packed as she went into the kitchen.

She pushed the "Start" button on a pot of decaf coffee, which she always prepared the night before so it would be quick in the morning. While it brewed, she showered and dressed for court. Then she picked up her files, a muffin, and her coffee cup and walked to her car. She didn't care much for apartment living, but her condo was being rebuilt after the fire had destroyed it. It would be ready in a few weeks and she could move back in.

On her way to court, Sabre phoned JP, who was kind enough to put her up when her condo burned. "Hey, JP, it's your old roommate."

"Hi, Sabre. Good to hear your voice. What may I do for you?"

"I have a case I need your help on. You may have read about it in the newspaper: 'John Smith, Stabbed to Death in His Bed.'"

"Yeah, I did read about that. Who's the perpetrator?"

"His wife, Betty. She's a good friend of mine, and I'm sure she's innocent."

"Oh, that's the worst kind. It's always a lot easier when they're guilty; not so much gets invested in the win. Hey, I'm sorry about your friends. I'll do whatever I can to help."

"Good, can you meet me at Las Colinas around twelve fifteen? I'll introduce you to my client and give you whatever information I have. I don't have the police report yet, but I want to get started as quickly as we can. She'll be arraigned on Friday."

"I'll see you there."

Juvenile court seemed more crowded than normal. Sabre plowed her way through the lobby toward Department One where Bob was waiting inside for her. She passed Richard Wagner in the hallway, where he was speaking with his client, Patricia Kemp. Sabre smiled. Blond-haired, blue-eyed Wagner was perfect for this case. She liked Wagner. He always made the cases more interesting, even though he irritated the court officers. He never seemed to be ready when the court was, and sometimes he would just walk off. The court officers evened the score by putting his cases to the bottom of their stack, which meant he was always the last case to be heard and often trailed to the afternoon. Of course, the other attorneys on his cases suffered as well, but at least Wagner was fun to be around.

When Sabre first came to juvenile court, she had only been practicing about six months, knew little about the system, and didn't know any of the attorneys. They all seemed to know one another and were rather clique-ish. Sabre felt like she was back in junior high. Wagner offered her help and gave her some insight on the different judges and the procedures, saving her several times from floundering. He showed her where the lounge was, where to file motions, and told her what she needed to go over with the clients at each hearing.

Wagner always went to bat for his clients in the courtroom, but he didn't pull any punches. On any given day, you could hear him chew out a client for doing something stupid. Most of the attorneys tried hard to be tactful with the clients and not rile them up. Wagner didn't seem to care if they acted out. Rather, he seemed to enjoy it. You could hear him say, "Hey, it's your life. If you want to screw it up more than it already is, that's fine with me. Now if you want to try to get out of this unscathed, then you better start listening. But if you want to act a fool, and don't care whether you get your kids back or not, that's your choice."

Inside the courtroom, Sabre sat down in the back of the room to review the file while Bob finished his conversation with the social worker. She read the allegations on the petition. It was filed under Welfare and Institutions Code 300 (c). A "c" petition was what the Department of Social Services used to remove children from what they determined were abusive homes. In these situations, there was no physical evidence, making it very difficult to prove. Kat's petition read:

> (c) The child is suffering serious emotional damage, or is at substantial risk of suffering serious emotional damage, evidenced by severe anxiety, depression, withdrawal, or untoward aggressive behavior toward self or others, as a result of the conduct of the parent or guardian or who has no parent or

guardian capable of providing appropriate care. No child shall be found to be a person described by this subdivision if the willful failure of the parent or guardian to provide adequate mental health treatment is based on a sincerely held religious belief and if a less intrusive judicial intervention is available...in that the parents have taught Kat to hate anyone of a different race, religion, or sexual orientation to such a degree it has resulted in fights at school on a regular basis.

Kurt's petition was also a "c."

...in that the parents have taught Kurt to hate anyone of a different race, religion, or sexual orientation to such a degree it has resulted in the child making statements of killing other human beings and the father has taught the child to aim a real gun at targets depicting other races.

Sabre knew the petitions to be true based on her one conversation with the children, but she also knew how difficult it would be to prove.

"Hi, Sobs," Bob said as he walked over to her.

"Good morning," Sabre said. "It looks like Wagner has the mother on Kemp. He's outside talking to her right now."

"Oh, good." Bob grinned. "This is going to be fun. And Wags and I are going to win this one. That will be one more jurisdictional win for me—the king of juvenile court!"

"Yeah, right. In front of Hekman? I don't think so."

The door opened and Wagner walked in. "You ready to send these kids home, Sabre?"

"I'm going to ask they be detained with you, Wagner, and Judge Hekman is going to make regular unannounced visits to your house. What do you think of that?"

"I think you're crazy," Wagner responded and walked off to let the court officer know he was ready.

"I'm going to tell them we're ready, too, before we lose Wags," Bob said as he followed Wagner.

Within minutes the attorneys and their clients assembled at the tables. The defense—Bob with the father and Wagner with the mother—and Sabre, representing the children, sat on the right side; County Council and Thelma, an African-American social worker three months away from retirement, sat on the left. Thelma, sixty-one-years old and carrying about fifty extra pounds, was a sharp woman with plenty of experience dealing with these cases, but she was tiring of the whole juvenile court thing and ready to move on to the next chapter of her life. She had lasted longer than most. The burn-out rate for social workers appeared to be fewer than ten years, and Thelma was still going strong some thirty years later. Sabre liked her as a worker and thought she was generally fair in her assessment, but she knew this one would be tough for her and didn't envy her position.

Judge Hekman took a seat on the bench. The case was called, and Wagner was officially appointed to represent the mother. "Also, Your Honor, a bit of housekeeping," Wagner said. "The petition reads 'Patricia Kemp' as my client's name. That's incorrect. I have a judgment here with a legal name change to Kelly K. Kemp." Wagner stood up. "May I approach the bench?"

"Yes, counselor."

Wagner walked up to the court clerk and handed her a copy of the judgment, which she in turn handed to the judge. Wagner then gave copies to each attorney at the table. "We're asking the petition be changed to depict her correct name."

"Hmpff…so ordered," Judge Hekman said.

Bob stood up, "Your Honor, we're asking the court to grant us a demurrer. We do not believe a legal cause of action exists for the facts stated in the petition. Even if the facts stated are true, and we're not suggesting they are, it doesn't constitute a cause of action under the W&I Code §300. We ask for the petition to be dismissed."

"Nice try, Mr. Clark, but I'm not granting your demurrer this morning. If you would like to file the appropriate motions, I'll hear it." The judge turned to county council. "The department is put on notice that this is a pretty weak petition."

Mr. Wagner stood up. "We'll be joining in Mr. Clark's demurrer and we're requesting a trial date on the merits should the court not see fit to grant the demurrer. We'd like the trial as soon as possible."

"We'll go off calendar and pick a trial date. But I want psych evals on both parents and the children," she demanded.

Bob jumped up. "My client objects to having a psych eval done pre jurisdiction. According to Laurie S. v. Superior Court (1994) 26 Cal. App. 4th 195, the court does not have the jurisdiction to order a psych eval until they actually have jurisdiction. If the department doesn't have the facts to support their petition, they can't order my client to do something to try to bolster their lack of facts."

"You're right, counselor, but I can order a psych eval for dispositional purposes, because it is relevant for placement of the children."

"That's true, Your Honor, but for the record we're objecting to that evaluation being ordered at this point in time."

"So noted."

"May I be heard on detention of the children?" Bob asked.

"I'm assuming you want the children placed with mom and dad. Is that correct?"

"Yes," Bob responded.

"I'm not going to do that, but we will pick as early a trial date as we can." The judge turned to the court clerk.

"When's the next available trial date?" She turned back to the court recorder. "We're off the record." The clerk gave the next date available, which was about three weeks out. Counsel all agreed to the date. "That was easy," the judge said. "The children will be detained in Polinsky pending foster care or detention with an appropriate relative, if you can find one." She turned to Sabre, "I'm sorry, Ms. Brown. Did you have anything to add on behalf of the children?"

"Only that I have concurrence for any relative detention."

"So ordered. Visitation will be supervised for both parents," the judge ordered. Mr. Kemp grumbled something to his attorney. Bob calmed him down and did not address the court. Judge Hekman continued. "And I don't want any relative supervision of visits. The department will supervise pending the trial. Psychological evaluations ordered for both parents and both children, assuming little Kurt is verbal enough to have one. The evaluations are for disposition purposes only. See you all in three weeks. Case is adjourned."

Wagner stood up. "There's one other thing, Your Honor. My client is requesting a different social worker be appointed on this case. She believes the social worker is prejudiced and cannot make a fair assessment of this case."

"Prejudiced?" the judge said as she snapped her head up.

"Did you just say prejudiced?"

"Yes, Your Honor, that is my client's contention. She just wants a fair trial."

Judge Hekman shook her head, never one to hide her attitude. "Request denied. Good day, Mr. Wagner."

7

As soon as Sabre finished her morning court calendar, she drove to Las Colinas. She checked in, showing her identification. "My investigator will be here shortly. When he arrives, would you please bring him into the interview room?"

"Sure, Counselor," the deputy responded.

Betty approached the interview room, escorted by a deputy sheriff. She sat down on the opposite side of the glass and picked up the phone. The sheriff said, "Ring when you're done," and walked off.

Sabre nodded, but the deputy left before he could see her response.

"Hi, Betty. You look tired."

"Yeah, not much sleep last night. The blankets are made of wool and they're scratchy. I'm allergic to wool." She raised her sleeve and showed the red bumps forming up and down her arm. "You know I'm not picky. I've slept in some pretty awful places, but this place is horrible. Are you going to be able to get me out of here?"

"The judge may hear bail arguments at arraignment. I don't know for sure what this particular judge will do, but it's always difficult to get bail in capital cases. You know I'll try."

"It doesn't matter if he does grant bail. I don't have any money or a house for collateral. I doubt if they'll take our old, beat-up trailer."

"Betty, if he grants bail, we'll find a way to get you out. Let's just take it one step at a time."

"Okay, so where are we?"

"Here's how it works. The police make the arrest, but the prosecuting attorney decides whether or not to file charges, and if so, which ones. Then they file the documents with the court alleging the charges against you. They set an arraignment hearing at which you are formally advised of your charges and your constitutional rights. Bail may be set at that time, but in this type of case, the judge often does not grant it. Your arraignment hearing is set for Tuesday." Sabre struggled with this process. She didn't want to be explaining these things to her friend. She took a deep breath. "Betty, I'm so sorry."

Betty raised her head slightly, her mouth turned down, and just nodded.

Sabre continued. "Look, I don't have the police report, so I don't know what they're claiming as probable cause for the arrest, but Nelson said he'd try to have it for me this afternoon. As soon as I know anything, I'll pass it on to you. In the meantime, I've hired a private investigator. His name is JP Torn. He's the best, and he's coming by this afternoon to meet you. He's going to help you through this, but you need to tell him anything he asks. It's all confidential, just as if you were talking to me. We need to know anything that might help us find the real killer. Something may not seem important to you, but it could be the lead that points us in the right direction."

"I'll do the best I can," Betty responded without looking up, her elbow on the table propping up her head.

The door opened and JP walked in, carrying his ever present black, felt cowboy hat in his hand, his boots clicking across the floor. Sabre realized these were two of her closest friends, and yet they'd never met. When she introduced JP to Betty, she noticed Betty sat up a little straighter.

JP said, "Nice to meet you, Betty. I wish it were under better circumstances. I want you to know you're in very capable hands with Sabre, and between the two of us we're going to find out who did this and get you out of here. Are you willing to help?"

"Yes," Betty said, looking into JP's calm, hazel eyes.

"Good, you'll need to answer all my questions. Some of them will seem inane, but humor me. I have a reason for every question I ask. I'll be starting with your background, where you lived before, who you knew, etc." Betty looked down, losing eye contact with JP. He continued. "I'll need to know everything I can about John as well. There's a lot at stake here."

"I know. And thanks for believing in me," Betty responded, still not looking JP in the eye.

"Hey, Sabre says you're innocent. That's all I need. Sabre doesn't lie." He glanced at Sabre and smiled.

Sabre said, "I need to get back to court. Are you staying, JP?"

"Yes, but I'll walk you part way." Sabre said her goodbyes, and they walked to the end of the hallway.

"She's holding something back," JP said as soon as they were out of earshot.

"You think?" Sabre was baffled by the comment. She truly believed in Betty's innocence, but she also trusted JP's instincts. Reconciling herself, she said, "Well, we all have our secrets, don't we? But I know she didn't kill John."

"Okay, that's the way we proceed. I'll call you later." JP returned to Betty and began his interview, asking about the details of the night of the murder, establishing her timeline, looking for anything they may have missed. Betty's responses matched Sabre's account of events. He was starting to agree with Sabre. Betty was hiding something, but he didn't think it was the murder. And he knew it must be big, or why wouldn't she share it with them and help get her off the hook? He continued his interview with Betty, asking probing questions and taking copious notes. An hour and a half later, he folded up his tattered notebook. "That's it for today. Would you mind if I look around your trailer to see if I can find anything to help our case?"

"What do you expect to find?" Betty pushed herself back in the chair.

"You can't know a horse until you ride it," JP said, throwing one of his granddaddy's lines at her.

Betty looked puzzled.

"I'm sorry…. I don't know what I might find or what I'm really looking for until I look. Do you mind if I go in?"

"I guess not. Sabre has the key."

"You've been very helpful, but you look beat. I'll be back if I need anything else." JP stood up, put on his hat, and rang for the guard.

JP left and the deputy escorted Betty back to her cell. It was a step up from the holding tank at the station. It felt more like a large dorm room than a cell, except Betty knew she couldn't leave. Rows of stainless steel bunks lined the walls, each covered with a thin mattress, flat sheets, and a wool blanket. A row of block wall shower stalls stood in the middle of the room. On the back side of the showers was a row of stalls for metal toilets and sinks, all with open fronts, allowing no privacy for personal bodily functions. The block walls on the showers and toilets stood low enough for the guards, or anyone else who chose, to look over. Everything had the same odor; the clothes, the bedding, and the rooms all smelled of cheap detergent.

Betty went to her bunk, lay down, and tried to sleep. The noise hurt her head and her mind raced. Her life, as she knew it, would never exist again. John was gone, yet the nightmare continued. She prayed Sabre would be able to help her. It all seemed so hopeless. She tried to sleep to avoid the guilt she felt, but the torment of the vision of John's bloody body wouldn't allow it.

Had she done the right thing?

8

Sabre left Las Colinas and drove to her office to catch up on a few things. Jack, another attorney who shared the building with her, walked out the door, briefcase in one hand and his suit jacket in the other.

"Hi, Sabre. How was your day?" He stopped on the step, his full head of blond and gray speckled hair glistening in the sun.

"I've had better. They booked Betty for the murder of her husband. I just came from seeing her."

"Little red-headed Betty?"

"Yup."

"I'm so sorry. Are you going to handle the case?" Jack asked.

"Yes. She can't afford anyone else, and I don't want her to have a public defender. I know she's innocent."

"Do you think that's wise? Representing her? It's difficult when you're so close to someone," he said, putting his hand on her shoulder.

"I know, but she needs me." Sabre's face lit up and her voice sparked. "Unless you want the case? I'd be glad to second chair."

"No thanks. It's not exactly my forte."

"Yeah, me neither," Sabre said, a little quieter.

"Oh, you can handle it all right, but aren't you a potential witness?"

"Yeah, but that shouldn't be a problem. I didn't really see the crime. They'll just want me to establish the time frame and attest that Betty was out of my sight for a period of time. The DA will probably let me stipulate to that and if not, Bob can cross-examine me. I just don't want to screw it up."

"Listen. Legally, you'll do a great job. I just worry because you're too involved. I worry about your state of mind. I'm not trying to tell you what to do, but I've been at this at least twenty years longer than you and I've taken cases I shouldn't have. I know what it's like." He gave her shoulder a little squeeze. "Sabre, what happens if she actually did kill him? Have you thought about that?"

"She didn't. I know she didn't."

"Well then, what if she's innocent and you lose? That's even worse. Are you going to be able to handle that?"

"Probably not." She paused. "I guess I better not lose."

He shook his head. "Well, if there's anything I can do to help, just let me know." Jack looked at Sabre, compassion visible in his eyes. Sabre knew he was concerned for her well-being. "And Sabre, please don't stay in the office too late. Elaine has already left and I still don't like your working here alone at night. I know that whole mess with the stalker is over, but there are plenty of other nuts out there besides him."

"I'll be fine. Just go on home. I'll be leaving here in less than half an hour. I have a date tonight." Sabre smiled. Thinking about Luke lifted her spirits.

After Jack left, Sabre checked her phone messages. Elaine, the tall, short-haired blonde receptionist, had them all sorted for her with the most urgent messages on top. Elaine had worked there since before Sabre rented the office space. She was Jack's personal secretary and the receptionist for the other two attorneys in the building. Her services were included in the monthly rent. Efficient as she was knowledgeable, Elaine always delivered messages accurately and timely. She ensured office supplies were readily available. Most importantly, she always treated clients with respect. Sabre would've loved to have her as a secretary, but Jack needed all of the time Elaine had to spare.

Sabre returned the urgent calls and flipped through the other messages, deciding they could wait. She gathered up the files she wanted to work on at home over the weekend. Since she started dating Luke, she didn't work at the office as much.

She often took her cases home with her and she'd toil over them while Luke worked on his computer, dealing with clients who needed glitches fixed on their programs from all across the United States. She wasn't quite sure exactly what he did. When it came to technology, she learned only what she had to know to do her work. Beyond that, she really had no interest. She tried to understand his work, but it didn't hold her attention long, and Luke didn't seem to mind that she wasn't interested. It was just one more thing she liked about him.

Sabre preferred leaving the office before dark, still not comfortable working late. For the most part, her life was good. She had always had good friends, and now she had Luke. It had been so long since she'd been this close to anyone. Luke could make all her problems fade away just by his presence.

As Sabre drove home to change her clothes for their date, she continued to think about Luke and how lucky she was to have him. For a few moments she was able to take her mind off John and Betty, but it didn't last long. Seeing Betty in prison garb behind the glass partition at Las Colinas was a vision she had a hard time erasing from her mind. She was convinced of Betty's innocence. She had known John and Betty for over four years, and in all that time she saw nothing but love between them. John's eyes always lit up when Betty appeared and Betty reciprocated with genuine smiles. They held hands when they walked. They sat next to each other whenever they could. When one of them spoke, the other looked and listened. They would fuss at each other now and again, but even that was never anything serious. Neither of them had eyes for anyone else.

Sabre stopped at a stoplight near her apartment. She tried to think about her date with Luke, but her mind kept going back to Betty. *What if Jack was right? What if she lost the trial?* Betty's life was in her hands. She tightened her grip on the steering wheel, feeling the ache in her stomach and the tension in her neck. The fear inside of her was interrupted by the ringing of the phone. "Hi Luke," she answered.

"Hi babe. Do you mind driving over here tonight? I have a little surprise for you," Luke said. "Oh, and bring your toothbrush."

"Is that the surprise?"

"No, I'm sure you're not surprised I want you to stay the night.

I've been asking you that for the past six weeks. Just bring your beautiful body over here. I miss you."

"What should I wear?"

"Nothing but a smile."

"Can I put a trench coat over my smile?"

"Sure, if you can stand the heat and don't expect to wear it long. It's coming off as soon as you walk in the door."

"I'll be there in about thirty minutes."

She wondered about the surprise. Luke had a very romantic side, although he didn't show it every day. When he decided to do something, he always made it special.

Sabre arrived at her apartment, parked in the stall, and hurried inside to change her clothes. She briefly considered wearing nothing but her raincoat, but the thought of what she'd do in an accident or some emergency changed her mind.

She took off her uncomfortable high heels and her dark blue Ann Taylor suit—not her most expensive suit, but one that fit well. Her silk blouse cost almost as much as the suit. She wouldn't have any of it if Bob, her personal male shopper—or PMS as she called him—hadn't gone with her on a shopping spree. Sabre, unlike most of her friends, didn't understand the art of shopping or enjoy it, so when she did make the effort, she bought as much as she could. When Bob had joined her at Nordstrom's and picked out the clothes for her to try on, it proved to be the most fun she ever had shopping.

She picked out a casual pink top to put over jeans and sandals, hoping that Luke didn't have anything fancy planned, and headed out the door. As she drove to Luke's apartment, her mind began to focus on Betty again. She knew Betty was innocent. She just had to prove it. She would receive the police report on Monday for the scheduled arraignment on Tuesday. Meanwhile, JP was already investigating. She hoped he'd find an argument for bail by Tuesday. Sabre was still thinking about Betty when she started looking for a parking spot on the street near Luke's apartment. She didn't like going there because the parking was so limited. Luke lived near Qualcomm Stadium in a complex that housed a lot of college students. The tenants had parking, but management only designated about twenty guest parking spots for two hundred plus units. After driving around the block three times without finding a space, Sabre called Luke.

"I can't find a parking spot," Sabre said without any of the pleasantries when Luke answered.

"I'm sorry, baby, I forgot to tell you to call me when you got here. I found out today that since I have a two-bedroom apartment, I'm entitled to two parking spots. They're end to end, so one car has to be parked in front of the other, but that's okay. You can park behind my roadster; you'll be leaving before me. Or maybe I'll make you park in front of me so you can't leave at all."

Sabre drove into the complex. Luke lived at the far end, so he had time to walk downstairs before she got there. He must've run down, though, because he met her just after she passed the first of three buildings. There he stood in the middle of the road, her tall, handsome, dark-haired man in ironed shorts and a t-shirt, waiting for her. Although he dressed casually most of the time, Luke was very particular about the way he dressed and how his hair looked. He took pride in his personal appearance.

"Hi, babe." He walked up to the car and gave her a quick kiss.

"Hi." She smiled, feeling her stomach giggle. She loved the feelings he aroused in her. "Where do you want me?"

"Anywhere and everywhere," he teased, "but you may put your car right there behind mine." He pointed to an empty space on the left about thirty feet away.

It had been awhile since Sabre had been in a relationship, and she soaked up the flirting and all that went with it. After parking her car, she met Luke at its rear. He put his arm around her and pulled her into him. "So, how was your day?"

"Not so great. I went to see Betty in Las Colinas this afternoon. It was really hard seeing her locked up in there. She's being strong, but I know she's scared to death. I just hope I can get her released soon."

"I'm sorry. It must've been awful seeing her like that. But I tell you what. I'm going to make you forget all about the outside world. Tonight, it's just you and me." He looked into her eyes, smiled, and squeezed her a little tighter.

Luke opened the door to his apartment. Only one dim lamp lit the room. The dining table contained two place settings, two candles flickering, and flowers in the center. Two other candles burned on the coffee table.

"Wow, Luke, this is really sweet." Sabre leaned backward into him, melting into his chest. He put his arms around her, pulling her even closer. She turned around and reached up, putting her arms around his neck, pulling his head down to meet her lips with a kiss.

"Hey, hey…. Wait 'til you see what else is in store for you. Come with me." He led her to the bathroom. Four more candles burned next to a full tub with bubbles. The aroma from the bath salts smelled clean, but not sweet, just the way she liked it.

"This is incredible. Is the tub for me or for us?" she teased.

"The tub is for you. I knew it was going to be a hard day because of Betty. So you just relax in the tub while I finish dinner."

"You can cook?"

"Of course I can cook. I love to cook, especially for someone special."

"You're amazing, you know," she said, as she turned and gazed into his eyes.

He put his hands on each side of her head and pulled her mouth close to his, kissing her gently, yet passionately. Then he let go and smacked her lightly on her butt. "There's a clean shirt on the back of the door you may use if you'd like. Relax and enjoy; I'll be in the kitchen if you need me."

Sabre watched him as he left the room, blown away that someone would pamper her like this. It was every woman's fantasy. She was tempted to go to him just to be with him.

Once he was out of sight she turned toward the tub with all its bubbles. It smelled clean and light, like melon or sweet peas. She peeled off her shirt.

9

Monday morning news in the paper was mostly about crimes committed both locally and nationally and the country's poor economy. Sabre had stopped receiving the paper for that very reason. It was only recently she started it up again. Robberies, bankruptcies, foreclosures—it was all depressing. She was about to lay the paper down when a picture of a nineteen-year-old young man caught her attention. He was found beaten to death and left on a hillside in Perris, California with the word "FAG" scrawled in the blood and dirt alongside his body, an obvious victim of a hate crime. The authorities seemed to think he was beaten and then dragged behind a pickup across rocks and brush, tearing off most of his skin. A pickup was reported leaving the scene near the north end of Perris, but no license number was obtained.

Sabre felt disgusted. It was crimes like this that made her consider working as a prosecutor But she knew her heart wouldn't be in most of it. She was working where she fit best. She tossed the paper on the top of a packed cardboard box and left for juvenile court.

After they finished their morning calendar, Bob and Sabre drove to the DA's office to pick up the police report on John's murder. Sabre read through the report, frowning and shaking her head as she read.

"What do they have on her?" Bob asked.

"The murder weapon has her fingerprints on it. It says she used a kitchen knife and left it in the sink. I didn't see a bloody knife when I was at her home."

Bob looked over Sabre's shoulder and read from the report. "It says the knife was found in the sink, but it had been rinsed off."

"That's strange."

"Yeah, she rinsed it off, but she didn't wipe off the fingerprints.

Why would someone do that?"

"I know. That doesn't work for me, either. And why would she just leave it in the sink?" Sabre paused. "Wait a minute. When I went inside to get some clothes for Betty, I saw the police officer put a knife inside an evidence bag. That must have been the murder weapon."

"That's another thing that doesn't make sense. If you're going to clean up a kitchen knife that you just used to kill your husband, and you're not going to get rid of it, why wouldn't you put it away with the other knives? Why would you leave it in the sink separated from the others so it stands out?"

"That might be enough to get her 'murder two' or 'manslaughter,' but it won't get her off the hook. It might take some of the sting out of pre-meditation," Sabre said as she shuffled through the pages looking for the coroner's report.

"What are you looking for?" Bob asked.

"I want to see what they say is the time of death. Ahh…here it is. They say John died between six forty-five p.m. and twelve twenty-one a.m."

"What time was she with you?"

"She arrived at the casino a little after seven o'clock and she left about ten thirty."

"So, conceivably, she could've killed him before she left or after she returned."

"Yup."

"I don't know. It still doesn't work for me." Bob cocked his head to the side and put his index finger to his mouth and mimicked, "Hmm…I guess I'll kill my husband and then go to the casino, play a few slots, and hang out with my friends. Then I'll come home, crawl in bed with the bloody bloke, and take a little nap before I call my friends to let them know. Oh, and while I'm at it, I think I'll wipe the blood off the knife and leave it in the sink for someone to find."

"Okay, that doesn't make much sense, but what if it happened after she got home?" Sabre tried to think like the prosecutor.

"That might be a little tougher, but let's think about that. What time did she leave the casino?"

"Well, we were still inside the casino at ten-thirty and she said she was leaving shortly."

"How long a drive is it to her house?"

"Not that long, maybe fifteen minutes. She lives on the east end of El Cajon."

"So, even if she left right away, she would've had to walk to her car and drive home. That would've put her there not much before eleven, even if she hurried."

"That's right, and it would've been at least ten thirty-five p.m. before she left, because we talked for a few minutes after I checked the time. We offered to walk her to her car when we left, but she said she was staying a little longer."

"So, it must've been at least eleven p.m. before she got home and probably even longer."

"That's true." Sabre wrinkled her forehead. "That still gives her an hour and twenty-one minutes to kill him. What's your point?"

"I'm just trying to see if the time works. Do they think she decided to go gambling and then come home, walk in, and stab her husband because he snored too loud?"

"Who knows what they think at this juncture, but you have a point. She couldn't have killed him if he were awake. She's a little, bitty thing and he's a good size man...and strong. He weighs about one hundred and eighty pounds. He's nearly six foot tall and he's pretty muscular." Sabre realized mid-sentence she was speaking as though he were still alive and changed her verb tense. "There's no indication of a fight. He would've had to have been sleeping and she would've had to get him on the first stab. What are the chances of that?"

"Not likely, but you're right. He would've had to have been sleeping. So, she had a maximum of eighty-one minutes to have an argument with him, wait for him to go to bed, and then kill him while he was asleep. And that's pushing the envelope of the time frame for his death."

"Can't they pinpoint the time of death more closely?"

"I think they can. We'll have to ask JP. He'll be able to clear some of this up for us, tell us how realistic it is."

"Perhaps Betty can shed some light on it, too. I'll go see her after we talk to JP. He's meeting us for lunch. We better get moving."

When they arrived at Pho's Vietnamese restaurant in the strip mall across from Kearny High, JP was there waiting for them.

"I'm glad you could join us for lunch," Bob said.

"Yeah, me too," JP said, as he picked up his file from his trunk and followed them into the restaurant. "I've never eaten here. How's the food?"

"Good," Bob said.

"Bob says it's good, but he really only knows number 'one-twenty-four' is good because he's never tried anything else. But, yes, the food is good," Sabre said as they walked in. Directly in front of the door sat a three-foot tall, gold-colored statue of a Buddha surrounded by fake yellow and white flowers and gifts of food. Sabre stopped for a second to admire the bright gold fish swimming in the aquarium just below the Buddha shrine before catching up to the guys. Once inside the main dining area they were seated at their usual table. In one corner of the rather long room was a karaoke machine playing American songs sung with heavy Asian accents.

"JP, have you seen the police report?" Sabre asked, always getting right to the point.

Before he could answer, Bob said, "Can we order before we start talking business?"

JP said, "Yeah, let's get some vittles into that cowgirl."

"Or we could just eat," Bob said. Sabre laughed.

"So, what's the 'one-twenty-four'?" JP asked.

"It's rice noodles with pork," Bob answered.

"Sounds good to me. That's what I'll have. This menu's too long to read."

Their favorite waiter, a young, witty man, came to the table.

"Hi, Binh," Bob and Sabre said at almost the same time.

"Hi, what you like to drink today?" he asked, carefully enunciating each word.

"JP?" Bob asked.

"Iced tea would be good."

"Just water for us," Bob said.

"Fine then, one iced tea and two Vietnamese Seven-Ups," Binh said with a little smirk. "And Mr. Bob, you want number one-twenty-four, and you ma'am, what you like today?"

"I'll have a one-forty, spicy, please," Sabre said.

"And you, sir?" Binh asked turning to JP.

"I'll have a one-twenty-four also."

"You just like Mr. Bob. I so sorry." Binh picked up the menus. "Rice paper rolls today?"

"Yes, please bring us two orders; we'll split them," Bob said.

"I didn't ask you, Mr. Bob." Binh winked at Sabre. Then nodding his head toward Bob, he said, "He think I care what he want." Binh tipped his head downward in a slight bow and stepped backward one step before turning. "Thank you. I be right back."

"Why is it he always remembers your name and not mine?" Sabre asked as the waiter walked away. Sabre and Bob ate at Pho's about three times a week and Binh always tried to work their table.

"Because I'm more memorable," Bob retorted.

"I don't think so," JP said, as he looked up catching Bob's eye and then Sabre's before his face turned dark red with embarrassment.

Sabre stood up. "Will you two please excuse me?" She walked off. JP kept his eyes on her backside as she walked away, her dark brown hair bouncing lightly on her shoulders, her short skirt showing off her shapely legs in her high heels. He watched until he couldn't see her any longer.

"Why don't you let her know how you feel? Geez, you've been smitten with her since the first time you saw her," Bob said.

JP knew that was true, but he really became enamored with

her when she stayed in his house with him for three weeks the previous year. Bob had asked JP to help protect Sabre when she was being stalked. Before they were able to find out who the stalker was, her house had been burned to the ground and she had nowhere to live. JP asked her to stay on indefinitely, but as soon as she felt safe, she found an apartment. He hated to see her go. "I'm too old for her."

"What's ten years when you're in love?" Bob dragged out the word love and rolled his eyes.

"Ten…I wish. I'm eighteen years older than she is, and besides, she's way out of my league. She deserves a smart, young buck like Lucas." He paused. "I hate that guy."

"No, you don't. Luke is an okay guy. You're just jealous."

"Yeah, he's alright, but I still hate him."

"Hate who?" Sabre asked as she walked up to the table.

"No one," Bob said. "JP's just giving me a hard time."

Sabre looked first at Bob and then at JP. Though curious about their conversation, she let it go. "So, JP," Sabre asked, "did you see the police report on Betty's case?"

"Yes, I did. Something doesn't add up, though."

"What's that?"

"Well, the murder weapon was identified as a kitchen knife with no blood on it, but it did have fingerprints. I'm thinking if you're going to wipe it off, you wipe off the whole thing. And why keep it in the kitchen sink afterward?"

"That's exactly what we thought," Sabre said. "JP, how do they determine the time of death?"

"It's pretty much about body temperature, but there are other things that are factored in, such as the victim's body weight, air temperature, whether the air is still or moving, if it's wet or dry. Also, whether the victim is clothed or covered, whether or not rigor mortis is setting in, and if so, to what extent. All that is plugged into a formula. They usually give you a time frame of about eight hours, but if all the information is correct, and if it's calculated correctly, the time is pretty close to the mid point of those eight hours."

"So, if John's death was calculated correctly, he would've died around…"

"Nine thirty-three p.m.," JP answered before Sabre could finish. "And wasn't she with you at the casino at that time?"

"Yes, she was." Sabre's eyes opened wide and with glee in her voice said, "So if the time is correct she couldn't have killed him." She paused and the light disappeared from her face. "But that's when I was playing bingo. I wasn't actually with her." She paused again, then continued to argue with herself. "But she would've had to move awfully fast to get home, kill him, and get back. That's preposterous."

Binh brought the drinks to the table. He sat JP's glass in front of him and said, "Iced tea for you." Then he placed the waters in front of Sabre and Bob. "Vietnamese Seven-Up for you two." He handed Sabre and JP each a straw. "You don't get one," he said to Bob and walked away.

"Okay, he always does that. He may remember me, but you always get a straw with your water and he won't bring me one. Why do you suppose that is?" Bob asked.

"Because you don't deserve one," Sabre said.

"Have you ever asked him for a straw?" JP asked.

"Yes, but he just smiles and says, 'Sure, Mr. Bob,' and then he won't bring it to me."

Sabre turned to JP again and asked, "Did you get a chance to start your investigation?"

"Yes." JP looked toward the karaoke machine and glanced around the room. He took a deep breath.

"Well, JP, what is it? Just tell me."

The waiter returned with the rice paper rolls and set them down on the table. He put a small, salad-sized plate down for each guest and a shallow bowl with peanut sauce in it for the rice paper rolls.

JP waited until the waiter left. "Did you know Betty was a widow before she married John?"

"I believe she mentioned it. Why?"

"Did you know when he died?"

"No, does it matter?"

"Well, it appears he died in Texas, about a month before she came to California with John."

"That's a pretty short mourning period. Was he sick for a long time or something?" Bob asked.

"No, he died of a sudden heart attack. And, by the way, there's no record of her marriage to John."

"So, maybe they weren't married. And maybe it was love at first sight. What are you getting at, JP?" Sabre asked, a little irritated.

"Nothing, yet. I'm just reporting the information. You can ask Betty for an explanation, or I can. Which will it be?"

"I'll ask her," Sabre said, unnerved by the information she had just received.

"She needs to start leveling with us, Sabre," Bob said. "She's jacking us around. I know you want to protect her and you believe in her innocence, but you have to wonder why she's keeping things from us."

10

As Sabre drove to Las Colinas her thoughts jumped around—her romantic weekend with Luke, her concern for how she would be able to protect the Kemp minors, and her questions for Betty. She focused on Luke. It had been a long time since she had someone she cared this much about. She and Luke were spending more and more time together, but he still wasn't smothering her.

The closer she got to Las Colinas, the more her thoughts settled on Betty. She was convinced of Betty's innocence, but if there was anything unusual, the prosecutor would use it against her. Sabre would need to explain everything amiss in Betty's life in court when the time came, and that could be so humiliating for Betty.

Sabre entered Las Colinas, showed her bar card and identification to the desk clerk, and asked for Betty to be put in an interview room. A guard walked with her down the cold, stone corridor where he opened the locked gates, let Sabre in, and followed behind her. The door clanged behind them, creating a cage. She felt claustrophobic and wondered how anyone could stand to be locked up, especially someone who hadn't committed a crime. To lose her freedom would be the one thing Sabre couldn't stand, which is probably why she chose defense work instead of prosecution. Sabre hated crime and criminals and was appalled by what they did to their victims, but was equally appalled by what the system could do when someone was innocent but still convicted.

She walked through the second gate. Clang. A shiver went down Sabre's back. She entered the interview room. "Your client will be right out. Just let us know when you're finished," the guard said as he walked away.

Betty was brought into the back side of the private interview room. The glass separating them formed a barrier between their friendship and the attorney/client relationship.

Betty sat down and gave Sabre a half smile. "Hi, Sabre. It's good to see you," she said.

"Hi, Betty. Is everything going okay in there? I mean, considering."

"It could be worse. They have me in a cell with one other woman. She's in here for murder, too. She claims she's innocent, but everyone in here says that, so who's to know? I'm sure they think the same about me."

Betty looked different. Besides being sad, she looked harder. Her eyes had lost their twinkle. "Are the accommodations pretty bad? I've never been in that part of the jail."

"I've lived in worse." Betty let out a little chortle. "They have metal toilets and sinks in the rooms, so there's no privacy. They say you get used to that after a while. I'm hoping I don't have to."

"You know I'll do whatever I can." Reticent to broach the subject of John and the knife, Sabre asked more questions about the facility. "Do they let you out of your cell?"

"Yeah, every day for a few hours, except on Saturday when they changed the bedding and gave us a change of clothes. They made us strip down and they gave me clothes that don't fit, a bra that's all stretched out, and a dingy t-shirt to go with my otherwise fashionable, orange jumpsuit. We had to stay in our cell that day and they gave us a really bad sack lunch. Normally, the food isn't that bad. No worse than most cafeteria food, anyway."

"Do you usually eat somewhere else?"

"Yeah, we usually eat in the Day Room. They send us through the line to get our trays and we sit at round metal tables with stationary benches. That's so no one can pick them up and throw them. We can go there for a few hours during the day. They have games, cards, and stuff like that in there. And they have a television, but it's controlled by the resident thugs. I'm not much into television, so I don't care. The big event in there, though, is mail time. That's the ultimate, especially for those who have been here awhile."

"How've they been treating you?"

"Fine. The guards are pretty civil. It's only a problem when you don't know the rules, but I'm catching on pretty fast."

Sabre took a deep breath and told herself it was time to act like an attorney. She had not known how hard it would be to represent a friend, but she had no choice.

"Betty, the police have the murder weapon."

"Good. Where did they find it?"

"In your kitchen sink." Sabre noticed the quizzical look on Betty's face.

"What do you mean, in my kitchen sink?"

"The perpetrator used a kitchen knife, which may or may not have been yours, and then cleaned it off and put it in your sink. Do you remember seeing it there when you came home that night?"

Betty thought for a second. "When I came home, I remember the door was closed, but not locked. That was kind of odd because John was careful about locking the door. I went inside and turned on the light in the kitchen, and I got myself a glass of water to take a pill. There was a cutting board on the counter with half of an apple on it. A knife was sitting next to it. I picked up the knife and cut the core out of the apple, sliced it, and ate the pieces. I rinsed off the knife and laid it in the sink."

"Did it seem unusual that the apple and knife were left out?"

"No, I'm used to cleaning up after John, especially things like that. He probably ate half the apple and then forgot about it. Sometimes he puts things away, but more often than not, he leaves them for me." Betty, in horror, cocked her head to one side. "Is that the knife they used?"

"It looks like it, and it has your fingerprints on it."

"Oh my God, this just keeps getting worse."

"There's something else I need to ask you about. I need to know about your last husband."

"Why?" Betty asked, looking a little surprised. "What does he have to do with this?" Betty shifted uncomfortably from side to side.

"Probably nothing, but there are unanswered questions and anything the prosecutor can use against you, he will. Even if it is to make you look like a liar because you didn't tell something."

"What do you need to know?"

"How long were you married?"

"I was married to Jim for sixteen years."

"You told JP he died six years ago, but the information he has indicates it was more like five years ago."

"I must've made a mistake. I haven't been thinking very clearly."

"I understand, but that puts his death about a month before I met you and that's shortly after you came to California with John." Sabre tried to pick her words carefully, "I'm not passing judgment on you, but a jury will, so I need to sort this out. Did you know John while Jim was alive? Sometimes it seems like you two go way back. You seemed to know each other so well."

"We knew each other for many years while I was married to Jim. We were all friends, just friends. When Jim had his heart attack, John was there to comfort me. He helped me through some pretty rough times. When I wanted to leave Texas, he decided to go with me. I wanted to get away from all the memories, and John insisted I not go alone. We grew closer and closer, and after a while we were a couple. We weren't married, but I used his last name because it seemed simpler. There you have it. I'm sorry if I misled you or JP. That wasn't my intent."

"It all makes sense now. Just be careful when you give me information, or worse, if you withhold information, because it'll come back to bite us. So, what is your last name?" Sabre asked. The tone of her voice made the question sound like a reprimand.

"It's Taylor."

"Did you tell JP that?"

"I don't remember, but I don't think I did."

"Is there anything else you think I should know?"

Betty paused for a moment, then shook her head. "Not that I can think of."

"Oh, by the way, JP asked me to get a photo of John from you.

Do you know where you have one?"

"I'm afraid I don't. I don't own a camera. I could never afford to develop the film, so I haven't owned one for years. And the new digital ones are just too technical for me. John never liked having his picture taken anyway, so I'm afraid I can't help you with that. I'm sorry."

Sabre found it very strange she didn't have even one picture of John. She looked Betty directly in the eyes, trying to see if she could read anything into her statement. Betty didn't look away. Sabre made a note on her pad about the photos. "I'll let JP know," she said. "Do you have any questions about court tomorrow?"

"What will they do at the hearing?"

"We'll enter a plea of 'not guilty' and the court will set a couple of court dates, a readiness conference, and a preliminary hearing. And hopefully we'll get a chance to argue for bail. If the judge doesn't entertain the bail issue, then a separate bail hearing will be set."

"How do they decide if there should be bail set or not?" Betty asked.

"Bail is used by the court almost like an insurance policy that you'll appear on future court dates. The amount is determined by the judge. Obviously, people with access to more money have to pay a higher bail and generally, the more heinous the crime, the higher the bail. There are really two factors in deciding if you should get bail: your risk of flight and whether you pose a danger to the community. So, in a nutshell, we'll argue you're no danger to society and you're not going anywhere."

"You said they'll set two other hearing dates. I know what a preliminary hearing is for the most part, but what is a readiness hearing?"

"The readiness conference is when we have a chance to speak to the prosecutor and negotiate your case. We can try to reach a deal that's best for you, a plea bargain. The judge may or may not be part of this process."

"But I didn't do anything. Why should I plea bargain?"

"Don't worry, we won't, but they'll set the hearing anyway." The lines seemed to grow deeper on Betty's forehead, and her eyes looked wet.

"Betty, keep your chin up. We're going to get through this. I believe in you." Sabre wanted to give Betty a hug, but was unable to because of the screen between them. She reached her hand up to the wire mesh and so did Betty, their fingers touching lightly. "I'll be back real soon," Sabre said. She saw tears rolling down Betty's face just before she turned to go.

Sabre left the detention center satisfied with Betty's explanations of both the knife and the death of her last husband. Betty was pretty distraught when she spoke with JP and could easily have made a mistake in time. And the knife would have her fingerprints on it if she handled it after the killer. The only thing Sabre really questioned was the fact that Betty didn't have a single photograph of John. It was also strange that she hadn't given JP her real last name.

Sabre called Bob to bounce it off him. He was a great sounding board. He could cut right to the chase. She needed him more than ever with this case. Sometimes it was difficult to see past her friendship with Betty.

"Hi, honey," Bob said when he answered the phone.

Sabre explained what she had just obtained from Betty. "So does that sound plausible to you?"

"Mixing up the dates is very believable. She's been pretty upset, and five years, six years, it's an easy mistake. And what difference does it make even if she hooked up with John right away? This is the twenty-first century and the guy was dead. Who cares?"

"So, what about the knife?"

"Well, that's more intriguing. It's a great way to get someone's fingerprints on the murder weapon, plant it in plain sight with an incentive for them to touch it. But you know what that means, don't you?"

"Yeah, it would have to be someone they know. Someone who knew Betty's habits and knew she would clean up before she'd go to bed."

"Any idea who that might be?" Bob asked.

"Not a clue. Neither of them seemed to have any enemies, at least not here."

"But it could be someone from his past. We don't really know anything about him."

"True. JP's working on it. He wanted a photo of John, but Betty says they don't exist. At least, she doesn't have one."

"You mean she has known this man for twenty-some years and she doesn't have one photo of him?"

"That's the story. But apparently Betty was never much of a photographer. I think her life was pretty rough sometimes in the past. She did say she could never afford to develop the pictures when she took them, so she quit taking any. She also said John didn't like his picture taken. So maybe there aren't any in her possession."

"Maybe," Bob said, but with little conviction.

"She's innocent, Bob, I know she is."

11

El Cajon Superior Court, built in the nineteen eighties, didn't have the traditional look of the courthouses Sabre so admired. It was more modern in its architecture, not giving her the feeling of grandeur and magnificence the downtown courthouse did. Sabre approached the metal detector, and greeted the bailiffs. Though she practiced mainly in Juvenile Court at Meadowlark, she occasionally went to court in El Cajon since it had a juvenile division as well. As a result, she knew some of the bailiffs who worked there.

Sabre laid her briefcase on the belt of the metal detector and walked through the door frame.

"Good morning, Sabre," said the tall bailiff with the thinning hair and wire rim glasses.

"Good morning, Jerry."

"Are you in delinquency or dependency this morning?" he asked.

"Neither. I'm here for an adult felony arraignment on a PC one-eighty-seven." She picked up her briefcase from the belt.

"A murder rap. You're moving up in the world."

"Or down, depending on how you look at it."

"True."

"Can you direct me?"

"Department Two on the first floor."

"If you see Bob Clark, will you tell him I went up to felony arraignment? He's supposed to meet me there."

"No problem."

Sabre exited the elevator and walked down the hallway to Department Two. She opened the door a few inches and looked inside. When she didn't see Bob in the crowd, she closed the door again. She took a seat outside of the courtroom and read the police report again. The only thing they'd do in court this morning is enter a plea and maybe argue for bail. She glanced through her notes for her bail argument. Sabre was not hopeful.

"Hi, Sobs," Bob said as he walked up.

"Hi. I'm glad you're here. I peeked in, but it's pretty crowded in there, and the judge hasn't taken the bench yet."

"Good. You ready to face the storm?"

"Sure, this is the easy part."

Sabre and Bob entered the noisy courtroom, walked past the gallery filled with defendants and their family members, and approached the bailiff. Sabre handed him two business cards, one of hers and one of Bob's.

"Hi. I'm Sabre Brown and this is Robert Clark. We're appearing on behalf of Betty Smith. I believe we're ninth on the calendar."

"Thanks," he said. "You may have a seat right there for now." He pointed to the front row of seats. "You're welcome to come in here when it clears out a bit and there's a little more sitting room."

"Thanks," Sabre responded. They took a seat where the bailiff had suggested.

"Do you know what that waist-high railing is called?" Bob asked quietly, although court was not in session yet.

"What railing?"

"The one right in front of you."

"No, but I bet you're going to tell me."

"It's called a 'bar,' and it's a wooden barrier used to separate the two parts of the courtroom. Apart from the parties in a case and any witnesses, only the lawyers may literally pass the bar. Have you ever noticed that even the court personnel and jury members usually enter through separate doors? That's the reason the term 'the bar' has come to refer to the legal profession as a whole."

"Well, aren't you just filled with useless information," Sabre teased.

"Hey, attorneys should know this crap. It's part of our...."

"Will the court please come to order. The Honorable Judge Lark presiding." The bailiff spoke in a strong, loud voice. A hush came over the courtroom as the black-robed judge entered and took a seat behind the bench. He stood about six feet tall and possessed a round belly and receding hairline. On the wall behind him was the great seal of the State of California; on either side of the seal hung a California state flag and a United States flag. Sabre was always impressed with the seal. It looked so important up there. She noticed it every time she entered a courtroom.

Bob and Sabre sat there while the court called three cases. A door to the left opened, and two bailiffs walked in with six female prisoners chained together. They all took a seat on a bench behind a glass wall. The bailiffs stood on either end of them. Betty was the third from the end. Sabre's heart skipped a beat and her chest constricted. She told herself to breathe, knowing she needed to be strong for Betty. She watched Betty closely until she looked back at her. Sabre nodded her head so Betty would know she was there for her. It seemed to help. Betty's droopy eyes and turned-down mouth seemed to level off a little when she saw Sabre. Sabre had trouble making sense of all this—how could she expect it of Betty? Betty shouldn't be there. It was bad enough her husband was dead, but she couldn't even imagine how she must feel being charged with his murder.

The court called a drunk driving case. The judge said, "How do you plead?"

"Not guilty, Your Honor," the defendant responded.

His attorney then spoke up. "Your Honor, my client is legally blind. He was not drunk."

"And that's better...how?" the judge asked. "Give him a trial date," he said to his clerk.

Four more cases were called before they heard the name "Smith."

Sabre stood up, and took her place at the podium. "Sabre Orin Brown appearing on behalf of Betty Smith and for the record, Your Honor, Betty's legal name is Betty Taylor."

"Thank you, we'll correct the file."

The bailiff brought Betty to the podium still in handcuffs. The judge informed her of her constitutional rights and asked her if she understood.

"Yes, Your Honor," Betty said.

"You're charged with murder in the first degree. How do you plead?" the judge asked.

"Not guilty."

"Before we set a preliminary hearing date and readiness conference, what is the District Attorney's position on bail?" he asked, turning to the short, thin prosecutor. Sabre had never had a case against him, but knew him by reputation. He was known to be hard on witnesses, even worse on defendants when they testified, but honest and a real seeker of the truth.

"We're asking no bail be set, Your Honor. The defendant doesn't have any real ties to the community. She does not own property here, she has no employment here, no relatives here, and the seriousness of the crime doesn't warrant release. However, should the court decide to grant bail, we would request a minimum of $500,000."

"Counselor Brown, argument?"

"We disagree, Your Honor. Although my client doesn't own real property here, she does have her mobile home which has been in the same location for four years. She has her own small business here, and there is no reason to believe she's a flight risk. My client does not have relatives here, but she does have a very close circle of friends in which I'm proud to be included. She has no prior criminal record. She has never failed to appear in court. In fact, she has never had a prior arrest. She's no threat to the community. She maintains her innocence, but understanding the court must consider otherwise for purposes of bail, then this would appear to be a crime of passion, and there is no reason to believe any other member of the community would be at risk.

"My client has just lost her husband and her only means of support is a small business, selling watches at swap-meets which she must now run by herself. She doesn't have property to put up as collateral, and as we argued before, she's no risk to the community. Therefore, we ask the court to release Ms. Taylor on her own recognizance."

"It looks like we're somewhere between nothing and a half million dollars. At this juncture, I don't intend to do either," the judge said. "I want to know a little more about this woman and about the evidence the prosecutor has against her, so I'll entertain arguments again at the preliminary hearing. The prisoner is remanded to custody."

"Thank you, Your Honor," Sabre said. She looked at Betty whose face was bathed in disappointment. "I'm sorry, Betty. I'll come see you tomorrow. Hang in there."

Sabre watched as the bailiff took Betty back to her cage. Her heart ached for her. She had to find a way to get her released. She turned to Bob with tears welling up. He squeezed her hand and murmured, "Keep it together, kid." He let go before they walked out of the courtroom.

"Damn, I hate seeing her like this. She looks like she's aged ten years. How long can she last in there?"

"She's tough. You said yourself you thought she's lived a pretty rough life. I wonder what she was like when she was young."

"She's never said much of anything about her past, other than she was once a hair stylist. That's why she's always so fussy about her hair and makeup. It's just little innuendos that make me think she has been through a lot. It's not like she ever complained or anything. I get the impression she spent a lot of time just trying to make a living. I know she'll survive jail time, but if she's convicted she'll go to prison. I don't think she could take that."

"We just have to see that it doesn't happen. But you knew going in that was a possibility."

"I know. It just upsets me. She's like an aunt to me. Not just an aunt…a favorite aunt. When I was having all that trouble last year, she baked me persimmon cookies. She invited me over for dinner and to play cards. She loves to play cards. So did John. Canasta was his favorite, but when we had four people we would play whist. You have to be from the Midwest to know that game…." Sabre stopped suddenly, realizing she had been rambling. "I'm sorry. I have to get going."

Bob gave her a hug before she got in her car to leave.

All the way back to her office, Sabre thought about Betty locked up at Las Colinas. She had to find who really did this. Hoping JP had made some progress, she dialed the phone.

"Hey, kid," he said, the way he always did when she called. "How you doing?"

"Fine. I'm just leaving the El Cajon Courthouse," Sabre said. "We had Betty's arraignment this morning."

"How'd that go?"

"I was really hoping to get her released on bail, but it didn't happen."

"I'm sorry, kid."

"Me too. How's your investigation going? Anything new?"

"I can't find any enemies of John, at least nothing recent. Everyone seemed to like him. He didn't have any real vices. I haven't been able to find anyone who had any reason to kill him. And either he left the door open that night when he went to bed, which Betty said was highly unlikely, or he knew the person and let him or her in."

"Betty said there was a key hidden. Do you know if it's still there?"

"Yeah, she told me, and I checked it out. It was still under the rock, but someone could have used it and put it back. It had been used recently, so that's a possibility."

"How do you know?"

"Well, not necessarily used, but I could tell it had been moved. The earth around it was disturbed, but I haven't had the chance to ask Betty how long it's been under there. She may not even know if John had used it recently." JP paused a moment before he continued.

"Anything else?"

"Not really. In fact, I'm hitting an inordinate number of dead ends."

"What do you mean?"

"I can't get past the last four years for either Betty or John. I'm trying to look into their backgrounds to see if there are any enemies lurking out there. But I can't find any schools either of them attended. No high schools. No grade schools. Nothing."

"What are you saying? That they don't exist?"

"I found birth certificates and social security numbers, but John's social security number has activity only for the past four years; nothing at all shows up before that."

"That's odd. What about hers?"

"There's nothing recent. She has worked the business with John the past few years, and they filed everything together. Betty said she hasn't worked outside of their swap meet business for a long time. I assume they filed everything under John."

"Is this normal?"

"Not really, but it happens. I'll keep looking and maybe you could speak to Betty and see if she can shed some light on this."

Sabre headed west on I-8 toward her office. She considered turning around and going back to Las Colinas to talk to Betty first, but then she realized she'd probably still be in lock up at the courthouse or in transit. She continued to her office.

"Hi, Elaine," Sabre said to the receptionist when she walked in. Elaine's hair looked even shorter than usual.

"Good afternoon," Elaine said as she handed her a stack of phone messages and her mail. "What happened to Betty?"

"She's still in custody. I couldn't get bail ordered."

"That's too bad."

"Anything urgent in here?" Sabre held up the bundled messages.

"You received a couple of calls on the Breton case for tomorrow. I think the father is back in custody and the mother tested dirty."

"Damn it." Sabre swatted the side of Elaine's desk with her mail. "I had such high hopes for those parents, and those kids really want to go home. Stupid, stupid people. If they loved their kids half as much as they did their drugs, the kids wouldn't have to go through all this."

She walked back to her office mumbling about the idiocy of parents. But that wasn't all that was bothering her. She was eager to talk to Betty about her background check, but that would have to wait until tomorrow. She set her files down and started through her mail. She threw away the junk, put the mail that Elaine would take care of in a bin, and set her personal mail aside to deal with later. She pulled out the Breton file and returned the phone calls from the social worker.

"What's Dad in custody for?" she asked the social worker.

"He was busted for possession."

"Possession of what? He's supposed to be the one who doesn't use. Was it the hard stuff?"

"No, he had a joint in his pocket. He claims it wasn't his, and I'm not sure it was."

"So, those kids aren't going home tomorrow, but this sounds like something that can be worked out down the road. Right?"

"I agree, but Mom can't handle those kids by herself and obviously she isn't ready anyway. They need to do this as a couple."

"So, you don't think Dad is going to be back?"

"He was with a hooker when he was busted. Not just any hooker, either. He was with Sunshine."

"That's the same one he was with before."

"Yup, and Mom isn't going to take this lightly."

"What the hell is the matter with these people? I'm so sick of their stupidity."

"You okay?" the social worker asked.

"Oh, yeah." Sabre picked up her briefcase and threw her files inside, slamming it shut. "I'm fine. Just lots of things going on with me and I'm very concerned for those kids. Did you see them today?"

"No, they don't know yet that they won't be going home, but I'll go by there in a little while and talk to them."

"Thanks, I'll see you in court tomorrow."

Frustrated, Sabre dived into the other cases she had on the calendar for the next day. She read over the report for the detention hearing on a molest case, the information for a disposition on a domestic violence where a three-year-old was shot, and several reports on old cases that were up for review. Sabre was deep in thought when Elaine rushed into the room.

"You need to take the call on line one. It's Las Colinas." Elaine looked frightened.

Sabre picked up the phone. A moment later, she hung up, grabbed her purse, and rushed toward the door.

"What is it?" Elaine called after her.

Sabre paused in the doorway and took a deep breath. "Betty's in the hospital."

12

The crowded emergency room smelled of medicine and body odor. The chairs were filled with people waiting to be treated, many of them with infants and small children. An hispanic man with a gash on his arm wrapped in a bloody towel stood up to let a feeble, old woman sit down. The line at the information window numbered about ten people, all sick or hurt or with someone who was. Sabre reached in her purse and took out a Zycam chewable and popped it in her mouth to protect her in the germ-filled room. A woman in front of her coughed without covering her mouth. Sabre turned to avoid her just as the man behind her sneezed. She felt a mist hit the side of her face. She shivered. She hated hospitals, nothing but sick people there. She couldn't afford to catch something and fall behind on her caseload.

Twenty-five minutes later, Sabre approached the information window.

"I'm here to see Betty Smith, uh…Taylor." Sabre was unsure under what name Betty would be listed.

"What is your relationship to the patient?" the receptionist asked.

"I'm her attorney." She handed her bar card and identification through the hole under the glass.

The receptionist looked it over, looked at Sabre, and picked up the phone. She explained who the patient was and gave Sabre's name and information. "Thank you. I'll let her know." She passed Sabre's cards back through the opening. "The doctor is with her right now. I'm sure it'll take a while. Please have a seat and wait for your name to be called. When you hear your name, check in with the guard over there," she said, pointing to a heavy-set, African-American man in a security uniform sitting on a barstool in front of the big swinging doors to the emergency room. "He'll escort you to her bed."

"Thank you," Sabre said, and walked toward the chairs in the crowded room. Sick people hugged the wall for support. An elderly gentleman there with his ill wife offered Sabre his seat.

"Thank you. I really appreciate the offer, but you keep it. I'm not sick. I'm just here to see a friend. Stay there with your wife. She needs you." The wife mustered a smile at her. "Besides, it's going to be a while before they call me. I think I'll step outside for a little fresh air."

Four smokers stood just outside the door, one of them right next to the sign that read, "Do Not Smoke within Thirty Feet of This Building." Sabre walked farther away to avoid the secondhand smoke. She was opening her cell phone to make a call when she heard a familiar voice say, "Hey, beautiful, I bet you could use a cup of 'Joe'."

A smile covered Sabre's face as she turned around. "Luke, I'm so glad you're here."

"Oh, you're just after me for my coffee." He handed her a tall coffee cup and kissed her lightly on the lips. "It's café mocha. I had it made just the way you like it."

Sabre took a sip. "It's perfect."

"How's Betty? Is she okay?"

"I don't know anything yet. They wouldn't give me any information at the desk, except the doctor is with her and they'll call me when I can go in." Sabre slouched in frustration. She knew the receptionist couldn't give her any information, but it still upset her. This was her friend in there, and she knew Betty had no one else. Sabre was her family.

Luke led her over to a concrete wall about two feet high. He set his coffee down and then took her cup and placed it next to his. He put one hand on each side of her head and pulled her mouth into his, lips slightly apart. He kissed her cheek and her forehead and then enveloped his arms around her in a long embrace. Sabre relaxed into his body; a feeling of belonging overtook her, and she allowed herself to forget about Betty. But only for a second.

"Do you have any idea what happened to her?" Luke asked, still holding her.

"No one has said anything to me, but I heard the nurse say something about the cardiac unit, so I'm thinking she must've had a heart attack." Sabre shook her head, rubbed her face, and stepped back out of the hug.

"Does she have a history of heart problems?"

"Not that I'm aware of. Maybe it's just anxiety. A lot of people mistake it for a heart attack."

"That's probably it," Luke said, as he put his arm around Sabre and walked her to the stone bench.

Sabre sighed. They sat in the chilly night air and finished their coffee in silence, Sabre comforted by Luke's warmth. "I guess we better go in so we don't miss our chance to see Betty," she finally said.

Luke kept his arm around her as he led her back into the emergency room where they leaned against the wall and waited. After about fifteen minutes, Sabre heard her name called, or at least what she thought was her name, the pronunciation butchered. They approached the security guard and gave their names.

"I'm sorry, sir," the security guard said to Luke, "but I'm afraid you can't go in. Only her attorney and immediate family are allowed, and even then only one may go at a time."

Sabre looked at Luke apologetically. She knew he wanted to see Betty, and she wanted him by her side.

"It's okay. You go, Sabre. She needs you. Just give her my love. I'll be here when you come out." He gently squeezed her shoulder and then walked away as she entered the emergency room accompanied by another guard. Once inside, a sheriff patted her down and escorted her into the hospital room.

Betty was hooked up to a heart monitor and an IV, and another machine was checking her blood pressure. Sabre was not surprised that Betty's heart had reacted to the stress of incarceration. Betty's face was ashen gray.

Just after Sabre approached Betty's bed the heart monitor went off. A nurse hustled in, checked the monitor, and yelled "code blue." Another nurse rolled in with a crash cart, followed by a doctor. Sabre stumbled back away from the bed, feeling a shot of adrenaline run through her body as she watched the staff surround Betty. Two more nurses and a respiratory therapist entered the room. Sabre stepped back against the wall, her heart fluttering. The noise from the machines and the attendants' loud voices echoed in her ears. Everyone rushed about the room, each doing their part while Betty lay there motionless; the machine screamed for help. Then, in what seemed like slow motion, Sabre watched the doctor put paddles on Betty's chest.

"Get her out of here," the doctor snapped at the sheriff.

Sabre felt the sheriff's hand on her arm. "Let's go," he said gently but firmly as he escorted her, disoriented, from the room.

"I...I'll be in the waiting room. Will you please have someone let me know what happens? She has no one else."

"I'll make sure," the sheriff said.

Sabre found herself in the hallway, not certain just how she got there, and then worked her way through the winding pathway to the waiting room where Luke waited for her.

"You look pale. Is Betty all right?"

"Her heart stopped, and they were resuscitating her when they chased me out. I wish I knew what was happening now. The sheriff said he would let me know."

"Come here." Luke walked her to a couple of seats in the far left corner of the lobby. "Sit. May I get you anything? More coffee? Water?"

"No thanks." Sabre looked down at her feet and shook her head. She sat down, put her elbow on the arm of the chair, and held her head up with her hand. "Luke, I'm worried about her— losing John, getting charged with murder, and now this."

"I know, honey. I'm so sorry." Luke put one hand on each of Sabre's shoulders and began to massage them.

"That feels so good."

He raised her hair and rubbed the back of her neck and her head. "You're in knots, baby," he said, as he continued to rub. "Try to relax a little. There's nothing we can do right now. We just have to wait." He reached with his left hand and pulled Sabre's chin up toward him. "She's going to make it through this. She's a tough old bird. And then you're going to help her through the legal stuff. She's lucky to have you."

Sabre leaned her head on Luke's shoulder and they sat there waiting for some news. About thirty minutes later, the deputy sheriff came out with a doctor.

"Are you here for Betty Taylor?" the doctor asked.

Sabre sat up. "Yes, how is she?"

"She's stable right now, but she needs a bypass. Are you related to her?"

"No, I'm her friend and her attorney."

"Does she have any family?"

"Not that I'm aware of."

"Okay, thanks." The doctor stepped back.

"Wait. May I see her?"

"She's being prepped right now. You'll have to wait until after the surgery."

"And someone will let me know?"

"Sure." The doctor and the sheriff started to walk away. The doctor turned back and said, "She'll be in surgery for four or five hours. You may want to go home and get some sleep."

"Thanks, but I think I'll stay. I'd like to be with her when she wakes up."

Sabre laid her head back on Luke's shoulder and after a few minutes looked up at him and said, "You can leave if you'd like. I'll be all right."

He tipped his head to the side and looked her in the eyes. "I'm not going anywhere. I'm staying right here with you."

"But I know you have work to…."

"Shh…." He put his finger over her mouth. "Work can wait. I'm not leaving you here alone. I want to be here."

She took a deep breath and snuggled back into his arms. She stayed that way most of the night, occasionally dozing off, waking with every announcement made in the waiting room, and praying

Betty would be all right.

It was nearly three o'clock before the doctor returned with any news about Betty. "She's out of surgery and she's stable. Now we just have to wait and see how she does."

"May I see her?" Sabre asked.

"Right now she's in recovery, but they'll move her to the cardiac intensive care unit in an hour or so. You'll be able to see her then. She probably won't be awake, however."

"That's okay. I just want to see her. Thanks, Doc."

The dawn was breaking by the time Sabre learned she could visit Betty. She walked into the room to find her with her hands strapped to the bed, an IV in her arm, and a tube in her mouth. Equipment monitored her heart rate and oxygen level. "Hi there, Betty Smith Taylor," Sabre said, as she took Betty's hand in hers. "You trying to keep me from doing my job?" Betty lay there unable to respond. Her gray roots showed through her bright red, dyed hair. Her pale skin looked ashen, her sunken eyes embraced dark circles, and her lips were cracked and slightly bleeding.

Sabre stepped back when a nurse came in and took Betty's temperature and scribbled on her chart. Then Sabre took Betty's hand in hers. "You sure gave us a scare. I'm not willing to lose you, so you better hold on. I need you around to keep me in line. You hear me? You have a lot of living left to do." Sabre rubbed Betty's hands. They felt dry and cold. Sabre reached into the stand by Betty's bed and removed the lotion. She gently applied it to Betty's hands. "I don't know if you can hear me or not, but if you can, you just rest. I'll sit with you and bore you with my day. You don't need to talk." Another nurse came in and checked Betty's EKG. The hospital room didn't feel as quiet or cozy as other hospital rooms she had been in. She assumed that was the nature of a cardiac unit. As nurses hustled around from one room to another, machines beeped for their attention.

"I'm sorry you have to go through all this. It just isn't fair. And

I know how much you miss John. I miss him, too." A third nurse came into the room, asked Sabre to step aside for a moment, took Betty's blood pressure, and checked her pulse and her breathing. Then she added something to the IV. "What's in the IV?" Sabre asked the nurse.

"She's receiving medications to regulate her circulation and her blood pressure."

"What's with the tube in her mouth?"

"The endotracheal tube allows her to breathe. She'll have that until the doctor is confident she can breathe on her own."

"Any idea how long that'll be?"

"No, sorry, but I do know she'll need to be awake before it'll be removed."

"Thanks." Sabre turned to Betty when the nurse left. "They just won't let you rest, will they? It'll be better when they move you to a regular room. They said that should be in a day or two." Sabre sat for a while longer, dozing on and off. She remembered Luke waiting in the lobby and she kissed Betty on the forehead. "You rest. I'll be back tomorrow." She looked at the clock on the wall. "Well, later today, actually."

13

Sabre returned home just in time to shower and leave for court, her eyes red and puffy. Bob met her at the door. "Geez, you look terrible. Sleep much?"

"I dozed once in a while between intercom announcements and hysterical people entering the emergency room."

"Yeah, I got your message. How's Betty doing?"

"She's relatively stable, but as of thirty minutes ago, she was still not awake."

Bob put his hand on her shoulder. "Bypass surgery is very common now, and most people do very well. She seems to be pretty healthy otherwise, right?"

"Yeah, at least she never complained about anything." Sabre paused. "Come to think of it, she never said much of anything about herself. I thought about that this morning while I sat with her…how little I actually know about her. But she's a good person. Maybe that's all one really needs to know."

"You're quite the philosopher when you're tired. Listen, why don't we get the Breton case done and then I'll finish your calendar and you go get some sleep."

"I don't think I can sleep, but I'll take you up on your offer. I'd like to go check on Betty."

"Okay, but if she's not awake, you go home and get some rest. Got it?"

"Yes, sir." Sabre saluted Bob.

Sabre finished her case and was driving to the hospital when her phone rang.

"Hi, it's JP. Are you busy?"

"I'm on my way to see Betty at the hospital. Why? What's up?"

"Is she awake yet?"

"She wasn't when I called, but I'm going to stop in and see what I can find out."

"Sabre, we need to talk. I went to Betty's trailer this afternoon.

I didn't find much, except a death certificate for Jim Taylor. I'm hitting a lot of dead ends, and I mean really dead ends. It's like their lives just stop about four years back. I need to know how far you want me to go with this."

"Can we meet after I check on Betty?"

"Sure, just give me a call when you're done. I'll be in my office working."

Sabre shut off her phone as she reached the cardiac unit, confused about Betty's lack of cooperation and concerned about her health. The noise level was louder than the night before, and there was so much activity. Nurses bustled in and out of rooms with medications, doctors huddled over charts, new patients moved in, and aides performed their tasks. Sabre walked directly to Betty's room. Betty didn't look much different than when she had left there a few hours before. Her hands were still tied down, the machines still connected, and the tube in her throat remained. A nurse was taking her blood pressure.

"Has she woken up yet?" Sabre asked.

"No, I'm afraid not." The nurse turned toward Sabre. "Her vital signs are good, though. Her blood pressure is good, and her breathing is steadier."

"Thanks." Sabre stroked Betty's hair. "Hi, Betty. I'm here. We all miss you." Sabre squeezed her hand. "You've slept long enough now. You need to wake up. You hear me?"

Sabre thought how silly she must sound and she wondered if Betty could hear her. She was always told to speak to people in situations like this, that your voice might help. "You know…" Sabre yawned. "…John would want you to beat this thing. He'd tell you the same thing I am: you need to get better."

Sabre sat down and held Betty's hand, rubbing it to warm it. After a few minutes, she rose and walked to the closet. Opening the door, she took out a blanket, placed it over her friend's legs, and pulled it up to cover her hands.

When Sabre left the hospital, she called JP and made arrangements to meet him at The Coffee Bean on Balboa. She stopped at a red light at the corner of Balboa and Genesee, and after a few seconds she heard a horn honk. She jumped, startled by the noise, realizing she had dozed off. She pulled into the parking lot and spotted JP's car parked in front.

JP sat in the front of the coffee shop in an overstuffed chair, alone in the room except for a man and a woman at a far end table. He stood up as she walked in. She saw his face light up when he saw her, but his smile turned serious as she approached. "You really look beat. Have you had any sleep?"

"Not really, unless you count dozing at the stoplights."

"You need some rest. Want to do this another time?"

"No, I'm here now, and I'm fine."

"Let me get you some coffee."

"Thanks. I'll have a medium decaf Café Mocha with less coffee, more milk, and an extra scoop of chocolate. There's enough caffeine in the chocolate to keep me awake."

Four young men with briefcases walked in and took their place in line before JP reached the counter. A woman pushing a baby carriage and a grandfatherly looking man walked through the door. They all seemed to be talking at once, but Sabre found the noise lulled her. By the time JP returned with her drink, Sabre had laid her head on the back of the soft chair and closed her eyes.

"Sabre?"

She jolted awake and sat up straight. "Sorry, I guess I'm sleepier than I thought." She took a sip of her coffee. "That's perfect. Thanks. So you said you were having trouble finding information. What does that mean?"

"Everything seems to just stop about the time Betty and John came to California. There's no record of social security activity. I can't find anything about their past work, education, insurance coverage, driver's licenses, or anything else. It's like their life just started here."

"So, what are you saying? Betty Taylor and John Smith didn't exist before then?"

"Maybe." JP stared at Sabre, head tilted, eyebrow raised.

"That's crazy. You must have something wrong, social security numbers or something."

"That wouldn't explain the lack of DMV records."

"Well, there must be an explanation."

"Oh, I'm sure there is." JP looked over his coffee cup as he sipped it. "Sabre, don't you think it's funny there are no photographs of John? I bet there are none of Betty either."

"Betty explained that."

"And you're satisfied with her explanation?" He paused, but Sabre didn't respond. "There's something very wrong here. Something Betty isn't telling you."

"She didn't kill him, JP. I know she didn't," Sabre said, raising her voice.

JP spoke softly. "Maybe she did, maybe she didn't, but either way she's lying to you because what she's telling you doesn't add up."

Sabre's leg started to shake. She held her coffee in one hand and rubbed her forehead with the other. "She didn't kill him," her voice louder.

"I know you want to believe her, but you have to wake up. She's hiding something." JP raised his voice to the same level as Sabre's.

"She didn't do it. I'm telling you she didn't do it," her voice rose.

"Sabre, listen to yourself. You can't even consider the possibility. So, do you want me to continue the investigation?"

"Of course, we have to, but read my lips." Sabre stood up, leaned in towards JP, and yelled out one word at a time. "Betty…didn't… kill…John." The chatter in the coffee shop stopped. Sabre looked around; all eyes focused on her. She moved toward the door. JP stood up, walked over to her, put his arm around her shoulder, and led her back to her chair.

"Okay, I'm listening, but you can't tell how deep a well is by measuring the length of the pump handle."

"Huh?" Sabre made a face of confusion. JP's Texas sayings always made her smile.

"I have to look at it from all sides when I investigate, or I'm going to miss something important."

"You're right." Sabre sighed. "So now what?"

"Now I need to go to Texas…Austin, Texas."

"Why Austin? I thought Betty told me they lived in Amarillo before they came here."

"Well, the address Betty gave me of their last residence was in Austin, and I found something in Betty's things indicating her last husband, Jim Taylor, died in Austin."

"Geez, what the hell is going on? Don't I know this woman at all?"

"I don't know, kid." He stroked her arm. "You go home and rest. I know it's only a few blocks, but no more falling asleep at stoplights. If you get sleepy, call me on my cell. I'll keep you awake." He squeezed her shoulder. "And I'm going to Texas."

14

JP stepped off the plane, his first time in Austin. He had been to Texas before. In fact, he was born there, but he'd never been to Austin. He picked up his suitcase from baggage and walked over to the Alamo counter to obtain the rental he had reserved the night before, his cowboy boots sounding like taps on the hard surface.

"Will an SUV be okay, or would you rather have a pickup?" the gray-haired, male clerk asked.

"Does the pickup come with a shotgun or rifle strapped along the back?"

The clerk laughed. "No, sir, but don't think it hasn't been suggested in one of those local Texas board meetings."

"You know, the pickup might be better. Maybe I'll blend in."

"Well, sir, you certainly look the part, with your boots and that mighty fine cowboy hat you're sportin'. It doesn't look like a costume, either; seems to have some wear. But if you're trying to blend in, your accent will give you away right off."

"I'll have to see what I can do 'bout that," JP said in his best Texas drawl. Having spent the first ten years of his life in Texas, the accent came back naturally.

"Not bad for a city slicker from California."

JP signed the papers, picked up his keys, tipped his hat, and strutted off cowboy style.

JP checked into the Embassy Suites on Highway Thirty-Five. He wanted to work out, but he needed to get to the government offices before they closed. He drove west on East Koenig Lane, just as the GPS instructed him to do. After several turns he reached the Texas Vital Statistics Office. He took the copy of the death certificate for Jim Taylor he had found in Betty's trailer and approached the desk.

"Howdy, ma'am," JP said to the attractive, fortyish, slightly overweight clerk.

"Howdy." She smiled. "What may I do for you?"

"I just need a little information, Stella," he said, reading her name tag. "My, that's one beautiful necklace you're wearing. Is it turquoise?"

"Thank you. Yes, it is turquoise. It's made locally."

"My name is JP Torn. I'm an investigator doing a little work for this lawyer out of California who's trying to see that a rather large inheritance gets delivered. But I need to verify the death, and so I'm here to do just that. The name is Jim or James Taylor. Here's the information," he said handing her a piece of paper. "Date of birth, social security number, date he died. Do you need anything else?"

"Actually," she hesitated, "I need a letter from the closest relative or a court order. Since you aren't immediate family I can't make you a copy of the death certificate."

"Dang." He raised his hat and scratched his head. "You see, here's my problem. We're pretty certain he died in Austin, but if that's not correct, then I need to go back to the drawing board and figure out where to start looking. If we're right, then the lawyer can get the court order."

"I'm sorry, JP."

He started to gather up his papers and then stopped. "Look, could you do this much for me? Just check to see if you have anything on file for him. Then at least I'll know where to start." He smiled at her. "I don't need any information about him; just let me know if I'm in the right place…please."

"I guess I can do that much."

"Oh, thank you, thank you."

"Give me the info." She took his paper and walked to another room.

JP sat down in a chair against the wall. He picked up a copy of "Texas Parks and Wildlife" magazine and thumbed through it, admiring the beautiful countryside. Stella was gone about ten minutes before she returned to the counter.

"JP," Stella called to him. "I'm sorry, but I can't find anything that'll help you. There are no deaths that day recorded for James or Jim or any Taylor. I spelled it in all the possible spellings. There was no one with that social security number or birth date. I even tried two days prior to his death and two days after. Nothing." She shook her head, "Sorry."

"Thank you very much. You've been a big help. At least now I know what I have to do and the heirs will just have to wait a little longer for their money. Thanks again."

Before he drove off, JP picked up his cell to call Sabre and then stopped. He didn't really have anything important to share yet. Although he'd like to talk to her, he needed a better reason to check in. He opened an envelope and retrieved the address Betty had given him of her residence in Austin and punched it into the GPS system. Nothing came up in Austin. He double-checked the address. "Damn it, that woman gave me the wrong address. What the hell is going on with her?"

JP pulled away from the government building. He turned right on to Sunshine Drive and then made a slight right on to North Lamar Blvd. He drove for three or four miles before he realized he was heading away from his hotel. He reached over to enter the address in the GPS system, but this model wouldn't work while he was moving. Trying to follow his instincts to get to the freeway he made several turns then spotted a coffee shop. The big red ball on top of the building had white letters that read "Jo's." He was ready for a cup of 'Joe.' He could regroup, figure out his next step, and maybe even find something—anything—about Betty before he called Sabre.

The quaint coffee shop welcomed him as he walked in. He picked up his hot, black, half-caf coffee and found a seat in the corner. He opened his envelope and shuffled through the papers until he found the death certificate he had confiscated from Betty's home. He had also taken a few other things he thought might help him, but it was difficult to find anything with Austin, Texas on it. He was starting to wonder if Betty ever lived in

Austin when he realized the death certificate had an address.

JP finished his coffee, walked to his car and typed in the address. The GPS guided him to a mobile park. He drove into the park past the garden setting entrance. Trees lined the driveways, providing shade to the campers and residents and lending a country atmosphere. There was no park space listed on the death certificate and JP didn't have any photos. He would need to be careful with his questions. He parked his car and walked until he found the area containing primarily permanent residents. He spotted a wavy, gray-haired gentleman in jeans and a t-shirt that read "Remember nine-eleven." He looked at least sixty-five and was sitting on an aluminum lounge chair in front of his trailer, drinking a bottle of "Lone Star" beer.

"Hello. How are you this fine evening?" JP asked.

"Finer than frog fur," the man answered without a smile. "You?"

JP hadn't heard that expression since his grandfather passed on. He liked using his grandpa's "Texas talk." It made him feel closer to him. "I'm good, thanks. Warm day, huh? Is this typical for this time of year?"

"'Bout normal."

JP wondered how he was going to obtain information about Betty out of these people if he couldn't even get a weather report. "You live here year around?"

"Yup."

"It appears to be a nice park. I'm thinking about renting a space here. Thought I'd look around a bit first."

"Yup, nice place." He took a long sip of beer.

"You lived here long?"

"A few months. I like it. Not so sure 'bout the Mrs., though."

"You have a good day, now," JP said as he walked off.

JP continued to walk around the park, receiving similar responses to his questions. He needed to find someone who was living there at the time of Jim's death. He came upon another gentleman who was outside smoking a cigarette. "Good evening," JP said.

"Good evening." The man smiled, looked JP over, and asked, "I don't recollect seeing you before. Are you a new resident or just a camper?"

"Neither. I'm thinking about renting space here and wanted to have a look at the place first," JP said, excited someone was actually having a conversation with him. "You lived here long?"

"Just over five years. It's quiet and comfortable."

"I had some friends who lived here a few years back, but I lost contact with them. I was hoping they were still here."

"What's the name?"

"Betty and Jim Taylor. Do you know them?"

"Hmm…maybe. What'd they look like?"

"I knew her better than him, but she's a little, short thing with bright red hair. At least it was red when I knew her. You never know with these women what color their hair will be from one day to the next."

The man chuckled. "There was a couple living a few spaces down, right over there," he pointed to a spot with a trailer and built-in porch, "when I moved in here. The woman who lived there was named Betty. She couldn't have been more than five feet tall, but I don't remember any red hair. They were only there a few months after I moved in."

JP sighed. "Well, thanks for your information. They always spoke highly of this place so I'm going to look around a little more and make my decision." JP turned to leave.

"Wait, my wife might have more information on your friends. She lived here for five or six years before we got married. She knows everything that goes on in this place. If she doesn't know them, then you have the wrong park." The man laughed at his own joke. "Let me get her."

"Thanks. I'd appreciate that."

"My name is Bill, by the way." He put his cigarette between his lips and reached out to shake hands.

"JP," he reciprocated.

The man walked up to the door and called, "Alice, could you come out here a minute?"

Alice stepped out of the trailer, a short, round woman with her gray hair pulled back in a bun and a white apron wrapped around her bright red dress. JP thought she looked like Mrs. Claus. "Yes, dear, what is it?"

"This nice gentleman used to have some friends who lived here. He was wondering if you remember them…Jim and Betty Taylor. Does that ring a bell?"

"Of course I do. They were delightful people. They lived right over there." She pointed to the same spot her husband had earlier. "How are they?"

"I'm not sure. I kind of lost track of Betty after Jim died."

"Oh!" Alice took a deep breath. "I'm so sorry. Jim was such a nice man, always so kind to everyone. What happened?"

"A heart attack, I believe." JP wrinkled his forehead. "Weren't they living here when he died?"

"No, they left together."

"I was hoping I could find some information that would lead me to them. Do you happen to know where they went when they left here?"

"I'm sorry, I don't." She shook her head. "Know one here knows."

"Why's that?"

"They left in the night, about three in the morning, actually. They never said a word to anyone. One of the neighbors saw them hitch up and leave, but he didn't talk to them, just saw them from his window. That was about four or five years ago. No one here in the park ever heard from them again."

"You're sure of that? Did they have other friends here, maybe?"

"Oh yeah, I'm sure. I was Betty's best friend. If she'd have contacted anyone, it would've been me. We were very close."

"So you knew their friend John?"

"There's a John who lives here. We were all friends, but he wasn't that close to them."

"No, this John knew them both for many years before they moved here."

"I don't know him." She rubbed her hand on her chin. "I don't remember them ever having anyone visit them from outside the park. We were their family."

JP thanked them for their information and left. He called Sabre and left her a message to call him. He needed to let her know this wasn't adding up. JP snapped his spiral notebook shut and shoved it into his pocket. Frustrated with Betty's lies, he drove back to the hotel, showered, changed his clothes, and went out to eat some dinner and have a drink.

The concierge gave him a recommendation for a restaurant/bar where they served ribs; after all, this was Texas. He ate his dinner, then went into the bar and ordered a Tecate. His watch said nine o'clock, but that meant seven in California. No wonder he wasn't tired. A band took the stage and began to play a Garth Brooks song. He thought of Sabre. Just then a tall, thin, closing-time attractive, thirty-something woman walked up.

"Hi, cowboy."

"Hi. How are you this evening?" JP said.

The woman smiled, showing sparkling white teeth against her deep red lipstick. "Yer not from these parts are you, cowboy?"

"California," he said.

"Wow, I've never been, but I hear it's beautiful. Do you know any movie stars?"

"No, I'm from San Diego. We don't see too many movie stars there." JP took a drink of his beer.

"Would you like to dance, cowboy?"

"I'm not much of a dancer." He felt badly turning her down. No one likes to be rejected. He added, "Maybe after a few beers."

She spotted someone else she appeared to know at the bar. "Okay, cowboy. I'll be back a little later." She flitted off.

JP thought about Sabre. He would dance with her if she were here.

15

JP awoke at five o'clock Texas time, too early to call Sabre. He donned a pair of shorts and a t-shirt and went to the hotel gym. The early morning workout was just what he needed to start him rolling. Still too early to call Sabre, he showered and then went downstairs to eat breakfast at the complimentary buffet. He went through the line, picked up some scrambled eggs, bacon, and country fried potatoes, put two slices of sourdough bread in the toaster, picked up a pack of butter, and then put it back down. He had enough cholesterol on his plate already.

Only a few people were sitting on the veranda, so JP found a seat close to the coffee pot. He filled his cup, all caffeinated, and sat down to eat. He poured catsup on his eggs and potatoes. Sabre used to tease him about his overuse of catsup, but she used it on her eggs and potatoes, too. She just didn't use it on everything else she ate, as she had often accused him of doing. He missed her living at his house, seeing her every day, smelling her cologne. He was sorry her condo had burned to the ground, but he was thankful for every minute he had with her because of it. Maybe Bob was right; maybe he should've let her know how he felt, but he was too old. She needed someone her age, like Lucas…but not Lucas. He didn't like that guy. He wanted to like him, for Sabre's sake, but he didn't. He knew he wouldn't like anyone who was with Sabre. It wasn't Lucas's fault. Who could blame the guy?

He finished eating and sat there awhile drinking his coffee. He made his second cup half-caf and his third all decaf. He went outside and took a little walk, killing time until he could call Sabre. At about nine o'clock, he decided he had waited long enough.

"Good morning, JP." She sounded so cheerful and close. He felt warm inside.

"You sound rested this morning."

"Yeah, I went home yesterday and fell asleep. I didn't wake up until about five this morning."

"How's Betty? Any word?"

"I called the hospital and spoke with the nurse. She seems to be stable, but very groggy and weak."

"But she's awake?"

"Yeah, but she still has the tube, so she can't talk yet. I'm going to court this morning, and after that I'll stop by and see her," Sabre said. "What've you found in Austin?"

"Well, there's no death certificate filed for Jim or James Taylor on that day or any day close."

"What does that mean?"

"Not sure, but I don't think he died where Betty says he did."

"I don't understand."

"Well, the address Betty gave me for where they were supposedly living doesn't exist; nothing is even close. There's no street by that name in Austin. But the copy of the death certificate for Jim that Betty had among her things listed his residence at time of death at a trailer park in Austin. I went there and spoke with someone who knew her, a woman named Alice. She said Betty and Jim left stealthily in the night, and no one ever heard from them again." Sabre was silent. "Sabre, are you there?"

"Yeah, just trying to make sense of it." She paused again. "So, where do we go from here?"

"I wouldn't say anything to Betty yet. I have a hunch I want to check out, but I need you to do something for me."

"Sure, what's that?"

"I need you to fax me a copy of John's photo from the police file. Since that's the only picture we have of him, it'll have to do. Also, I'd like you to go through Betty's cell phone, get me her most recent calls, and write down the names and numbers of anyone in her contact list you don't know."

"May I ask why?"

"It's just a hunch. Let me play this out. If I come up with anything, you'll be the first to know."

"I don't know." Sabre hesitated. "This makes me uncomfortable, but I guess you're right. If she's hiding something we need to find out what it is."

JP walked to the business office of the hotel and picked up his fax from Sabre with the information he had requested. Not much in the phone numbers looked too promising; no phone numbers appeared for anyone in Texas. He put the faxes in his envelope and drove back to the trailer park to see Alice.

"Good morning, Bill," JP said as he walked up. "Is Alice around?"

"Yup, she sure is." Bill took a puff on his cigarette, dropped it on the ground, and stepped on it. "I'll get her." He walked up to the door. "Alice, that feller, JP, is here to see you."

Alice walked outside with another woman about the same age. "Hi, JP. Nice to see you again. This here's Rose. She lives five doors up." She nodded in the same direction as Betty's old lot, then turned to Rose. "JP here is friends with Betty and Jim Taylor. He was wondering if anyone knew where they moved to. I told him no one here knew; the last we saw was them moving out in the middle of the night."

"That's right," Rose said. "Don't have any idea where they went to."

"Did you know their friend, John?" JP asked Rose.

"Nope, didn't know no one named John." She shook her head and then looked down at her feet, avoiding eye contact with JP.

JP observed her body language. "Do you mind looking at something for me? It's a little bit morbid, but I came across something that concerned me and I want to make sure Betty isn't in trouble." He took out the photo of John's dead body Sabre had faxed him and showed the two women. "Do you know this man?"

"Yes, that's Jim," Alice answered, her eyes wide at the sight of the dead man in the picture. "So he did die. What a shame!"

JP watched Rose as she saw the photo. Her face turned somber, tears starting to well up in her eyes. She swallowed and took a breath, composing herself. "You okay?" JP asked.

"Yes, just surprised. I had no idea Jim was dead. He was such a good man, always there to help everyone."

"Did you know them well?"

"Not that well, just trailer park buddies," Rose said.

Alice wrinkled her brow at Rose. "Yeah, she's right. Betty was really my friend. She spent a lot of time with me." She shook her head. "Poor thing, losing her husband."

"I better be going," Rose said, as she took a step toward her house.

"What's your hurry, Rose? You were going to help me with that crochet stitch, remember?"

"I'm sorry, Alice, another time. My stomach is acting up again." She walked off.

"I think the photo upset her." Alice said, as she turned to JP. "She has a weak stomach."

"Yeah, I'm sorry I brought it out. I better go, too. Thanks again."

As soon as JP left he called Sabre. "Do you still have Betty's cell phone?"

"Yes, why?"

"I want you to check it in the next ten or fifteen minutes and see if she received a call. If so, get me the number."

"Okay, but what's going on?"

"I think I may have found someone who knows the scoop on Betty and John. I'll catch you up as soon as I follow up on this."

"Wait, I'm turning her phone on now." She paused. "A call came in about two minutes ago with a five-one-two area code."

"Bingo! That's it."

"How did you know a call was coming in?"

"Just a hunch. I'll call you back." JP hung up and walked toward Alice's trailer, counted five down, and stopped near Rose's place. He dialed the number Sabre had given him but didn't push send. Keeping his finger on the send button of his cell phone inside his pocket, he walked up to her front door and knocked.

Rose came to the door. "Hi, Rose. We need to talk about Betty."

"I told you everything I know, and I'm really not feeling well. Could we do this another time?"

"I'm sorry, but it's very important, and I know you called her after you left here."

"I don't know what you're talking about. I didn't call anyone." JP pushed the send button on his phone. "There's my phone now. I need to get that." She started to walk away.

"That's me calling, Rose. I got the number off Betty's phone."

"Look, I don't know anything." She turned and faced JP, but stayed back from the door. "I don't know where she is. I didn't know Jim was dead. I don't know anything." Rose trembled as she spoke. "Please don't hurt me. I really don't know anything."

"I'm so sorry," JP said through the screen. "I'm not here to hurt you. I'm not here to hurt anyone. Come out here and sit down, outside here where everyone can see us, and I'll tell you what I know. Maybe we can help each other…and Betty."

Rose came out, still shaking, and reluctantly sat down.

"You didn't know John…er…Jim was dead, did you?"

Her voice cracked when she spoke, "No, I didn't. What happened?"

"He was murdered." JP didn't want to blurt it out, but there was no other way.

"Oh, my God." Rose gasped. "And Betty, is she…?"

"No, she's alive, but she's in the hospital. She had a heart attack. She's stable now, but we haven't been able to talk to her since she had her surgery two days ago."

Betty sat there, shaking her head in disbelief. "Who are you, anyway?"

"I'm a private investigator. I work for Betty's attorney."

"Why does Betty have an attorney?"

"She's been charged with Jim's murder."

"That's ridiculous. She wouldn't kill Jim. They loved each other more than anyone I've ever met. They gave up everything to be together."

"What do you mean? What did they give up?"

"I don't know exactly. I just know they had another life they had to walk away from, and then one day they had to leave this one. She told me that day she was leaving, but I'm sure she didn't tell anyone else. And she never told me what she was afraid of, just that they had to go, that their lives were in danger."

"Did you know where they moved to?"

"No, she didn't want me to know in case someone came looking for her. She didn't want me to be in danger. I was so scared when I saw you at Alice's."

"I didn't handle that very well. I'm sorry," JP apologized. "I'm thinking her past caught up to her, and Jim was killed because of it. We don't even know if they were after her, or him, or both of them. Did she ever say anything that might give us a clue where to start looking?" JP paused. He looked at Rose pleadingly. "The only way we're going to clear Betty is to find who really killed her husband."

"What has Betty told you?"

"Not much. She's apparently still afraid of what might happen if she talks. I don't know if she's afraid for herself or someone else. Did she have any family?"

"Not that I know of. When they first moved here, they said they were from West Virginia, but I don't think they were. She didn't seem to know that much about it, and she always changed the subject when it came up, so I didn't pry. Her past was her business. We all have a past, things we regret in life. I just know they're good people."

"Thanks, Rose." She was breathing easier now, as JP handed her his business card. "Please call me if you think of anything else. I apologize again for upsetting you."

As JP started to walk away, Rose called out. "Wait. There's a possibility she spent some time in Wisconsin."

"Why do you say that?"

"Because once we were talking, and I mentioned the place where I was born, a place called Klondike Corner. When I said that, she said, 'In Brighton?' Jim gave her a very odd, stern look and Betty looked surprised, as if she suddenly realized what she'd said. When I said it was in Wisconsin she tried to say the one she knew was in West Virginia. I tried to pursue it but she clammed up. Klondike Corner is an unincorporated area in Brighton, Wisconsin. Brighton itself has a population of fewer than fifteen hundred; Klondike Corner has way less than that. It's a very small place. What are the chances of another town with the same 'corner' in another state?"

"I suppose it's possible. She never brought it up again?"

"No, she didn't. But I asked her about it once when Jim wasn't around. She said I must've misunderstood, but I know what she said. And she had such a strange reaction, even then with Jim not there. She stammered and said she had to go."

16

"Thanks for picking me up at the airport," JP said as he and Sabre walked across the parking lot to the IHOP on Balboa. JP reached around Sabre and opened the door for her.

"My pleasure. Besides you said you needed to talk to me about Betty. Do I want to hear this?"

"Probably not." They walked to a table on the patio and sat down. Sabre placed her briefcase on the seat next to her.

"Do you have any good news to tell me? If so, maybe I could have that first."

"Yes, I do. The good news is you don't need to be suspicious about the death of Betty's last husband, Jim, because he didn't die from a heart attack in Texas."

"So, he's not dead?" Sabre tipped her head to the side and curled her lip up.

"Well, actually he is dead, but he wasn't dead when Betty told you he was dead."

"What the hell are you talking about?"

"Jim and John are the same person. Jim didn't die like Betty said. Jim was very much alive when they sneaked out of Texas in the middle of the night."

"So, why did they do that?"

"I don't know. Betty's friend, Rose, thought they were afraid of someone, but who knows. They could've been running from the law. What do you know about Betty before she came to California?"

"Nothing really."

"Right, and there are no photos of anyone. No mention of family or friends. There's something very odd going on."

Sabre shook her head. "I don't get it. She's just a nice, sweet lady. What could she possibly have done?"

"I'm still working on that. I have a lead I need to follow up on, but I don't know if it means anything or not; it's something I got from Rose."

"What's that?"

"She mentioned another place Betty may have lived. I'll check it out and let you know if it leads anywhere."

The waiter took their order. Sabre sat in silence mulling over what she had just heard. When the food came, they ate with little conversation.

"We'll get to the bottom of this, Sabre." JP took a drink of his coffee.

Sabre nodded her head. "I'm sure you will, JP. I just don't know whether to be angry or sad. I still don't believe she had anything to do with John's death, but frankly, she's starting to annoy me." Sabre sighed. "When I confront Betty with this, hopefully she'll give us some straight answers."

"That would certainly make my job easier. How's she doing, by the way?"

"She's more alert. They think they can take her tube out this afternoon. I'm going to the hospital to check on her as soon as I leave here."

"Good. Do you want me there with you?"

"No. I think I'll try it alone first. She may be more willing to open up. Besides, I want you to do a little investigating into another case for me." Sabre opened her briefcase, removed a file, and handed it to JP. "This is the Kemp case."

"What am I looking for?"

"I need a background check. Their criminal record is already listed. There's nothing for the mother, but Mr. Kemp has a trespassing charge in Charleston, West Virginia. See what that's all about."

"Is that it?"

"See if there are any other criminal charges the department might have missed. And see if there's anything else unusual that might help me determine what level of protection these children need."

"I'll get right on it."

Sabre reached for the check, but JP picked it up before she could. "I've got it."

Sabre didn't fight with him. She knew it was no use. "Thanks." She smiled.

They left the table and walked outside toward the car. JP put his arm around Sabre's shoulder. "I'm sure there's some reasonable explanation for all this," he said, as he gently squeezed her arm.

"I expect so," Sabre responded. She found some relief in JP's confidence. "Thanks."

Sabre dropped JP at his house and drove to the hospital where she found Betty sitting in her slightly elevated bed, with her tube gone. "Hi, you're looking a lot better today."

"Thanks, I am." Betty, still in her hospital gown, hair uncombed, and no make-up spoke weakly.

"And she speaks," Sabre announced. "Good to see you're doing better. You had us all worried."

Betty forced a smile and in a hoarse voice said, "Sorry I'm so much trouble."

"You're no trouble." Sabre took a deep breath, wondering if she should question Betty.

"What's the matter?"

Sabre shook her head. "Nothing that can't wait. We'll talk tomorrow if you're feeling up to it."

"Thanks." Betty laid her head back and scooted down. "Could you lower my bed for me? I'm really tired."

"Sure."

Sabre sat at the bedside until Betty fell asleep. She drove back to her office and attempted to prepare for the next morning's hearings. She had a trial to prepare for. She had to stay focused, but Betty and John, or Jim, whatever his name was, kept creeping into her thoughts. *She's afraid of something. I hope she didn't commit a crime. God, I hope she didn't kill John. No way. She couldn't have.*

The phone rang, startling her. It was Luke. "How would you

like to go out on the town tonight?"

Sabre smiled, welcoming the distraction, and giddy at the thought of spending time with him. "Sure, I'd like that. Where do you want to go?"

"You just go home. I'll pick you up. Dress nicely, but casually. Oh, and wear comfortable shoes. We both know you have plenty to choose from," he teased.

Sabre put on a nice pair of black slacks, a light-weight red and black sweater, and a cushy pair of black boots. She was ready when her date arrived. "You look scrumptious," Luke said, nibbling at her neck.

Chills ran down Sabre's back as she reached up and put her arms around his neck. He worked his way around her face, kissing her gently, until he reached her open lips. "Hmm...you taste scrumptious, too." He swooped down and picked her up and started toward the bedroom.

"I thought we were going out."

Luke swung her around. "Right, and I have reservations. I lost my head for a moment. I guess we better go."

"So, where are we going?"

"You'll see."

Sabre picked up her new leather jacket and slipped it on. It fit her form perfectly, stopping at her waist. She zipped it up about six inches. "Well, at least tell me if I'm dressed all right?"

"You're perfect...in every way."

Sabre smiled at him. They walked to his car. He opened her door, and then closed it behind her. When he got in the car he reached over and squeezed her leg, then started the engine and drove off. *Maybe I've finally found the man of my dreams. Heaven knows, I've waited long enough.*

"What are you thinking and smiling about?" Luke asked.

"Just happy to be here with you," Sabre said, unable to wipe the smile off her face.

Luke winked at her. He drove south on I-163 until it ended,

continued on Tenth Street until he reached Market, and turned right.

"Dick's Last Resort?" Sabre asked.

"Nope."

"Good. Last time I went there, I was in a food fight. I don't want to ruin my new jacket."

"You?" He looked at her curiously, emphasizing the word "you." "You had a food fight?"

"Yeah, it's a pretty crazy place. The table next to us started it, but we joined right in. We were there for Bob's birthday and almost everyone had had too much to drink. Marilee, Bob's wife, got hit in the back of the head with a French fry, and she turned around and slung a spoonful of cole slaw at their table. The food really started to fly after that. I was a designated driver, so I didn't have an excuse for acting like the drunks, but I got caught up in it just the same."

"You amaze me. I don't think I've ever been in a food fight... certainly not in a restaurant...and not since I was maybe ten... no, not even then. I flicked a spoon full of ice cream at my cousin once at the dinner table. I thought my dad was going to kill me. He said I couldn't have ice cream for a month, so I gave it up for Lent and figured I'd kill two birds with one stone."

"So, you do have a wild streak?"

"I was ten."

"We'll have to go to Dick's sometime when you feel like letting your hair down."

"Maybe...or not." He drove on Market until it ended, then turned right past Kansas City Barbecue.

"That's where they filmed *Top Gun*."

"I love that movie, but I've never been to that restaurant. You'll have to take me there sometime." Luke signaled a left turn.

"Seaport Village? This is one of my favorite spots in San Diego!"

"I know." He smiled. He looked content in his choice.

They parked the car and walked up the hill to The Harbor House, a restaurant in Seaport Village. The maitre d' seated them at a table next to the window with a view of the water. "Is this okay?" Luke asked.

"It's perfect." Sabre looked out at the beautiful Pacific. An elderly couple walked by on the boardwalk holding hands. She wondered if they had been together for a lifetime. A caricature artist sat on the grass drawing a picture of a young girl with knee-length hair. Next to him stood a clown making balloon animals. He handed a little boy a balloon giraffe almost as big as the boy.

Luke reached across the table and picked up Sabre's hand, lacing his fingers through hers. "I want you to tell me about your day, and then let's set work aside for the rest of the evening and just enjoy each other."

"Deal. You go first. How was your day?"

"Uneventful, mostly. I have a company I work with in Dallas that's having some program glitches. So far I've been able to deal with it from here, but I may have to go there for a few days if I can't get it all solved."

"Does that happen often, where you have to go onsite to fix something?"

"Actually, it does. I've been lucky the past few months in not having to go anywhere. I generally average at least one trip a month." Sabre was pleased Luke was sharing more of himself with her.

"How long are you usually gone?"

Before he could answer, the waiter came to their table and Luke placed the order for both of them. "That's what you wanted, right?" He said to Sabre.

"Exactly, special requests and all."

"The length of the trips depends on a lot of things. Most of the time it's only for a day or two, but it may be as much as a week or so. I think the longest was about three weeks, but that was a real mess." He reached across the table and caressed her hand. "How's Betty doing?"

"Not ready to run a marathon yet, but she's doing much better. They took her tube out and she was able to talk to me for a bit."

"But?" Luke looked at Sabre with compassion. "Something else is bothering you. What is it?"

Sabre wrinkled her forehead. "Do you think Betty could've killed John?"

Luke's head snapped up. "Sabre, what is it? Why would you ask that?"

Sabre shook her head from side to side and shrugged her shoulders. "It's just that the investigation is turning up some unusual stuff. I can't really talk about the details. I'm just wondering what your gut feeling is?"

"No. My gut says 'no'. You certainly know her better than I do, but I don't think she has it in her. She's just a sweet, old woman… spunky, but not mean or malicious. No, I don't think so." Luke paused. "Have you found evidence that she murdered him?"

Sabre shook her head. "No, nothing like that. Just some things in her background that don't add up."

"Hey, we all have stuff in our past we're not proud of."

"Yeah. What do you have in your past besides flicking ice cream at your cousin?" The waiter brought them warm brie and a basket of bread.

Luke waited until the man turned away from their table and then said, "I stole a microscope from a science lab in high school on a dare."

"Well, lock you up and throw away the key."

"The stupid part is I got caught returning it."

Sabre laughed. "You're right; that wasn't too smart."

"Look, sweetie, I know you're used to using your mind on your cases, but this is Betty. You know her. Maybe you have to go with your heart on this one. I think it'll make your job easier."

"You're right."

The waiter returned with a tossed salad for Luke and a California spinach salad with avocado, berries, and toasted sunflower seeds for Sabre. She dug right in.

"So, enough about work?"

"Yeah, just you and me now. Tell me, is there anything else

in your past I should know about? Any other heinous crimes you've committed? Now is the time to unburden yourself." Sabre snickered.

"Nothing I'm ashamed of. I went to Catholic schools all my life, so the guilt was instilled in me. I'd be haunted if I did anything the church didn't approve of."

"So, you were a little angel in school?"

"I wouldn't go that far. I never smoked or did the drug scene. I got drunk at my senior prom, but I didn't drive. I got good grades. I played a lot of sports; that kept me focused and out of trouble. How about you?"

Sabre thought back to a simpler time. "I never did anything really awful, but I could never seem to make it home on time. My brother, Ron, used to drag me off the dance floor at parties to make curfew. He was the mischievous one, always doing something he shouldn't, but he never seemed to get caught. He used to tell me not to bring attention to myself with the small stuff, like curfew." Sabre leaned back in her chair as a passing busboy reached across the table and whisked away their empty salad plates. "My parents always thought I was the troublemaker because I spent so much time grounded for silly things. Ron never seemed to get grounded. I guess he was a smarter delinquent than I was."

Their waiter appeared with a plate of mixed, grilled seafood for Sabre and cioppino for Luke.

"Wow, that looks good. What's in it?"

"It has fish, shrimp, mussels, clams, and scallops. It also has tomato, wine, and olive oil. We call it an Italian fisherman's stew. Some places serve it in a bowl; here they put it over linguini. Want a taste?"

"Sure."

Luke picked up his fork and cut off a portion of his stew for Sabre. She leaned over the table and he fed her the bite. A noodle hung down the side of her mouth. She slurped it in and Luke laughed. "Done like a true Italian."

The cartoonist and the clown with the balloons were still doing a good trade as Sabre and Luke reached the boardwalk after dinner. They strolled along the water, stopping to breathe in the cool ocean air, and snuggling and kissing at every opportunity. Sabre breathed deeply when they passed Upstart Crow, taking in the sweet aroma of the coffee. They stopped for a few moments to watch the ducks swim under the little bridge, and then they meandered through the unique shops that made the area so appealing to tourists. Stopping at the hat shop, they tried on a few hats and laughed at the sight of Luke in a bright pink stovepipe.

They reached the middle of the village just as a juggler was about to start his show. They took a seat on the rock wall. A crowd gathered—old people, young people, some sitting, most standing. The juggler started talking as he warmed up, encouraging the people to form a circle. "Come up a little closer." A few moved; most stood still. "Just move your feet and your body will follow," he said. The crowd lingered, bringing more people together around him until he was completely surrounded. The juggler talked as he threw his balls in the air, making jokes. Everyone laughed. He threw three balls up in the air, first in a column pattern, then in a shower, and finally in the traditional cascade. The crowd cheered as he added additional balls to the shower and the cascade, first four, and then five. They applauded. When he reached six balls, his hands moved so fast they left a blur. The group cheered even when he dropped one. "Part of the act," he said, and then picked up four juggling pins and started again. The noise stopped as the crowd watched him take out three machetes and toss them in the air, "Don't try this at home," he said, as he tossed the machete under his leg. He lit three torches and juggled them. A man started to walk away. "Hey," he yelled at him, "where are you going?"

"Uh, home…."

"I didn't leave when you came," the juggler chided and the crowd clapped.

The juggler continued with his performance. Just before the end of the show, he placed a top hat on the ground for tips. Luke walked up and put a twenty dollar bill in his hat. Sabre smiled, impressed with his generosity.

"I'd like a cup of coffee. You interested?" Luke asked.

"Yeah, and my favorite coffee shop slash bookstore is here at Seaport." They walked around the corner past The Hat Shop and The Christmas Store to Upstart Crow. "I even love the name of this place," Sabre said as they walked in. It smelled of brewed coffee, cinnamon, chocolate, and newly bound books. "Yumm…."

They ordered their coffee and took a seat at a table for two in a corner. This was Sabre's favorite part of a relationship. The part where you're comfortable enough to speak freely, loving enough to touch a lot, yet new enough to still have some mystery.

After coffee, they took another stroll to the end of the boardwalk and then to the carousel. "Want to ride?" Luke asked.

"Love to."

Luke took her hand and led her past a horse-drawn chariot, a dragon, several horses, and a teddy bear. He stopped at a beautiful dark stallion with its head high in the air and its mane blowing in the wind. He made sure she was seated and then mounted his gray mare next to her. The music box began, the horses moved up and down, and around and around they went. Sabre felt so free and childlike. There was nothing quite like a carousel ride. She looked to her left, and out of the corner of her eye she saw Luke staring at her with what appeared to be admiration. She turned toward him and looked him directly in the eye. Up she went. He reached his hand out and touched the side of her face, taking hold of her chin and keeping her face directed at him. Down she went. When they met in the middle he spoke softly, "I've fallen in love with you, Sabre Brown."

Sabre was unsure for a moment what he had said, startled by the words. Her stomach churned with emotion, a mixture of happiness and fear. She sat there looking at him, unable to speak. The horses slowed down and then came to a stop. Luke's horse was a little higher than hers. He leaned down and gave her a deep, lingering kiss. When their lips separated, Sabre opened her mouth to speak. Luke put his finger over her mouth, "Shh…you don't need to say anything. Just know I love you."

17

Sabre woke with a headache from lack of sleep. She had been restless ever since Luke brought her home. She was glad Luke went home to pack for his trip and didn't stay the night. Sabre couldn't decide which bothered her most—the news about Betty, or Luke professing his love for her. She turned over on her side. Her stomach felt queasy.

She stepped out of bed and dashed to the bathroom, flung up the toilet seat, and plopped herself down on the floor. She leaned her head over the toilet, and her stomach convulsed until she threw chunks into the bowl. She sat on the floor until she was certain she had finished. Then she stood up with determination and walked to the sink where she aggressively brushed her teeth and washed her face.

Sabre felt better after she had taken her shower, but her mind still raced. Luke was gone, Betty might be guilty of killing John, the Kemp children were probably going home to learn more hatred, and she had to get to court.

Bob greeted her when she walked in. "You look like hell. What happened to you?"

"I love you, too," Sabre replied.

"No, I mean you look really tired. Didn't you get any sleep?"

"Not much."

They walked toward Department Four. Bob put his arm around Sabre's shoulder. "What's the matter, snookums?"

"Betty's been lying to me, I don't know who she is; John is Jim; Luke says he loves me; Betty may be a murderer…."

"Whoa. What was that?"

"I said, 'Betty may be a murderer.'"

Bob stopped. He grabbed Sabre's arm and stopped her, turning her around to face him. "No, the part before that, about Luke."

"Oh, that." Sabre shrugged. "Luke told me he loved me last night."

"So? What?" Bob raised his right hand, palm up. "You don't believe him?"

"No...I mean, yes...I guess I believe him."

"So, what's the problem?"

"I don't know what to do with that information."

"What do you mean? You don't know what to do with it? Do you love him?"

"I don't know. Maybe. I don't know."

"Sabre, stop it. You're acting like a girl."

"Bob." She paused and looked at him with her head cocked to the side, rolling her eyes. "I *am* a girl."

"I know, but you don't usually act like one."

"Is that supposed to be some kind of back-handed compliment?" Sabre took a step forward and then stopped. "Because it sounds like an insult to me."

"You know what I mean. You always look at everything so logically. You can detect a problem, organize the facts, figure out an answer, and solve it before most people know what the problem is."

"Thanks, honey. But it sounds to me like you just described a woman. Besides that only works in my professional life. In my personal life, I suck." Sabre started to walk again. Bob followed. "Anyway, enough about me. We need to figure out what to do about Betty."

"I spoke with JP last night and his report is a bit disturbing, but there may be a reasonable explanation. It doesn't mean she's a murderer," Bob said.

Sabre stopped before entering the courtroom. "Yeah, you're right. I'll go talk to her this morning. Can you finish my morning calendar? All I have are a couple of reviews and you're on both of them."

"Sure. Do you have trial this afternoon?"

"I do. You want to meet for lunch?"

"Pho's?"

"Pho's it is." Sabre took her hearing cover sheets out of her files and gave them to Bob. "Please just fill in the hearing dates and put them in my box. And thanks for taking care of this for me."

Sabre hustled out of the courthouse and drove directly to the hospital. Betty moved her bed up into a sitting position when Sabre entered. "You're looking much better today," Sabre greeted her.

"Yeah, maybe I'll be able to go *home* soon." She snickered. "I've never been sick before where I wasn't eager to get well. Damn, I don't want to go back to that jail cell."

Sabre patted her hand. "I'm sorry, Betty. I know the future looks bleak right now, but we're going to solve this thing."

"That didn't sound very promising."

"Betty, we need to talk." Sabre removed her hand. "Actually, I need some answers."

"About what?" Betty seemed hesitant. She pulled back and seemed to stiffen up.

"JP's investigation brought up some unusual information. First, of all, we know John and Jim are the same person." Betty sighed and nodded her head in affirmation. "We also know you left the trailer park in Austin in the middle of the night, the trailer park for which you gave us the wrong address, by the way." Betty sat there in silence. Sabre watched her friend's face tighten when she said, "Why did you lie to me, Betty?"

Betty pursed her lips. "I was afraid."

"Afraid of what or whom?"

Betty sighed again. "The IRS. We owed a lot of back taxes and we just got in so deep, we couldn't get caught up. Then we started running, and I was afraid to say anything different than the story we'd been telling."

"You were running because of back taxes?"

"Yes, I know it's stupid, but we just got in a bind."

"How long have you been running?"

"It started in West Virginia, about six or seven years ago. That's why we left there."

"And that's where you lived before Austin?"

"Yes."

"Where were you born?"

"Cabin Creek, West Virginia."

"I thought you said you were from Charleston."

"Cabin Creek isn't far from Charleston. Unless you're a die-hard fan of Jerry West, the basketball player, you probably never heard of it. Most people haven't. So, it's easier to say Charleston. Besides, we moved to Charleston when I was very young. I'm sorry if I misled you; things have been so confusing since John died."

"Did you ever live anywhere else?"

"Not for long. We lived in a few different cities in West Virginia and once in Tennessee for a while, but that's about it."

"Never in Wisconsin?"

"No," she answered quickly. "No," she shook her head. "Not Wisconsin." Betty tried to lay her head back, but her pillow was bunched up. Sabre took it out and fluffed it up for her.

"There, is that better?"

"Yes, thank you." Betty nestled into her pillow. "Sabre, I'm really tired. Do you mind if I rest for a while?"

"No, you go ahead." Sabre leaned over and kissed her on the forehead. "I'll come back later."

Sabre left the hospital and drove to court. She was out of time and would have to go see JP after her trial.

Sabre's client, Merriam, a mousy woman with a huge scar on the side of her face, was waiting for her when she reached the courthouse. She escorted her client upstairs to an area where they could have some privacy and went over the social worker's reports with her.

"They're willing to return the children to your care, but the attorney representing your children thinks you'll let your husband back into the home. We have to show you're serious."

Merriam handed Sabre some papers. "Here, I filed the divorce papers, along with a restraining order. That ought to mean something."

"That'll help."

"I'm not letting that son-of-a-bitch back into my home. It's one thing how he scarred me, but the scars he left on my daughter are unforgivable."

"A lot of women say that, and they really mean it at the time, but then they weaken and let the abuser back in."

Merriam raised her voice, "I'm not going to lose my children. Not for any man."

"Okay. You just speak the truth when you're on the stand and please, when I ask you a question just answer the question that's asked. Don't volunteer anything extra. Understand?"

"Yes."

"And when county council or the other attorneys ask you something, don't be too quick to answer. Just take your time. It's okay to pause and it gives me time to object if I don't want the question answered. And do the same with them; don't volunteer any extra information. The more you say, the more that can be twisted or misunderstood. Got it?"

"Yeah."

"Okay, let's go." They stood up, walked downstairs, and Sabre entered the courtroom. Merriam waited outside while the attorneys met to try to resolve some of the issues and shorten the length of the trial.

After some negotiation, the clients were summoned and the matter was called to order. Sabre whispered to Merriam. "We've settled. The children are going home with you." The woman's eyes lit up. She smiled and squirmed in her chair.

While the judge reviewed the stipulations to the settlement, Sabre's stomach began to feel queasy again. Her chest tightened.

"Is your client in agreement?" the judge asked. So many things were weighing on Sabre. She had to figure a way to keep the Kemp children safe and find John's real killer. "Ms. Brown?"

Sabre looked up, bringing her mind back to the case. "Sorry, yes, Your Honor. My client agrees."

"All other orders remain in full force and effect." The judge tapped her gavel and left the courtroom.

"So when do they go home?" Merriam asked.

"This afternoon. The social worker will help you with the arrangements."

"Thank you. Thank you." Merriam reached up and hugged Sabre. Her wet cheek rubbed against Sabre's face.

"Just take care of those kids."

"I will. I promise. I'll keep them safe."

Sabre walked to the parking lot, got in her car, and started to back out.

"Honk! Honk!" Sabre slammed on the brakes to avoid hitting a dark green Chevy Suburban. The driver honked and screamed obscenities at her. Sabre waited for a few minutes, took a deep breath, and then drove out of the lot.

She drove to JP's home office, calling him on the way to make sure he was in. He made a new pot of coffee and was waiting for her when she arrived.

"Coffee?" he asked.

"Decaf?"

"Of course. I know your weaknesses."

"I'd love some. Thanks."

JP poured each of them a cup of coffee, adding lots of skim milk to Sabre's. He picked up both cups and led her out on the veranda. "It's too nice to be inside," he said. "So, what's up?"

"I spoke to Betty about your investigation." She sat down at a small, white wrought iron table. "She said they were running from the IRS."

"Do you believe her?" JP placed her coffee in front of her.

"I want to, but I think she's still holding back."

"Well, that should be easy enough to check out. I can find out if they owed back taxes. Is there something else?"

"She denies ever being in Wisconsin, but she was a little too quick with her response, and then she didn't seem to want to talk anymore. I don't know, maybe she was just tired. She said she lived in West Virginia before Austin."

"Well, so far I haven't found anything in West Virginia, but I'll keep checking."

Sabre remembered. "Oh, and she was born in Cabin Creek, West Virginia, not Charleston."

"Okay, I'll try that. She said her maiden name was Johnson. So, I'll see what I can find for Betty Johnson in Cabin Creek, West Virginia. And I'll check the tax records for Jim Taylor."

Sabre sipped her coffee in silence, then looked up at JP. "What do you think, JP? Do you think she's telling the truth about the tax thing?"

JP turned toward Sabre. "It's plausible. People get really afraid of the IRS and often do stupid things. She's definitely afraid of something. What bothers me is her ease at lying. She's very comfortable with it, like she's done it a lot. That throws up red flags for me." JP picked up a report from his desk and handed it to Sabre. "Speaking of red flags and Charleston, West Virginia… that trespassing charge on Kemp had all kinds of them."

"Like what?"

"The property he trespassed on belonged to an African-American who was killed in a drive-by shooting while Kemp was on his property."

"What?" Sabre looked puzzled glancing at the police report.

"The police couldn't find any evidence that connected the two incidents, but knowing Kemp's background, I'd bet there's something there. And actually, his being there gave him an alibi."

18

JP propped his feet, encased in his favorite cowboy boots, up on the stool under his desk and pulled his computer onto his lap. His goal was to find out who Betty really was. He needed to find out for Sabre today; the sooner she new the truth, the easier it would be for her. He had spent most of the morning on the phone trying to come up with some trace of Betty and her husbands, and then the entire afternoon looking for delinquent tax records. He had settled in, knowing it would take a while, but was frustrated with the results. The window beckoned him. He wished he were outside watching the sun set instead of glued to the computer and telephone.

Ding, dong.

JP stood up, stretched his back, and walked to the door, relieved to be interrupted after hours of sitting and glaring at the screen.

"Hi, Bob, come on in. You just come from court?"

"Why else would I be wearing a suit and tie? You know it comes off as soon as I can get rid of it. Besides, not all of us get to work in jeans and cowboy shirts." He tugged at his tie to loosen it.

"Like you would wear them even if you could."

"Hey, I have a pair of boots—nice ones, too. I bought them at Marshall's for twenty bucks."

"That's a little over your limit for shoes, isn't it?"

"Yeah, I usually won't pay over fifteen, but these were special."

"You cheapskate."

"Hey, I buy Florsheims for that price. You just have to find them on clearance, a sale upon a sale. It's all in the shopping."

"Well, you can have the shopping. Want a drink?"

"Sure."

JP walked over to the bar and poured Bob a vodka on the rocks, more vodka than rocks. He took a bottle of Coors out of the refrigerator for himself. He tipped his head toward the sliding glass door. "Let's go outside. It's nice out this evening."

"I see you're still drinking Coors."

"I always drink American. I'm not a traitor like you, drinking that Russian garbage." They sat down at the little, white, wrought iron table on the deck.

"How's your investigation going?" Bob asked.

JP took a drink of beer. "Lots of holes in Betty's story. For starters, there are no delinquent tax records. At least not for the social security numbers I have for John and Betty Smith. John's social security number matches his name but only goes back four years. There are lots of tax records for John's alias, Jim or James Taylor, but none with the social security number John was using."

"So, John found a way to not only get a new name but also a new social security number. That's kind of sophisticated for the 'country bumpkin' he supposedly was, don't you think?"

"Sure is. I found one 'James Taylor' in Austin in the tax records, but the age wasn't even close, so I don't think that was him. Nothing in West Virginia quite adds up, although it's difficult to say without a social security number and such a common name."

"What about Betty's birth certificate? Did you find that?"

"Yes…no." JP shook his head in confusion. "I don't know."

"That was perfectly clear."

"I found a Betty J. Johnson, born in Cabin Creek, West Virginia on the same birth date as our Betty."

"That must be her then. What's the problem?"

"She died."

"Well, that must just be a mistake." Bob looked up, eyes opened wide. "Wait…you don't think she killed her and took her identity, do you?"

"No. I mean she died at birth."

"That's crazy. There must be another child with the same name."

"Born the same day?"

"I guess that's not likely." Bob sighed.

"No, not likely. And Cabin Creek is a very small town."

"There just must be some mistake in the records back then. Remember, everything was done by hand. Maybe a wrong box was checked or something. What do you need to do to verify it?"

"I requested some paperwork from West Virginia, but I don't know how soon I'll get it, or if it'll really tell me anything."

"What about Jim Taylor? Find anything on him?"

"No, nothing. No birth records, nothing around Charleston anyway, but he changed his name once. Maybe he was someone else before he became Jim Taylor."

Bob squeezed his lips together in agreement, nodding. "It might've even been before Betty met him. She may not even know his real name."

"That's possible."

"What's next?" Bob asked.

"I think I'll check out something Betty's friend, Rose, told me when I was in Texas. She mentioned a town in Wisconsin that Betty denied having any knowledge of, but Rose seemed to think she'd been there."

"It's worth a shot. Since our client is obviously keeping something from us, I guess we need to go around her." Bob hesitated. "Between you and me, do you think she murdered her husband?"

JP shook his head. "I don't know. I want to think she didn't for Sabre's sake. I mean, if it were a crime of passion, I'd be quicker to believe it, but this looks like premeditated murder. Yet, she has lied to us at every turn. She's definitely involved in something besides tax evasion. Is it murder? I just don't know. I do know that the closer we get to the truth, the guiltier she looks."

"Yeah." Bob sat back in his chair and looked out at JP's backyard, taking a drink of his vodka. "So, how about those Padres, huh?"

"They're actually on a winning streak. We might have a good season this year—that is, until the Dodgers come to town."

"Oh, you and your Dodgers."

"Sabre would agree with me. She likes the Dodgers, but then she has better taste than you."

"Yeah, and you like Sabre. You better make your move pretty soon. Luke's getting awfully sweet on her."

"No. I've decided to let it go. She deserves more than I can give her. Let her see if Luke is the one for her…but if that jerk ever hurts her, I'll kill him."

"Yeah, you're a tough guy." Bob stood up. "I have to go. Marilee's expecting me to be on time for dinner tonight. I've been working late everyday this week, so I better get a move on."

"No problem. I think I'll go have a chat with Betty before visiting hours are over."

"That's probably a good idea. Maybe she'll tell you something she wouldn't tell Sabre."

"Unlikely, but worth a shot."

"Thanks for the drink." Bob walked toward the slider. JP followed him inside and to the front door.

"Anytime. Next time you visit, though, I'm going to have some nice American vodka. No more of that foreign stuff."

JP sat in the waiting room chatting with the guard until he saw the nurse leave Betty's room. When he walked in, she smiled uncomfortably.

"Hi, Betty. How you feeling?" JP asked.

"A little better than I did yesterday."

"You're looking good. Lots of color in your cheeks."

"Thanks."

"You getting lots of rest?"

"Yes, that's all I do."

JP tried to follow what he knew would be Sabre's wishes and go easy on Betty, but he was too frustrated. "Look Betty, I'm sorry, but I'm going to get right to the point. You've got to start leveling with us."

Betty's face turned red. She looked around. "About what?"

"About everything." JP remained calm. "I need the truth if you want me to find John's…er…I mean Jim's killer."

"What's not the truth?"

JP raised his voice a little and tried to keep eye contact with her. "Well, for starters there is no delinquent tax problem with either you or John Smith, at least not under the social security numbers you gave us."

Betty shifted in her bed, but didn't look away. "I'm sorry, but that is the problem. Jim used a different social security number when he changed his name to John Smith."

"How did he get another number?"

"I have no idea. He said something about a friend getting it for him. He didn't really want me to know stuff like that. He said the less I knew, the better. He was trying to protect me."

JP leaned in a little closer. "From what?"

"From the IRS."

"So you had delinquent taxes under the names Jim and Betty Taylor?"

"James, but yes."

"So, it should show up under *your* social security number then?" She hesitated. "No, Jim changed mine too."

"That's easy. I'll check under your old numbers, the ones for Jim and Betty Taylor. What are the numbers?" JP picked up his pen and opened a notepad ready to write.

Betty was offended, or afraid and acted offended. JP couldn't tell which. "I don't know them by heart. I'd have to look them up," she said.

"You tell me where they are in your house and I'll go get them for you."

"Actually, I don't know if I even have them on anything. We destroyed all our old papers and such when we took on the new identity."

JP sighed, taking another tack. "Betty, I need a little help here."

"I'm sorry," she said. "It's all I've got."

JP looked at his notes and then said, "Okay, let's talk about your birth records. I can't find anything on Jim or James Taylor in or around Charleston, West Virginia. Are you sure that's where he was born?"

"That's what he told me, but they were dirt poor. He was born at home; maybe nothing was recorded."

"Well, what about you?"

"What about me?"

"I checked Charleston. I checked Cabin Creek. I checked all around there. The only thing I found was a child named Betty J. Johnson on your birth date born in Cabin Creek to Ed and Virginia Johnson."

Betty perked up. "That's me. Those were my parents."

"No." JP shook his head. "That baby died."

"That can't be. I'm obviously here. That's me. There must have been a mistake made back then. Maybe I was sick or something. Maybe the authorities thought I died and I didn't." Betty's voice escalated. "Maybe someone just screwed up the paper work or mixed up the names. Johnson is a pretty common name. I don't know, but I'm here. That's me."

"Okay, calm down." JP patted her arm. "I'm sorry I upset you. I'm just trying to keep you out of prison."

Tears welled up in Betty's eyes. "I don't care if I'm in jail. John's gone."

JP pressed on. "So, just level with me. Tell me what you're hiding."

"I can't." Betty said loudly. Her eyes opened wider, seemingly surprised at her own words. "I mean…I've told you all there is."

19

Sabre woke up Friday morning about six o'clock, cursing because she could've slept in. It was the first weekday she hadn't had court in months. Her body seemed heavy and in need of some serious sleep. She had tossed most of the night dreaming about Luke, Betty, and John. She had a nightmare about John coming to life and Betty attacking him, while Luke stood behind them saying, "Forget them, Sabre, because I love you. That's all that counts." Her stomach was churning and her mouth tasted like rotten avocados. She ran to the bathroom but was unable to vomit. She lay back down and tried to stop the room from spinning. After a few minutes she fell back to sleep. When the sun started to come in through the window, Sabre arose with a start. She quickly dressed, grabbed her files, and started off to visit the minors' homes she had scheduled earlier in the week. She needed to accomplish something, not sit at home dwelling on things.

Her first stop was to see a twelve-year-old girl in a group home. She'd been doing so well in her foster home up until about a week prior. She had lived in that home for over five years. A few years back, they even spoke of adopting her, but her addicted mother and her petty-crime committing father managed to have enough involvement in her life to prevent losing their parental rights. Last week the foster parents announced their intention to leave the state, and their plans didn't include taking the girl with them. She ran away before she could be placed in another home, stole some clothes from a department store, and landed in the group home. Sabre stayed with her for over an hour, listening to her rant about how she hated all the adults in her life, and how she couldn't wait to leave the system and live on her own. All Sabre could do for her was to listen and assure her she'd make every attempt to find her a better placement. This was the part of her job that was so hard, but it was also a driving force to keep her going, to keep her protecting the silent voices of children.

From there Sabre drove to see a one-week-old baby born addicted to drugs, three siblings who had been physically abused by their step-father, a five-year-old whose father thought the child was a Chihuahua and was feeding him dog food, and a three-year-old whose baby brother was knocked out of the crib and suffered a broken neck when their parents got in a fist fight.

You'd think I'd be used to all the violence, Sabre thought, as she drove from one foster home to another, *but when those kids tell me what happened, I still get that sick feeling in my gut.* Sabre realized the feeling she had in her stomach had turned from nausea to an emotional ball. She hurt for the kids. Although she was still very tired, at least she didn't feel like throwing up.

Colin Raye's song, "If You Get There Before I Do" played on her telephone. Luke had programmed her phone with the song so she'd know by the ringtone when he called. She had not answered his last two calls, and she wasn't exactly sure why.

Sabre took a deep breath. "Hi, Luke."

"Hi, are you okay?"

"Yeah, I'm sorry, I haven't felt that well the last two days and I've been crazy busy. I should've called you back last night, but by the time I got home I was exhausted. I just fell into bed."

"I'm sorry you're sick."

"I'm doing better now, thanks."

"Are you up to having a visitor tonight? I'm leaving Monday morning for Dallas and would like to spend as much time with you this weekend as I can before I go."

Sabre decided she needed to face him and deal with her feelings. She couldn't keep hiding. "Sure, that would be great. So, you got that assignment you were talking about?"

"Yeah, it looks like a good one. I'll tell you all about it when I get there. How about four o'clock? We can catch an early dinner and then maybe just stay in and watch a movie or something."

"That...."

"Better yet, I'll bring you some chicken soup."

Sabre thought how thoughtful he was and felt better about her decision to see him. "Wonderful. That's just what I need." She started to hang up. "Wait, I have to start moving my things into my condo this weekend. And you said you'd help, remember?"

"I didn't forget. It'll just give us an earlier start tomorrow morning."

Sabre finished her home visits; drove to the hospital to check on Betty, who was sleeping; and then stopped at The Coffee Bean for a meeting with JP.

"You feeling okay? You look pale," JP said when Sabre walked in. He handed her a cup of decaf mocha.

She smiled at him. "Thanks, that was very sweet of you."

They walked to the big stuffed chairs in the front of the coffee shop and sat down facing each other. "Yeah, that's what Aunt Opal always said."

Sabre laughed. He knew how to make her smile. She looked at his rugged, sincere face and thought he'd make some lucky woman a good mate. Wondering what brought on that feeling, she shrugged it off and said, "What do you have for me?"

"Well, I received the copy of the birth certificate on Betty J. Johnson from Cabin Creek. It lists Betty's parents, but it says the baby was stillborn."

"Couldn't they have made a mistake?"

"I suppose. Not exactly sure how, but anything is possible. And Betty swears that's her."

Sabre took a drink of her coffee. "I went by the hospital to see her today."

"Did you get any more information?"

"No, I went as a friend. I just wanted to see how she was doing."

"And, how is she?"

"She's getting a little better every day. I almost don't want her to recover because she'll have to go back to her cell."

JP stroked her arm. "I'm sorry, Sabre."

Sabre nodded her head and tightened her lips. "I know." She blew out a short breath. "So, where do we go from here?"

"I need to go to Wisconsin."

"Why? Betty said she never lived there."

"She also said her husband's name was John and she's running from the IRS."

Sabre looked at him, puzzled. "What do you expect to find?"

"I have no idea, but it's all I've got. Rose was pretty convinced Betty had a connection there. And Betty gets befuddled whenever we bring it up."

"She does that, for sure."

"I've made a reservation for Monday morning, but if you think it's a waste of time, I'll cancel it."

"No, I trust your judgment. And like you said, what else do we have? Do you want a ride? Luke is flying out Monday morning also. He's going to Dallas on a consulting job. If you're going early enough, I could take you both at the same time."

"Thanks, but I'll take my car and park it at the Park and Ride. I won't be gone long and then no one has to pick me up."

Sabre visited with JP until their coffee was finished. They walked to the car and JP opened her door for her. "Always the gentleman, JP. Thanks."

"My daddy would turn over in his grave if I weren't. We don't want that now, do we?" He laid his hand gently on her back just before she entered the car.

20

Sabre walked to the door wearing her gray sweats with "P-I-N-K" in block letters across her butt. With her wet hair and make-up-free face, she peeked through the peephole in the front door and saw Luke standing there with a bowl in one hand and a bag in the other. When she opened the door, he quickly kissed her on the lips, stepped back and said, "You look beautiful."

"Right...thanks. Come on in, sorry about the mess."

He handed her the bowl. "Chicken soup, just what the doctor ordered." He held the other bag up and waved it as he walked to the freezer. "And Haagan-Daz...Vanilla Swiss Almond."

"Yummy, now that's what the doctor ordered!"

Luke put the ice cream in the freezer, placed the bowl of chicken soup on the kitchen counter, and walked toward Sabre. He reached down, picked her up, and carried her into the bedroom, walking around packed boxes as he nibbled on her neck. He gently set her down on the bed, pulled her sweatshirt up over her head, and kissed her passionately, working his way down her neck and shoulders until he reached her breasts, then slowly lowering her until she was in a prone position. He stepped back for a moment while he removed his shirt. Sabre watched as he unbuttoned each button, revealing his sculptured chest. He tossed the shirt, lowered himself onto her, and placed his open mouth on hers. He kissed her gently and raised his lips slightly, just long enough to whisper, "I love you, Sabre." Then he covered her mouth again with his, not giving her time to respond. She was relieved. She didn't need to say anything. She wanted to. She thought she loved him, but when she tried to say the words, they stuck in her throat.

When they finished making love, they lay there in each other's arms, her head on his chest. He stroked her hair. Sabre thought how right it felt. She wanted to tell Luke how she felt. It was time. "Luke?" Her stomach gurgled.

"Let me guess…you're hungry. You need some of my famous chicken soup."

Sabre chuckled. "Sounds good."

They got up, dressed, and went into the kitchen. Luke took a pan out of the cupboard, poured the soup in it, and lit the burner.

"May I help?" Sabre asked.

"No, you just sit there and look beautiful."

Sabre reached up to her damp head. "Oh, my hair. I must look awful. I'll go dry it while you warm up the soup."

"You look perfect to me." Luke caught her arm as she walked past him, swung her around, and kissed her. "There, now you may go."

Sabre returned, still wearing her sweats but with her hair dry and fluffed and light make-up applied. The soup was ready, and Luke was looking through Sabre's four DVDs sitting on the stand by the television. "Is this all you have? They're all chick flicks. Don't you have any macho movies? Maybe a little Clint Eastwood? And not *Bridges of Madison County.* That doesn't count."

"Most everything is packed, but I just happen to know where there is one." Sabre walked over to one of the boxes that hadn't been taped shut yet, rustled through it for a bit, and pulled out a DVD. "Here you go, *Gran Torino.* Have you seen it?"

"No, is it good?"

"You'll love it."

They finished their soup, cleaned up, and Luke put the disc in the DVD player. Then he took Sabre's hand and led her toward the sofa. He sat down but Sabre remained standing, looking around at her boxes.

"Do you need help packing?"

Sabre nodded. "I should finish this." She shook her head back and forth. "No. I've been doing this all week." She sat down next to Luke just as he started to stand up. "There's not that much left. I'll finish it in the morning while you're loading the truck."

"Deal." Luke wrapped his arm around her and started the

movie. About halfway through, they took a break and ate their ice cream. They lay back down on the sofa, and before the movie ended Sabre was asleep in his arms.

Sabre woke with a start when her iPhone blurted out Waylon Jennings singing "Bob Wills is Still the King." JP's ringtone was his favorite classic country singer, Waylon, while Bob liked Leonard Cohen. Those two close friends didn't exactly share the same taste in music. Sabre pushed herself up and reached for her phone, knocking it off the coffee table. It had rung four times by the time she was able to answer it. "Hi, JP."

"Hi. Did I wake you?"

"No…well sort of. I just dozed off. What's up?"

"I just spoke with one of my buddies in the police department and they have more evidence against Betty."

"What could they possibly have?" Sabre sat up.

"A neighbor says he was out walking and saw a man and a woman get out of a 2003 gold Honda Accord and enter her trailer the night of the murder…about nine-thirty."

"That's a good thing. What does it have to do with Betty?"

"He thought the woman was Betty, but he didn't see her very well. He got a real good look at the man. He was about six feet tall, short brown hair, clean shaven, around forty- or forty-five years old."

"So, if he didn't see the woman very well, then he can't be sure it was her, right? Besides, she was at the casino."

"The woman fit the same general description as Betty, same height, weight, and short, red-spiked hair. The clincher is the witness saw Betty talking to this man earlier that day at the park, around ten in the morning. He was driving a 2003 gold Honda Accord, and he swears it was the same man."

21

O n Saturday morning, Bob arrived at Sabre's apartment with JP's truck and trailer. He walked in and looked around at the stacks of boxes. "How did you accumulate so much in such a short time?"

"There's not really that much."

"How many of these boxes are shoes?"

Sabre put her head down and spoke just above a whisper. "Only four."

"You have four boxes full of shoes? It's only been seven months since your stuff burned. How does someone who hates to shop accumulate so many shoes?" Bob asked.

Luke laughed. "Yeah, that's a lot of shoes."

"It's not that many. They're still in their original boxes, so they take up a lot more room. Only about six pairs fit in a box."

"Only six? That's still twenty-four pairs of shoes."

"Just load the damn things. I'm going to finish packing." Sabre chuckled and walked into the kitchen to pack the remainder of the food and dishes. Luke and Bob commenced carrying out furniture and boxes and loading them in the truck.

Sabre put the few remaining clothes from her closet in the back seat of her car and followed Bob and Luke to her home. As she pulled up in front of her newly rebuilt condo, she reflected on a cold, southern California December day a few weeks after the fire. John had taken her by to see the rubble.

Sabre had been out of the hospital for less than a week. Everything around her was black. Her house, her furniture, and all her possessions were reduced to a dark, cold pile of ashes. She stood there shivering and crying, but not ready to leave. John had taken a blanket out of his truck and wrapped it around her. "You need to keep warm. You're going to catch pneumonia."

"Thanks." Sabre sobbed.

"I know it doesn't seem like it now, Sparky, but life will get better."

He put his arm around her shoulder. She felt the strength and love he had for her.

"You're strong. You'll pick up the pieces and move on."

"But I've lost everything. Every photo of my brother, every memento of my childhood, everything I've ever owned...my furniture, my clothes, my shoes...." *Sabre sobbed.*

"But think of all the fun you'll have shopping for new shoes." *He gave her a quick hug.* "You know how much you like to buy shoes."

Sabre mustered up a smile, but it disappeared quickly. "It's like... like my past has been erased."

"I know a thing or two about that. I've lost my past on more than one occasion."

Sabre looked up at him, eyes still full of tears, not quite sure what he meant. "I came to realize material things just aren't that important. And no matter how many 'things' are destroyed, no one can take your memories. Even if some of them fade a little, you'll remember the love. And you have oh so many people who love you. Betty and I love you like you were ours. You have brought a ray of sunshine into Betty's life and for that I'll be forever grateful."

"She's a good lady. She does so many little things for people. You both do. Always helping people in the park fix things, making food when someone is sick, hauling in groceries and cleaning the cat litter box for old 'Mrs. Pain-in-the-butt' on the corner."

John smiled. "She's not so bad."

"Not so bad....She screams at you every time you try to help her." *Sabre spoke in a high pitched, shaky voice mimicking the old lady:* "Be careful with that milk. You're gonna drop the bag. Don't put it there. Can't you remember anything, you old fart? Take that cat poop to the dumpster. I don't want it stinking up my trash can...yadda, yadda, yadda."

John laughed. "She's just old and in a lot of pain. She has no one. I don't let it bother me. Betty taught me that."

Sabre looked into John's weather-worn face. "You two are very lucky to have each other."

"I'm the lucky one." *He looked into Sabre's eyes.* "Someday you'll *have someone like my Betty. Someone who loves you unconditionally. Someone who sticks by you through all the bad times because the love is so strong it transcends everything else."*

It all seemed unlikely at the moment to Sabre. *"I hope so."*

"You will, Sparky. Just don't settle for anything less." He tilted her head up to force her to look in his eyes. *"But sometimes you have to open yourself up, be a little vulnerable to find what you're looking for. And remember to give back just a little bit more than you get. If you both do that, it works. It's a two-way street, you know."* He kissed her on the forehead.

"What are you waiting for, Sobs?" Bob yelled from the back of the truck. "You need to open up the condo." He threw his hand in the air. "I don't want to make a career of this."

Sabre quickly wiped the tears from her eyes, exited the car, and walked up to her "new" home. She hadn't seen it since they finished painting and laying the flooring. She dashed in, spun around, waving her hands in the air. "Wow, it's beautiful." She walked from one room to another observing the similarities and the differences to what she'd had before. Luke remained downstairs answering a phone call. Bob followed Sabre as she climbed the empty staircase where her collection of stuffed animals used to sit. Sabre's demeanor changed.

"You okay?" Bob asked.

"Yeah."

"There are no demons here, you know."

"I know, but please don't let anyone buy me stuffed animals. I don't want them moving around in my house this time."

Bob chuckled. "Fair enough."

They walked into the master bedroom. Sabre slipped off her shoes at the doorway. Her feet sunk into the cream-colored carpet. She liked the contrast of the slightly darker cream walls. It was different enough to make a new start, yet familiar enough to feel like home.

Bob glanced around at the empty room. "When's your furniture going to arrive?"

"It'll be delivered on Monday. Meanwhile I'll use an air mattress."

"You could stay in your apartment until then."

"No, I'd rather be here. Luke will be here tonight and tomorrow night, and by then I'll be comfortable again."

"You sure?"

"I'll be fine. I'm not going to let a bad memory run me out of my home. And quit acting like my mother." She pushed Bob lightly on the back. "Go help Luke bring my stuff in. I need to start putting things away."

It was mid-afternoon by the time everything was unloaded. Sabre directed the men as they came in, although she had each box labeled for each room and its contents. She had the boxes with perishables and items she needed to help her through the first few nights marked with a green marker. The things she needed next were marked in red, and the stuff that could wait indefinitely she had marked in black. By the time the boxes were all in the condo and in their proper rooms, Sabre had all the "green" boxes unloaded and put away.

"I hate to run off, but I need to return JP's truck," Bob said as they all walked outside. "I'm having a little barbecue at the house tomorrow around three. You two want to come?"

Sabre looked at Luke. He nodded his head. "We'd love to. I still have a lot of unpacking to do, but I think we'll be ready for a break. What should we bring?"

"Nothing. We're all set. There'll only be a half dozen people there. I want to show off my new deck."

"See you tomorrow," Luke said and walked in the house.

Sabre lingered for a moment. "You talked to JP about the new evidence against Betty?" she asked.

"Yes. What do you make of it?"

"I don't know. It just keeps getting worse. I'm going to run by the hospital and talk to her this afternoon."

"Good idea," Bob said as he got in the truck.

After he left, Sabre and Luke tidied up a little before each took a shower. Then Luke settled in with his computer, and Sabre drove to see Betty.

Betty muted the television when Sabre walked in. "I didn't expect you today. I thought you'd be too busy with the move."

"It's coming along, but something came up I need to talk to you about."

Betty's face looked strained. Sabre was sorry she had to bring it up. She hated putting more stress on her, but she needed some answers. "What is it?" Betty asked.

"The police have an eye witness that saw a man and someone fitting your description at your trailer about nine-thirty the night of the murder."

Betty's eyes widened. "That wasn't me. I was at the casino. You know that."

"I wish I'd stayed with you the whole night because the timing just stinks."

"Honest, Sabre, I wasn't there," she pleaded. "The witness is wrong."

"This same witness says he saw the man earlier that day in Hayden Park talking to you. Were you there that day?"

"Yeah. I go to the park nearly every day around ten o'clock and take my walk."

"Did you talk to anyone?"

"I said hi to people as they passed." Betty rubbed her forehead and then her chin, her face wrinkled with thought lines. "I don't remember talking to anyone." She nodded her head. "Yeah, there was a man who got out of his car with a map in his hand and asked me for directions to Jamacha Road. He said he was visiting someone in the trailer park. He said the name, but it wasn't anyone I recognized."

"Did he say anything else?"

"Not really, not that I can remember. He commented on our nice weather. He said it was so much nicer than Tucson. That's about it. We didn't talk very long."

"What kind of car was he driving?"

"It was a gold color, I think. I didn't pay any attention to what it was."

"And you didn't know this man? Had never seen him before?"

Betty's voice, somewhere between anger and frustration, said, "No. He was a complete stranger." Then fear appeared in her voice. "Sabre, this looks real bad, doesn't it? Why would someone say they saw me that night? And why did that man single me out to ask directions? Do you think I led him to John?"

Betty was either really afraid, or she was doing a great job of covering. "I don't know. I was hoping you could tell me."

Sabre and Luke went out to a local café for a bite to eat and then settled in for the evening. Sabre had expected to feel anxiety her first night back in her home, assuming the memories of its burning would be too much for her. Instead, she felt a calm she could only attribute to Luke's presence. She lay next to him, wrapped in his arms, her head on his chest. She could feel his torso rise and fall with the light sound of his breathing. She felt safe. She was home. She wasn't alone, and she wasn't settling. Maybe John was right. Maybe she had found her "Betty." But was John's "Betty" the person he believed her to be? Could Betty have murdered him? No, it was all too crazy. She had to let it go and think about Luke; she had to enjoy the moment.

She nudged him. "Hmm…?" he asked.

"Would you like to move in here with me?"

"Sure," he mumbled, as he pulled her closer, burying his face in her hair.

She wondered if he'd remember it in the morning—and if she wanted him to remember it. Her feet felt cold. She tucked them under his leg. He rubbed the top of her foot with his. *Yeah, she wanted him to remember.*

Sabre and Luke drove to Einstein Bagels the next morning for a quick bite before they started working in the house. When they returned, Luke found a quiet corner, carried over a couple of sturdy boxes, one to sit on and one for his computer, and started to work. Sabre continued to put things away, sneaking a peek every once in a while at Luke, and thinking how good it felt to just have him in her home. Luke hadn't mentioned anything about the conversation they had last night, or rather the conversation she had about him moving in. *Did he not remember, or had he thought better of it? Should she ask again?*

By the time they drove to Bob's for the barbecue, Sabre was convinced Luke either wasn't going to say anything or just didn't remember. It was starting to drive her crazy. Should she bring it up again?

Corey ran up to Sabre when they walked into the backyard. He gave her a big hug. "Hi, Auntie Sabre."

"Hi, sweetheart." She tousled his hair. "How's the sax playing coming along?"

"Good, and I'm playing soccer, and I made a goal yesterday."

"Whoa! Good for you. I want to come to one of your games."

"Snap." Corey spotted another guest and ran off to greet him. Sabre watched Corey and thought how different his life was from the Kemp children. He ran and played with an innocent freedom they never had.

Luke walked over to the ice chest for some drinks. Sabre spotted JP leaning against the magnolia tree. He smiled when she walked up. "I wanted to thank you again for letting us use your truck yesterday. We managed to get everything in one load."

"Anytime…I mean…I hope you don't have to move anytime soon, but…."

"I know what you meant. I appreciate it. So, are you all set for your trip tomorrow?"

"Yeah."

Bob walked up and interrupted. "JP, can you give me a hand? I need to move the grill onto the new deck."

"Sure."

Sabre started to walk away, but stopped and turned back around. "By the way, Bob, your deck is gorgeous." She thought she saw JP quickly turn his eyes away from her butt. When she caught his eye, his face turned red. She smiled to herself and walked off.

The barbecue was a big success. Bob's spicy sausages were a hit. Sabre drank about four bottles of ice water. Luke put away just as many bottles of Goose Island Oatmeal Stout. Bob's wife, Marilee, had made a huge pasta salad that had all but disappeared. Sabre and Luke mixed some with the other guests, but mostly they stayed close to each other, watching and laughing at Bob's antics all afternoon.

They stopped at Luke's on the way home so he could finish packing for his trip. His bag was ready except for a few toiletries. He packed those up, and put the suitcases in the car to take to Sabre's so they could leave from her house in the morning.

By the time Sabre and Luke arrived home, cleaned up, and added a little air to the mattress, they were both ready to call it a night. Luke's flight left at five minutes after seven in the morning, so he had to be there by at least six. And since it was their last night together indefinitely, they wanted to spend it making love.

Sabre wondered if she should bring up the invitation to move in again, but felt uneasy if he had heard her and just wasn't responding. They talked about the day, about how much they'd be missing each other, and agreed to call each other every day. They lay there with their naked bodies becoming one, Luke's arm under Sabre's head, which was nestled on his chest. She could feel him breathing but knew he was still awake. Luke breathed in, then exhaled. "What would you think about my moving in here with you?"

Sabre sat up, slapping him lightly on the chest. "You brat! You did hear me last night."

He grabbed her, pulled her down, rolled her over, and kissed her longingly. "Yeah, I think it's a great idea." He relaxed his body, moving it into sleep mode, still holding her tightly. "We'll figure it out when I return."

22

The shuttle bus from the Park and Ride pulled up to the curb and JP stepped out just in time to see Sabre driving away. He waved. She lowered her window and yelled, "Have fun."

JP rolled his single bag into the airport, stopped at the kiosk to print his boarding pass, and then rode up the escalator toward his gate. As he passed Starbucks, he saw Luke standing in the coffee line. He chose not to stop. Since he was not a real fan of Luke, chatting with him wasn't high on his list of things to do this morning.

When he reached the gate, he sat down, pulled out a mystery novel, and read until they started to board. He was seated at the rear of the plane and was one of the first to board through the back door. JP liked this airline. It was one of the few that had planes that loaded from the rear so people weren't climbing over one another to reach their seats. Nearly every seat on the plane was filled. He was lucky to get an aisle, even if it was in the last row. JP hated the middle seats. He was just too tall and felt claustrophobic sitting in the middle. And he never failed to be seated between two hefty people, leaving him no room to put his arms or his legs. But today the middle seat next to him was empty allowing him to stretch his legs.

JP took out his novel and read until he got too restless and the seatbelt sign went off. He stood up, stretched his legs, and went to the restroom located almost directly behind him. When he came back he started to walk a little ways forward to keep his muscles loose and fill his boredom, but when he got about halfway up the aisle he saw a man step out of his seat in first class and go into the front bathroom. It looked like Luke. He even walked like Luke. JP quickly turned around and went back to his seat. He kept his eye up front waiting for the man to come out and take his seat. The flight attendant started down the aisle with the drinks blocking his view as the man returned to his seat.

Why was Luke on the flight to Chicago? He was supposed to be going to Dallas. He wouldn't be flying to Dallas via Chicago. That didn't make sense. Why would he lie to Sabre?

JP remained in the rear of the plane where he was confident he wouldn't be seen. He didn't really expect the guy in first class to be slumming it in coach. He envied Luke a little for having a more comfortable seat, but he was probably dealing with a big corporation with deep pockets. Sabre had a client with nothing, which meant she probably had to pay for the flight herself. He knew she could petition the court and she might obtain some funding, but he also knew that didn't work much of the time. *Maybe I shouldn't be doing this. After all, it's a long shot. I'll donate my time, that's what I'll do; then at least she'd only have to pay for the expenses. After all, that's what she and Bob are doing.*

When the plane landed in Chicago, JP hustled off as quickly as he could, trying to catch a glimpse of Luke. By the time he was able to leave the plane, the man in first class was no longer in sight. JP didn't have to go to baggage pickup, but hopefully "first-class guy" did. JP moved quickly through the airport, following the signs to baggage pick-up. He found the carousel with his flight number flashing in neon above it. There was no luggage out yet. He looked around. There was Luke, standing at the end of the carousel.

JP didn't have time to pick up his rental car. Luke would be gone before he was able to process the paperwork and find his way around to where he would exit the building. So he slipped outside, hailed a cab, gave the driver some extra cash, and asked him to wait until he was ready. The young, long-haired cab driver wore a baseball cap with a big "C" on the front, and had patches of stubble where his beard was supposed to be. He twitched and bobbed as he watched the traffic control officers walk up and down asking people to move along. He kept stepping out of the vehicle and rearranging the suitcase in the trunk. Just as an officer started walking toward him, JP yelled, "Let's go. Let's go."

The cab driver jumped in and breathed in deeply. "Where to?"

"Follow that car, the black Lexus."

The driver looked at him through the rearview mirror, his eyes lighting up in anticipation. "You're kidding, right?"

"Do I look like I'm kidding?" JP said loudly. Then he lowered his voice. "Do you know your way around this city?"

"Lived here all my life." JP thought that would be about twelve years. "All twenty-three years. Been driving or riding my bike around here for most of that time."

"Look, kid, I'm sorry I yelled at you. It's just very important I know where that car goes."

"You a cop or something?" He followed the car as it left the airport weaving in and out of the lanes.

"Or something."

The cab driver turned to look at him, taking his eye off the street. "Are you FBI or CIA?"

"Please watch where you're going." JP reprimanded him. "No, nothing like that."

"You're a PI then, aren't you? That's what you are. What's that guy done? Did he murder someone?" The driver whipped around the corner as the car turned right.

"No, I'm afraid it isn't anything that exciting, just a cheating husband."

"Oh." The driver sounded disappointed. "You probably get a lot of exciting stuff, though, huh?" He made another quick turn.

"Sometimes. What's your name?"

"Jerome. But my friends call me Romeo." JP was certain he saw him puff up his chest as he said it.

"Well, Jerome, maybe you could try not to draw too much attention to us. Perhaps make the turns a little slower."

"Sure, just didn't want him to get away."

The traffic was heavier and moved more slowly as they drove through the city. Cars kept cutting in and getting between them, but Jerome always managed to find his way back, keeping one or two cars in front of him. Finally, the Lexus pulled over to a curb and stopped. Luke and his driver, a man about ten years older than Luke, stepped out and went into a restaurant. The neon light over the door read, "Paceco's."

"I need to follow him inside. Can you wait for me?"

"Sure, but the meter keeps running."

"Look, how about if we shut off the meter, you loan me your cap, and I'll pay you fifty dollars an hour for down time. You okay with that?"

"You bet. I'll watch their car for you, too. No extra charge."

"Thanks."

JP exchanged his black Stetson for the cap, slipped out of the cab, and walked to the restaurant. It was crowded enough inside to not be noticed. He spotted Luke heading towards three gentlemen sitting at a corner table. The men greeted each other with kisses to each cheek. *That's a behavior you'd never see in Texas—California maybe, but never Texas*, JP thought. He positioned himself at the bar where he could see the table but not be noticed, ordered a beer, and nursed it. Luke and his three companions sat and ate dinner, drank wine, and conversed for nearly two hours. JP hoped his cabbie and his Stetson were still waiting outside for him. When the men appeared to be leaving, JP left five dollars on the bar and slipped out before Luke could see him. He looked around, but didn't see his cab; then he heard a slight honk of a horn. He glanced across the street and spied Jerome parked on the far corner. The cabbie had rolled down his window and was now waving one hand frantically. JP darted across the street and jumped into the car.

"Is he with another woman?"

"No, just a couple of guys."

"Dang, I was hoping you caught him on my watch."

"Any activity at the car?"

"Nope."

It was another twenty minutes before Luke and his driver came out of Paceco's restaurant. They walked directly to the car, got in, and drove off. Jerome eased out into the traffic and stayed a couple cars behind them, not making too many sudden moves.

"I think you're getting the hang of this surveillance thing, Jerome."

Jerome smiled and sat up a little straighter.

Following Luke's car, they drove a few miles, passing stores, office buildings, and restaurants, and entered a residential area. The homes were mostly two-story brick and well maintained. The traffic grew more and more sparse until there appeared to be only Luke and the cab left on the street.

"Drop back and slow down or they'll see us." JP saw the brake lights come on as Luke's car slowed way down. "Pull over in front of that house, the one with no lights. And act like a cabdriver."

Jerome chuckled as he opened his car door and stepped out. He walked around to the passenger side and opened the back door. Luke turned right, into a driveway. Jerome got back in the car and they drove slowly past the gated area where Luke had entered. The gate was about one-quarter of the way closed, and the tail lights on Luke's car left a trail of red leading up to a three-story mansion situated on acres of trees and manicured lawn.

"You want me to follow? I can make it," Jerome said, as he started to turn the steering wheel.

"No," JP yelled. "No!" Then more calmly he said, "Just go straight." JP couldn't see any numbers on the fence or the curb, but he jotted down the number of the house just past the mansion. It couldn't be too hard to find out who lived in the house Luke was entering.

"So, where to now, boss?"

JP shook his head and smirked. "Just take me back to the airport, Romeo. I need to pick up my rental car."

Jerome let JP out near the rental cars, removed the bag from the trunk, took the money JP offered him, and was counting it as he walked back to the driver's side of the car. Apparently pleased with his earnings, he looked up with a smile and nodded before driving off.

JP rented his car, then walked over to the gift shop and purchased a Cub's baseball cap. After picking up the car, he drove to his hotel and checked in. It was late and he felt bushed. He took a shower, channel surfed until he found a cop movie on television, rested his head on the pillow, and fell asleep before the first commercial ended.

He woke just before his alarm went off at four-thirty the next morning. He quickly dressed and drove back to the mansion where he had last seen Luke. JP parked far enough down the street to not be conspicuous. Within fifteen minutes, Luke drove out of the driveway and towards him. JP crouched down in his seat below the window. As soon as the car had passed he sat up, made a u-turn, and followed Luke's car. About ten minutes later, Luke pulled into a parking lot in front of a fitness gym, took a gym bag out of the trunk, and went inside.

JP waited outside, parked so he wouldn't miss him when he came out of the building. An hour and a half later, Luke emerged looking clean and shiny, his head wet. JP surmised he had taken a shower after his long workout. He thought Luke worked awfully hard at looking good. He deserved that body. JP knew he couldn't keep up that pace. He worked out from time to time but never with the same dedication Luke seemed to put into it. JP would work out for a few months, and then he'd get bored or something else would seem more important and steal his time. He just wasn't motivated, and although he had a decent body for his age, he didn't have the desire to work any harder to keep it in shape. He walked a lot and played basketball in the neighborhood, but even the basketball seemed to be getting more difficult. His aches and pains were greater and took longer to go away. His knees would ache after he played for an hour or so. He was getting old. Too old, he thought, for Sabre anyway. And she had a decent enough young buck chasing after her, unless he was in Chicago on some shenanigan, in which case he didn't deserve her.

Luke pulled out of the parking lot, drove a couple of blocks, and turned into a drive-through coffee shop. JP drove past him and into a gas station on the corner, positioning his car so he could still keep an on eye on Luke and drive any direction. When

Luke pulled out JP edged his way into the traffic, keeping enough cars between them to avoid any suspicion. A few blocks later Luke stopped near a Wells Fargo bank, walked up to the ATM, and made a withdrawal. He dropped the cash in his jacket pocket and returned to his car.

From there JP followed him back to the mansion, dropping back as they approached. JP pulled off the street before Luke reached the gate. He saw him turn and disappear into the vast estate. JP drove around until he found a spot near a little neighborhood park where he could be less conspicuous but still see if anyone left or entered the estate. JP remained there for nearly two hours before he saw any activity. A dark green jaguar with two men inside it drove past his parked car. He watched it turn toward the wrought iron gate. About fifteen minutes later, a black Rolls Royce with a chauffeur did the same. The tinted windows were too dark to see if anyone sat in the back seat. Two black Cadillacs followed closely behind. Each Cadillac had a male driver and a male passenger in the front seat, and one of them had passengers in the backseat. Three more expensive, black cars later, the procession stopped.

Frustrated and bored, JP waited another two hours before he decided he had better start to work. After all, Sabre wasn't paying him to tail her boyfriend. JP heard tires screeching just as he reached to turn on the ignition. He looked up and saw a Cadillac speed past him. Then the Rolls Royce drove out of the gate at a speed of about fifty miles per hour. By the time it passed JP, he estimated the speed at eighty-five or ninety miles per hour. He couldn't see who was in it. Another black Cadillac whizzed past and he tried to catch a glimpse of the passengers, but they were moving too fast. The car Luke drove that morning was mixed among the others. He thought he saw Luke at the wheel, but he couldn't be certain. JP counted nine cars, all breaking the speed limit and turning off on different streets, scattering throughout the neighborhood. He tried to watch which way Luke went. Although he was anxious to pull out, he didn't want to be seen, and it would've been dangerous until all the cars had passed. After the last car, JP peeled out and headed in the direction he thought Luke had taken. He followed the taillights until he got close enough to realize it wasn't Luke or any of the cars he had seen leave the mansion.

Giving up the chase, JP drove toward his hotel, stopping to pick up a hamburger at a Sonic he had passed earlier in the day. When he reached the hotel, he sat down to eat his dinner. He hadn't realized how hungry he was until he started to eat.

When he finished, he picked up his cell phone and opened it to call Sabre. He closed it. What would he tell her? That he'd wasted a day chasing her boyfriend who was supposedly in Dallas? All he really knew was he was staying in a fancy house in Chicago. He rubbed his hand through his hair, walked to his cooler and took out a bottle of beer, twisted the top off, and sat down in front of the television. He finished his beer and rose to get another. After a few swallows he muted the television, picked up his phone, and pushed the button on speed dial for Sabre. He took a drink of beer while it rang.

"What's up, JP?"

"Hi. I hope I'm not disturbing you and Luke."

"Luke's in Dallas, remember?"

"That's right; I forgot. I was just checking in, but don't have anything to report. I'll call you tomorrow."

He hung up feeling awkward and uncomfortable, and wondered again why Luke was lying to Sabre.

23

The next morning, JP checked his email for a response to a computer whiz friend of his who worked for the government. The friend was checking birth records for the town of Bristol, Wisconsin. JP had pegged Betty for around fifty-eight, though her identification said sixty-three. He had his friend search the birth records for any child born five years before or after her estimated birth date. After all, how many could there be in a town that had a population of eight hundred fifty-seven.

The email was there, indicating a pretty busy time for births in the small town. The population boomed as all the men came home from the war. He checked both males and females, since he wasn't sure if he was looking for information on John or Betty. He had discovered thirty-two births during that ten-year span. Three of them were stillborn and two more died within the first year, leaving twenty-eight to investigate. He eliminated two more who died in Vietnam and eight others who died of cancer or heart disease. JP knew those were risky because, after all, John had died twice already, but he had to start somewhere. His list consisted of ten females and eight males. He obtained addresses for some who still lived in the immediate area and hoped to get some information from them. If someone lived in the town Betty's entire life, they would likely know if she'd been there at one point.

JP hand wrote the names on another piece of paper with the words KLONDIKE CORNER, WISCONSIN written across the top. To the right he wrote May third, nineteen fifty-two. Then he tore off the fifty-two, wrinkled the paper into a ball, opened it back up, poured a little coffee on it, and then flattened it out again. He walked outside, picked up some dirt, and rubbed it across the paper. Then he folded it in eighths, opened it up, and refolded it over and over for the next hour while he drank coffee and watched the morning news.

Armed with his list he started his trek to Brighton. He had

only one stop to make along the way: a local Chicago library. Walking in, he surveyed the librarians until he found the oldest person working there. She was a thin, gray-haired woman in her seventies, fresh from the beauty salon and wearing a color-coordinated suit-dress.

"You look lovely today," JP said as he stepped up to the counter where she was sorting some books.

"Thank you. I'm giving a speech later today to the Historical Society. I don't know if they want me to speak because I have access to the information here in the library or just 'cuz I'm so darn old. They probably think I saw everything first hand." If she was joking, she didn't smile at her own joke.

"But I'm sure you still know a great deal, regardless," JP suggested.

"Truth is, I do remember a lot of stuff, and what I didn't see, my poppi told me. I loved to sit and listen to his stories. We'd sit out on the porch in the early evening and watch folks pass by. He'd tell me stories about everyone he knew. He could talk for hours. Not sure anyone else ever listened to them. But I did. Don't know if they were all true for sure, but some of it I've been able to verify and most of the time he was right on. I'm thinking I might write a book someday…when I retire, perhaps." She picked up a couple of books and placed them on a cart. "Sorry, I do go on. I guess it comes naturally from my poppi. So, what can I do for you, young man?"

"I think you're just the person I need to see. I passed a house, a mansion really, this morning. It was huge and had a block wall around it with a big, wrought-iron gate like a castle. Looked like acres of land surrounding it. I was wondering if there's a story behind it."

"You must be talking about the 'Chateau Dumas,' or 'Paceco Villa' as it is now called. That's the only place in Chicago that fits that description." She set more books on the cart.

JP stepped up closer. "May I help you with those, ma'am?"

"No, I'm fine. I only need to move a few." She checked another book and placed it on the cart. "The Chateau Dumas has an interesting history. A love story, really." She sighed. "The building of the mansion commenced in early 1900. It was completed about 1920, I think…no, 1919…or was it eighteen? I better look it up. No, I remember. It was 1919. That's right. Built by a wealthy Frenchman named Adrian Dumas. He shipped and railed every bit of wood and glass from Europe to build that house. I hear it has more stained glass than the Vatican. He brought in the best mahogany and cherry wood. There are twenty-four bedrooms in the main house and eight guest houses on the property. The guest houses are larger than any home I've ever owned. Monsieur Dumas wanted to build the perfect house for his young bride, and I believe he did." She stopped and looked up at JP for a second. "But even the rich can't stop fate."

"What happened?"

"Shortly after the house was completed, his wife and child died in a fire while visiting a friend. Monsieur Dumas was a mess. He started drinking and cursing the Almighty. He stopped tending to his business, and then the Great Depression raped him of his fortune. He died in 1949, homeless and penniless. The house was purchased in the thirties by a man named Lucia Marangelli, and it has remained in his family ever since. If you check the property records, you'll see the surname was changed to Marang somewhere along the line. It's now owned by Marcus Paceco. He would be Lucia's grandson, I believe. When Marcus' mother married Mr. Paceco, they changed the name of the mansion to Paceco Villa."

"Wow, that's quite a story. Thank you for that bit of history."

"You're quite welcome. Where are you from anyway, lad?"

JP smiled. He couldn't remember being called a lad since Granny O'Rourke died. "San Diego, ma'am."

"That's a lovely place, or so I've heard. I've read a lot about it. The temperature there is about the best you can get in these United States, most temperate anyway. Pretty mild compared with this windy city." She snickered. "I don't know why I'm telling you that.

You ought to know. You're the one who lives there. Hmph…there I go, rattling on. Is there anything else I can do for you?"

"No, thank you, ma'am. You've been very gracious."

The old woman leaned in toward JP, looked to her left and then to her right, and whispered, "Rumor has it the Pacecos are in the mob." Then she stood up tall again, wrinkled her nose, and said, "But how could anyone on the outside know that for sure?"

24

"You look like hell," Bob said as Sabre walked into juvenile court. "Your face is real pale. Are you all right?"

Sabre picked up her files from the metal detector. "Thanks. I feel like hell. Don't get too close to me. I've been fighting a bug of some sort. It's been nearly a week now, and I can't seem to kick it."

"Maybe you ought to see a doctor."

"Nah, I'll be fine. I usually feel better once I vomit in the morning." They walked together toward Department Four.

Bob looked at Sabre with a wrinkled brow. "So, you only feel bad in the morning?"

Sabre stopped. "Don't look at me like that." She lowered her voice. "I'm not pregnant."

"Okay."

They went into Department Four and informed the bailiff they were ready for their cases.

Sabre tried to concentrate, but Bob's reaction to her throwing up kept coming back into her mind. Maybe she was pregnant. She hadn't even thought of that. But they'd been so careful and always used protection. She decided she'd stop and pick up a test on the way home.

When she finally finished her court calendar it was nearly 12:30 p.m. She waited in the lobby for Bob.

"Hi, Sobs. Are you feeling better?" Bob asked as he walked up.

"Yeah. I feel much better."

"Lunch?"

"I don't have time. We have the Kemp hearing this afternoon and I'm meeting with the CASA worker a little ahead of time." She nodded her head toward the front door. "It looks like you don't have time, either. There's your buddy, Mr. Kemp."

Mr. Kemp, pacing and snorting outside the courthouse, threw down his cigarette and approached Bob as he walked out. "Who the hell is this CASA person who's brainwashing my kids?"

Bob spoke in a soft voice. "Calm down, Mr. Kemp. Come over here and sit down. We'll talk." He led his client over to a concrete bench. Kemp took out a pack of cigarettes, removed one from the pack, started to put them back in his pocket, and then stopped and offered one to Bob. "No, thanks. I quit." Bob sighed. He still wanted to smoke, wanted the taste, the sensation. "CASA stands for Court Appointed Special Advocate. Among other things, her job is to interview everyone, determine the child's feelings, and report back to the court with recommendations of services. It would really help to have her on our side. So, what's the problem?"

"Her name is Weinstein. She's a Jew!" Kemp stood up, flailing his arms in the air, his voice loud enough for everyone to hear. "The social worker is a damn nigger and the CASA worker is a kike! How am I, a white American, supposed to get justice?"

A crowd had gathered outside the courthouse. People walking up the stairs stopped to listen to the ranting—people of all colors, some laughing, some angry. Bob said, "Sit down and lower your voice before you start a riot."

Kemp remained standing. Two African-Americans in suits suddenly looked menacing as they stepped toward him. Kemp turned around. "I'm not talking to you. You don't like what I have to say, then get the hell out of here." The noise alerted the sheriffs. Four deputies dashed out of the courthouse and stepped between Kemp and the two men. Noise from the sheriff's radios blared. Bob scooted back a little on the bench, bracing himself. He had been punched in court before. Still, rather than being afraid, he was more astonished at the ignorance of his client and embarrassed at his behavior. Bob scooted over a little more, giving the sheriffs room to block him if his client were sucker punched, which Bob secretly hoped would happen.

"If you have a hearing, go on inside; otherwise please move along," one of the deputies said to the crowd. Two of them herded the bystanders forward. The other two—Michael, thirty-something and fit, and Ernie, a little older and a little heavier—stayed next to Kemp until the crowd had dispersed. Kemp stood there huffing and puffing like a bull about to take on a matador.

Michael said, "You okay, Bob?"

"Yeah." Bob remained seated.

Michael looked Mr. Kemp in the eye and said quietly, "You need to settle down or we'll have to cuff you and take you in."

Kemp raised his voice once again and leaned into the deputy's face. "You can't arrest me for talking." Then louder. "This is America. I have a right to say what I want when I want." He whipped around to Bob. "You're my attorney. Tell them about free speech. These morons don't seem to know about it."

Bob stood up, moved very close to his client, and spoke softly, but sternly. "Look, Mr. Kemp. I think you need to know that 'freedom of speech' excludes what they call 'hate speech,' which if you haven't reached already, you're very close to doing."

Mr. Kemp puffed up his chest. "But...."

"Ehh...," Bob said as he raised his right hand and waved it in front of his face. "I think these officers are more concerned about keeping the peace right now, which brings up a whole new issue. But if you continue, I won't be able to stop them from making an arrest." Then in a flippant tone Bob said, "I could, however, help defend you once you are arrested." Mr. Kemp sighed, deflating his chest; his shoulders dropped. Bob continued more seriously. "But I don't think you want that. More importantly, we have a good shot at winning this trial today if, and that's a big 'if,' you can calm down and do as I say. So, if you want your kids back, I suggest you control yourself and let me do my job. Either way, I'm walking out of here today a free man. You decide how you want to play it." Bob picked up his files and started to walk off.

Kemp reached out and grabbed Bob's arm. Bob turned around to face him, shaking him off, and saw a tear in Kemp's eye. "All right," Kemp said. "I just want my kids back. I'm going crazy without them."

Thelma Barnes, the social worker, hobbled into the courtroom and took a seat next to County Council at the far left of the table, her arthritic knees slowing her down as she walked. On the right side of County Council was Robin Weinstein, the CASA volunteer. Next was Wagner, sitting by his client, Mrs. Kemp. Then there was Sabre, minor's counsel without the children present. Bob sat next to Sabre and on his right, at the far end of the table, was Mr. Kemp. The judge was on the bench, the court clerk sat at the desk next to the judge, and the court reporter was on the other side of the judge near the counsel tables. Two bailiffs stood in the back about ten feet from Mr. Kemp.

"I'll hear arguments on the demurrer," Judge Hekman said.

"Thank you, Your Honor." Bob stood up, hands folded in front of him, and stated matter-of-factly, "I've provided counsel with copies of my motion to dismiss for failure to state a cause of action. My client is not disputing the facts in this case." Bob looked at his client, his voice taking on a political speech tone. "In fact, he is proud of his American heritage, his right to free speech, his freedom of religion, and his right to bear arms. He readily admits he's teaching his children at an early age to handle guns." Mr. Kemp sat up straighter in his chair, puffing up his chest. "The guns are never loaded; the ammunition is locked up. This is not a safety issue, Your Honor. In fact, it's quite the contrary. He believes if his children learn to respect and handle guns they will be safer in the long run. As far as his choice of targets, it's ludicrous to think it affects the safety of these children." Mrs. Kemp was nodding her head in agreement.

"The petition states these parents are teaching hatred which results in fights, putting the children at risk. There is no evidence indicating my client has in any way taught his children to fight. He is a peaceful man with very strong beliefs. And yes, he gets angry when other people don't allow him to express those beliefs. He's not angry, Your Honor, because they think differently than him." Bob's voice grew louder and with more indignation. "He's angry because they try to infringe on his rights, his constitutional right to free speech, his right to raise his family as he sees fit, his right to bear arms, and his basic right of freedom of religion.

These are fundamental rights granted to us by our forefathers." Mr. Kemp balled up his fist and struck it in the air in front of him. Bob lowered his voice. "All parents teach their children their religious beliefs and their heritage. Some parents teach their children Catholicism, or Judaism, or the teachings of Buddha. My client finds this appalling. He believes the only true church is 'The White Church.' This is his heritage. His birthright. Furthermore, it is his religion.

"The petition alleges facts that are undisputed by my client, but his position is basically, 'So what?' These facts have not resulted in any physical harm to his children and there is no real reason to believe that it will."

Both parents nodded in agreement.

"According to the Welfare and Institutions Code 300 (c), the department needs to show *'The child is suffering serious emotional damage, or is at substantial risk of suffering serious emotional damage, evidenced by severe anxiety, depression, withdrawal....'* There is no evidence of any severe anxiety, depression, or withdrawal. The department will likely argue the petition also talks about 'untoward aggressive behavior toward self or others,' but there is no evidence of that, either. The fights Kat was involved in were provoked by other students. She merely protected her space."

"That's right," Mrs. Kemp said out loud.

The judge said, "Mrs. Kemp, please refrain from commenting."

Wagner leaned into his client and whispered in her ear, then nodded to the judge, who said, "Please proceed, Mr. Clark."

"And, in addition, it is my client's contention that this is a strong and sincerely held religious belief and therefore not covered by this code section. In fact, this goes to the very core of his religion. We're asking the court to dismiss this petition for failure to show an underlying cause of action."

Judge Hekman cocked her head to one side and looked out over her glasses at Mrs. Kemp and her attorney. "And Mr. Wagner, I see you filed on behalf of the mother as well. Would you like to add anything?"

"Yes, Your Honor," Mr. Wagner said before he stood up. "I agree with the comments made by Mr. Clark and would add that my client is very dedicated to her religious beliefs, so much so that she went to the trouble to change her name."

"Excuse me. You say she changed her name for her church?"

Mr. Wagner waved his right hand in a circular motion. "You know, like the Buddhists or Muslims obtain a new name. Or even the Catholics are expected to choose some kind of saint's name."

The judge shook her head in disbelief. "Mr. Wagner, are you saying you have to change your name to be a member of this church?"

"No, and I don't think you're actually required by the Qur'an to have an Islamic name, either, but I'm not entirely sure about that. I do know that when you're confirmed in the Catholic church, you receive another name. But my client did in fact change her name from Patricia Kemp to Kelly K. Kemp and…."

The judge held her hands up, palms up. "Whoa. Just a minute. I'm almost afraid to ask this, but are you suggesting everyone in this church has the initials KKK?"

The mother shook her head signifying no and her attorney said, "No, Your Honor."

"Well, that's a relief," the judge said rolling her eyes.

Mr. Wagner continued. "I just point that out as an indication of her true dedication to her religion." Looking forward toward the court, Sabre rolled her eyes up in her head. The court reporter saw it and smirked.

"I can see how dedicated she is, Mr. Wagner, by the tattoo of her initials on her bicep." The judge looked at Sabre. "What is your position, Ms. Brown?"

Sabre stood up. "Your Honor, the petition speaks only to religion as a defense if the parent fails to provide adequate mental health treatment. That is not the case here. This is not about the treatment of mental health at all. In fact, if anything, this is about creating a need for mental health treatment. This clause does not give parents the right to beat their child for religious reasons, or neglect them, or put them at risk in any fashion such as these parents have done. I believe there is sufficient cause of action stated and the court should hear the case on the merits."

The judge said, "County Council?"

It took a few seconds for the attorney for the department to stand up. When she did, she leaned on the table supporting her weight and pushed herself up. She was so heavy her skirt appeared shorter in the back than the front, and Sabre noticed her ample nose had a mole with a whisker growing out of it. "I join in the remarks of minors' counsel and submit on our response to the demurrer," she said.

"Very well," the judge said. "We'll take a fifteen-minute recess, and when we return I'll have my decision."

The County Council waddled out of the courtroom with the social worker and the Kemps. After everyone else exited, Bob, Sabre, and Wagner remained. Wagner threw the papers in his folder, dumped it in his briefcase, and slammed it shut as if he had completed a good day's work. He put his briefcase upright on the table, leaned his elbow on it, and asked, "So what do you think Hekman will do?"

Bob hesitated, waiting until everyone had left the courtroom. "Well, she's considering it, and that's more than most juvenile judges would have done," Bob said. He turned to Sabre. "Do you think she's going to grant the demurrer?"

"I don't know. It is a weak petition and I'm not sure there's a cause of action stated." She sighed. "But I'm sure those children need something besides a constant diet of hate fed to them every day, and for that reason I'll continue the fight." Sabre shuffled toward the door. "By the way, Wags, your argument sucked."

"Hey, Bob had said all the good stuff. It's all I had left. Besides, you never know about Hekman. Sometimes that crazy old coot buys this nonsense."

25

Sabre walked upstairs with the CASA worker, Robin Weinstein. "So, how did you get so lucky as to get this case?" Sabre asked.

"Just next in line on the rotation. They offered to pass on me because of my last name, but I told them no. I wasn't about to back down from these people. But now it's looking kind of futile because, since the parents got wind of my name, the children won't talk to me anymore."

"I know, even though the visits are supervised, it doesn't keep the parents from saying exactly what they want to say. They don't even try to hide the racist slurs, even now while they're in the system."

Robin threw her hands out, palms up. "The funny part is I'm not even Jewish. I'm probably more white Anglo-Saxon than the Kemps. But I guess since I'm married to a Jewish man, I'm suspect anyway."

"It may all be moot after Hekman's decision today." They stopped at the top of steps. "If she grants their motion, the case is over."

"Do you think she'll grant it?"

"You never know with her. She won't want to, but if she feels the petition's not legally sound, she'll have to grant it." Sabre walked over to a bench in the hallway and took a seat. Robin followed her. Sabre turned to her with a sympathetic voice. "Did you visit much with the children before you got the cold shoulder?"

"Yeah, I talked to them a few times and was able to spend a little quality time with them. Kat was starting to open up."

"Did Kat say anything about what they do, where they go, what her parents do? Anything that might lead us to something?"

"She said something about going to Perris."

"California or France?"

"California. Actually, I was talking about Paris, France, and Kat told me she had been there. After a few questions, I realized she was talking about Perris, California."

"Really? What did she say exactly?"

"She said there's a beautiful castle made of stone that sits on top of a hill in Perris. She said they go there a lot."

"To the castle?"

"Not to the castle itself, but I had the impression it was somewhere very near there because she could see the castle—even climb the hill to reach it if she wanted to and if it wasn't dark."

Sabre leaned into Robin and said, "Think. Did she say when they go there? What day of the week, maybe?"

"I think it's on Sunday because they go after church. They have services twice on Sunday in their 'white church.' I'm thinking they go after the evening service because she said it's usually dark."

"Thanks," Sabre said. She leaped up, then reached down and hugged Robin. "By Jove, we just might have something." Sabre darted downstairs to seek County Council. "See you in court."

Back inside the courtroom, everyone was seated when the judge came out and took the bench. Mr. Kemp sat up straight and confidently, almost in defiance of the robes before him, his attorney next to him. Mrs. Kemp whispered something to her attorney as the judge took her seat. "I'm ready to rule on the motion," she said. The courtroom became very still. "First, I want to say something to the parents." She looked directly at the father and then the mother. "You ought to be ashamed of yourselves for teaching those children to hate and to be hateful. You've planted seeds they'll carry with them for a lifetime and most likely make their lives miserable." Bob caught Wagner's eye. Wagner winked. Sabre saw it and sighed. She knew Hekman wouldn't be giving them the lecture unless she was cutting them loose. "You've taken the innocence away from your children."

Mr. Kemp's face turned red and he half rose from his chair. Bob grabbed his arm and pulled him back down. "Sit," he said, a little louder than he probably intended. Then he leaned over and whispered something in his ear. Mr. Kemp nodded, took a deep breath, and squeezed his lips tightly together. Wagner spoke to his client as well, most likely in anticipation of her outburst.

The judge continued, "I see a lot of cases come through here. Every day I deal with parents who lose control and beat their children, sometimes to death, or neglect their children because of their sick addictions, but I have to say this case disgusts me even more than some of those. Although I'm not excusing their behaviors, those people need help with their tempers, with their addictions, but you two you are making a conscious choice to teach your children to hate. And you do it in the name of religion. That is just wrong on so many levels." Her voice had risen almost to a shout. She shook her head and lowered her voice. "I don't think there's any hope for you. No amount of therapy is ever going to teach you anything. You'll never believe you've done anything wrong, and when one of your children gets killed because you taught them to put themselves in impossible situations, you'll blame the minority, and it'll just boost your sick beliefs another level."

The judge took a deep breath, blew it out, closed her eyes as if she were meditating, and then said, "The parent's motion is granted. The petition is set aside...."

Mr. and Mrs. Kemp both stood up. Mr. Kemp threw a clenched fist in the air shouting, "Yes!" He turned and faced his wife, and each reached up with their right hands and clapped it against the other's.

The bailiff walked over to Mr. Kemp, tapped him on the shoulder and said, "Sit down." Another bailiff entered from the back and stood on the opposite side of Mr. Kemp. Another who had entered from the hallway stayed directly behind Mrs. Kemp, keeping a vigilant watch on her movements.

The judge spoke over the confusion. "Enough, Mr. Kemp, or I'll hold you in contempt."

He snapped his head up toward Bob and asked, "Can she do that?"

"She sure can. You might want to just sit down and be quiet."

"What about my right to free speech?" The bailiffs stepped in closer.

"What about quitting while you're ahead?" Bob said quietly. "Now please sit." Mr. Kemp grumbled as he sat down.

Judge Hekman continued, purposefully ignoring the outbursts. "I do not believe those children are safe in your home, but I also don't believe the department filed a worthy petition. So, I'm not sending the children home today."

Mr. Kemp started to rise from his chair shouting, "What the f…" when the bailiffs each put their hands on his shoulders and arms, and pushed him back in his chair.

Just then Mrs. Kemp jumped up and began to climb across the table toward the judge yelling, "You bitch!"

County Council slid her chair out of the way, making room for the bailiff to react. Mrs. Kemp put one foot up on her chair and flung the other one up on the table, kicking Sabre in the head as she stepped up. Sabre let out a yell as Bob tried to catch her, but she fell to the floor with a thud, knocking the wind out of her. Gasps resounded throughout the courtroom. The bailiff grabbed Mrs. Kemp by both arms and pulled her back into him, falling against the railing and almost going down with her. "Get your hands off me," she hollered, as her legs flew up in the air and came back down on Sabre's chest.

Bailiffs rushed into the room from both directions. Mr. Kemp tried to take down two of them by himself in a frenzy to reach his wife. He yanked away and lunged toward her, but a bailiff slapped the handcuffs on him before he reached her.

Sabre heard Judge Hekman bang her gavel on the sounding board. She looked up from the floor to see two bailiffs on either side of Mr. Kemp, another two surrounded Mrs. Kemp, and both parents in handcuffs. Sabre saw Bob on his knees bending over her as she started to stand. She held on to him. "I'm okay," she said, "really." She rubbed her chest. "She whacked me pretty good, but I'm fine."

Bob helped her to her seat. "Are you sure?"

"Yup." She looked up at the judge and gave her a half smile, cleared her throat, and said, "I'm ready, Your Honor."

The judge shook her head and her whole body trembled with it. She looked directly at the parents. "Hmmph….As I was saying, the children are not going home today. And instead of ruling on the motion this afternoon, I am now taking it under submission and we'll continue this hearing next Wednesday." She shifted her gaze to County Council. "The department needs to give serious consideration to a new petition or be prepared to let this case go," she paused, "depending, of course, on my ruling on the demurrer."

The bailiffs walked the parents out the back door into the holding tank. The attorneys left through the front. Bob said, "Those kids are staying at Polinsky. Damn it, we had that one won until they flipped out."

Sabre said, "Do you think they'll keep the parents?"

"They might let my guy go, but I think they'll keep the mom. She went too far," Bob responded.

Wagner growled. "The stupid woman deserves it. We had won, and then she blew it. They don't listen to a damn thing we tell them." Wagner was still grumbling when Sabre and Bob left him and walked out of the courthouse toward their cars.

As Sabre entered her car, she felt the discomfort in her chest where Mrs. Kemp had kicked her. She drove directly to Long's Drug Store and bought a pregnancy test and two ice packs. She'd use them tonight and see how she felt in the morning.

From there she drove to her office to check her phone messages and pick up some files for court the next day. While she was packing up her files her cell phone rang. "Hi, sweetie," Luke said. "Can you pick me up at the airport tomorrow evening?"

"Sure." The sound of his voice made her breathe easier, surprised to hear he was coming home so soon. The last time they talked he hadn't mentioned it. "What time?"

"My flight arrives at ten minutes to seven. I'll meet you outside in front about seven o'clock."

Sabre smiled and then took a deep breath, but the stretch hurt. She placed her hand on her sore chest. She knew she had discomfort to look forward to for a few days.

She still had to run that test. She didn't want it to be positive. She wasn't ready. She wasn't sure she'd ever be ready. It was such a responsibility, and did she want to bring children into this world of destruction? A world with Kemps spreading hate. She couldn't stand the thought of her children, or any child, living with such hatred. *The test will be negative. It has to be.*

26

JP's hands were dry and his face chapped from the wind as he drove into Brighton, Wisconsin. He drove past miles of trees along the highway and acres of land with old wooden fences enclosing animals or defining boundaries. The trees glistened with moisture, interspersed with green fields of wheat. He knew that, within a few months, the fields would be brown and bales of hay would be spread out across them. He liked the Midwest. The people were easy to talk to and generally quite helpful. Life here was quiet and uncomplicated. A cow mooed.

"Are you agreeing with me, or insulted because I think your life is too simple? Just like a woman," JP said aloud. "Wow, I'm talking to cows. I better get back to the city."

Once in town, he spotted a coffee shop and decided it would be a good place to start asking questions. If that didn't work, there was always a bar.

When JP walked into the coffee shop, there were only three people inside, likely left over from the breakfast crowd. He took off his cowboy hat and hung it on the rack by the door. Lunch was approaching. If he had coffee, then lunch, and coffee again with dessert, he could spread it out long enough to maybe speak to several people. He took a seat at the counter next to an old man with white whiskers, leaving the seat on the other side open for another possible informant.

"Morning," JP said.

"Not much left," the old man said, as he took a bite of his food.

"Of your breakfast?"

"Nope, of the morning."

"True enough. Have you eaten here before?" JP asked.

"Yup, lived here all my life. Best place in town for breakfast, except when Pearl burns the toast." JP thought he was joking, but saw no smile on the old man's face.

"I heard that, Charley," a voice rang out from the open kitchen directly behind the counter. "I don't burn the toast. You're just too damn fussy."

"She's got hearing like a bat, that one." Still no smile.

The middle-aged waitress, with mousy brown hair pulled back in a ponytail and wearing a beige dress and brown apron, approached JP. "Coffee?" she asked.

"Yes, for now. And could you leave a menu. I may want to eat in a bit."

She laid the menu down, poured a cup of coffee. "Cream?"

"No, thanks."

"What are you doing in these parts?" the waitress asked.

"Looking for the people on this list." JP opened his list of names. "I found this among some stuff in my dad's belongings. He died when I was pretty young. My mom had a box of things that belonged to him, and I found it after she passed away last year. She would never talk about my father, so I know very little about him. I was hoping I might find some answers here in this town."

"Let me take a look at that." The old man took the list and held it at arm's length. "What was your pa's name?"

"Jacob Johnson."

"Can't say as I recall anyone by that name." He moved his coffee cup forward for the waitress to fill it. "But I can tell you a few things about some of those people on yer list."

"That would be great." JP took out his pen to make notes. The cafe was starting to fill and the noise level had picked up.

"The Jones boys have all passed on. Mary Lou's still here. She's married to Jerry Tollefson. His sisters, Ruby and Mabel, went off to college and stayed away." He paused as if he were trying to remember. "Don't know where they are, but I expect Jerry would. The Gerstner girls passed on, one just a few months ago, the other a few years back. Charles still lives here, but he's been a little tetched since Vietnam. Don't think he'd be much help." Charley read through the list again. "Don't remember anyone named Paul." He looked around the restaurant and raising his voice asked, "Anyone in here remember someone in this town named Paul or Yvonne Marticello?"

"No, nah…," the crowd responded half-heartedly. The waitress came over and filled his coffee cup.

Big, round Pearl stepped out of the kitchen, wiping her hands on the bottom right corner of her stained, white apron. Her white hair was in an old but stylish do sprayed so no hair moved; she wore light makeup except for the bright red lipstick. She smiled a sheepish smile. "I remember Paul Marticello. Best looking kid in school, especially by the eighth grade. He was in my class. He moved away the summer before high school. Too bad, too. He was just starting to notice me." She pretended to swoon.

Two men, one in overalls, the other wearing a plaid shirt, Levis, and a Detroit Tigers baseball cap walked over to Charley and looked over his shoulder. "What's going on?" the man in the overalls asked.

"This young man's trying to find these folks to see if they can tell him anything about his pa." Charley stood up and turned toward the tables, most of which had filled up. "Does anyone in here remember a guy named Jacob Johnson?"

"He would've probably been here in the late fifties," JP added.

The crowd murmured, "Nope."

Charley, still standing and facing the crowd, more of whom had gathered closer to the counter, asked, "Anyone know what happened to James Herold?"

"Nope."

"How about Roger Torvinan?"

Mumbles could be heard around the cafe. "Roger joined the Army. After he did his tour, I heard he moved to California," the man in the overalls said.

Charley asked, "What about Martha Broden or Edith Underdahl?"

Pearl, still standing there with the crowd, said, "The Broden girl married a guy from Milwaukee and moved there. Edith left in high school. She and her mom moved somewhere. No idea where to, but Mary Lou might know. They were best friends."

The waitress was taking orders and putting up order slips for Pearl, but Pearl didn't seem to be in a hurry to read them. Charley handed the paper back to JP. The crowd meandered to their seats. Pearl was still standing there when Charley spoke up, "Don't you have some cookin' to do, woman?" She waddled off to the kitchen.

The waitress took JP's order for the meatloaf. Charley paid his check and left a dollar tip. He stood up to leave. "I hope you find what yer looking for…about your pa, I mean." He smiled and walked out. JP wondered if he knew he was after something else, the smart old goat.

JP finished his lunch, obtained directions to Mary Lou and Jerry Tollefson's house, and went on his way. Pearl had called ahead to see if anyone was home and if it was all right for him to drop by.

When he arrived at their home, Mary Lou graciously invited him inside, appearing delighted to have company. JP removed his hat as he walked in, but kept it in his hand. Jerry offered him a beer, which he declined. Mary Lou brought him some iced tea. "What can we do for you?" Jerry asked.

JP handed him the list. "As Pearl explained, I found this in my father's things and I was hoping to find someone who could tell me something about him. Both of your names are on the list. Did either of you ever meet a man or boy named Jacob Johnson? That was my father's name."

Mary Lou shook her head. "Not me."

"Me neither," Jerry said.

"Perhaps you know something about the people on the list. If I could find them, maybe someone will remember." JP fiddled with his hat. "The folks at the diner were very helpful, but there were a few they didn't know about. I've marked them with an X."

Jerry handed Mary Lou the list. She picked up her reading glasses off the end table and put them on. "Let me see….I have no idea what happened to James. He left here shortly after high school, but I don't know where he went." She turned to Jerry, "Do you, Jer?"

"Nope. He left for Chicago the first time. He stayed there a few months and then came back. A few months later he just left without telling anyone, and he never returned."

Mary Lou looked at the list again. "I'm not sure where Gladys went, but she ran away in high school." She shook her head, and made a tsk sound with her tongue. "Her father used to beat her. One night he came home and caught her with a boy from Bristol. She had been seeing him for a while. All the kids knew about it, but when her father found out, he beat her real bad. She didn't come to school, but Edie and I saw her the next day at the store. She looked awful. She sneaked out that night and never came back."

Then Mary Lou's face lit up when she spoke. "Ah, Edith. I called her Edie. She was my best friend all through grade school and in high school. She and her mom moved to Chicago in our junior year. Edie was pregnant by Gary Herold. Edie's mom took her and moved so no one would find out."

"Maybe Edie and Gary got married," JP suggested.

"No. He wanted to, but Edie didn't. She fell in love with someone else after they moved."

"So you'd hear from her?"

"Yeah, she wrote me letters almost every week. She had it pretty good there. She lived in a big house; she called it 'the castle.' It wasn't their house, though. Her mom took a job as a maid for some rich Italian guy."

"Why did she call it the castle?"

"It was huge. It had twenty-some bedrooms and acres and acres of land around it. She drew a picture of it for me and sent it in one of her letters. She could draw real good."

"Are you still in touch with her?"

"No. She wrote for about a year. She had Gary's baby. It was a boy. And as I said, she'd fallen in love with someone else. The guy was someone who lived in 'the castle,' and I don't think he was part of the hired help."

"Why?"

"Because she was real secretive about him. She said she shouldn't be seeing him, but she did anyway. She told me not to write anything about him in my letters back to her in case someone else got a hold of them. Then one day the letters stopped. And the last two letters I sent her came back."

"Does Gary still live around here?"

"No, he lived here for a long time raising his son, Neil."

"Gary raised their boy?"

"Yes, he got him when he was maybe about six months old. He said Edie gave the boy to him and disappeared. He said he had no idea where she was."

"Do you think he was telling the truth?"

"No, I didn't, at least not at first, because I couldn't believe Edie would leave her son and never see him again. But some years went by and she never came back, so maybe he didn't know where she was."

"Is Neil still around here?"

"No, he and his father left here after Gary's mother passed. Neil was about ten years old then. Gary was just a kid himself, only about twenty-eight. Anyway, they moved on and never came back. Rumor had it they moved to somewhere in Texas, but I don't know if that's true or not." Mary Lou stood up, "Wait, I still have that picture Edie sent me." She walked into another room and returned with an eight-by-ten drawing in a cheap picture frame and handed it to JP.

"Villa Paceco," JP said.

27

JP approached Chicago just as the rush hour traffic hit; he wished he had left earlier to avoid the mess. This was when he longed for Texas or places like Montana or Wyoming. He knew he was a cowboy at heart, but he needed the city to make a living. A car inched its way into the space in front of him. He looked to the left. A car passed him on the shoulder, and horns honked. He could see the rage building on the face of the man in the car next to him and a child crying in the backseat. The man yelled, and the woman in the passenger seat cowered as he bellowed.

He worked his way back to the mansion just in time to see Luke leaving in a limo. He dropped back and followed him into the city traffic, which was still moving slowly. Luke's driver approached Paceco's, the same restaurant the cabby had taken him to the night before, and pulled in behind a car that had just parked near the front door. The short, round driver opened the car's passenger door. Two slender legs in high heels stepped out of the car, attached to a tall, dark-haired woman in a slinky, red cocktail dress. Luke stepped out and the man drove off. Luke put his arm around the sexy woman and they walked together into the restaurant.

JP felt his face heat up with anger at seeing Luke with another woman. When he finally found a parking spot four blocks away, he removed his cowboy hat, put on his new Cub's hat, and walked into the restaurant, mingling with several other people as they entered. Once inside, he slipped away and found his way to the bar. He looked around but didn't see Luke.

"What can I get you?" the bartender asked.

"Coors Light, please," JP said, thinking the bartender didn't look old enough to be serving drinks.

He returned with the beer. JP laid a ten-dollar bill on the counter. "Which way is the restroom?"

"Right around there, past the bar, at the end of the hall." He pointed behind the bar.

JP pulled his cap down and cautiously walked around the bar, past booths on his left and barstools on his right. He kept looking around to see if he could find Luke. He didn't see him or the girl. Once past the bar, he saw another dining area to his left. A rather wide gentleman was standing just inside the doorway. He stepped in just behind him and glanced quickly around the room. No Luke.

He walked back and into the hallway. He could see the men's room about ten feet in front of him. Just as he came to a pay telephone booth on the wall, he saw the men's room door open and Luke exit. JP stuck his head inside the phone booth, picking up the phone and putting it to his ear. He heard another door open and footsteps coming toward him from the direction of the restrooms.

"You promised," a female voice whined.

"Look, babe, I'm trying here." Luke sounded exasperated. "But this is just the way it is. You know that."

They were right behind JP now. He kept his head buried inside the wooden phone shelter, turning slightly as he heard the footsteps pass him. He could see Luke and the girl turn toward the private dining area. JP gave them ample time to walk inside the dining room, and then he walked straight out past the bar and outside.

JP stepped into the light crowd on the sidewalk and moved in the direction of his car. Two huge goons followed him out of the bar and walked in his direction. One had a sculpted face and square jaw; the other had a shaved head. He felt like he was being followed by "The Terminator" and "Mr. Clean." As he moved past a blue mailbox on his right, he picked up his pace and tried to blend in with other people. He walked between an elderly couple hobbling along, who cursed at him, and passed a woman walking an Irish setter, who nipped at his leg. He glanced back, hoping he had lost them, but they stood like tree trunks above the crowd and were gaining ground. With his car still a good three blocks away, he knew he'd never make it. He crossed the street, dodging cars, but they followed. When he spotted a taxicab coming, he stepped out in the street and waved for the cab, but it kept going. He had lost time hailing the cab. He felt for his gun in his holster under his jacket. The cold steel gave him comfort. As he looked back, he saw "The Terminator" using his cell phone. They both outweighed him, and they were younger and in better shape. He was way too old to outrun them.

JP kept walking, faster now, past a nightclub and some condos. Two skyscrapers stood tall, one on each side of the street. He crossed the street. Another tall building was on his right and a parking lot was across the street. Two more blocks to go. Another skyscraper, perhaps a bank with offices. Certain it would be locked, he made no attempt to enter. Trees lined the street for the next block; the street lights shone down like a spotlight on him, keeping him visible to his stalkers. He looked back. They were gaining, but it seemed they intentionally kept their distance. He could see the parking lot on the next block, but he knew he couldn't reach the car, get inside it, and drive away without the two goons catching him.

He spotted a Catholic church on his right just across the intersection. Cars filled the spots in the church parking lot. Noise emanated from the lighted church as the service proceeded. He ran across the street, dodging the traffic, and up the steps of the church. He ducked inside. People were kneeling, Celine Dion was bellowing "Because You Loved Me," and JP could see an elderly bride and groom at the altar. He pulled off his cap, stepped quickly and quietly around to the side behind a pillar, and stood where he could see if anyone entered. The church was quite large and the pews nearly filled, but only a couple of teenagers sitting in the back rows seemed to notice him.

The church door flew open. The priest stopped talking and looked at the two intruders. All heads turned to the back of the church.

"Sorry, Father," Mr. Clean said. His bald head sparkled in the light. He made the sign of the cross, stepped back out, and closed the door behind him.

JP remained behind the pillar until the service ended. The priest announced, "The bride and groom would like you all to join them in the church hall for their reception." Then Dean Martin came loudly and clearly over the PA system singing, "That's Amoré" as the newly married couple hobbled down the aisle and left the church. JP walked out behind a tall gentleman, staying close behind him as the crowd threw birdseed on the bride and groom.

He blended into the crowd as they walked to the hall adjoining the church. He looked around for the two men, wondering why they were after him. Had Luke spotted him? He walked into the reception hall and tried to mingle without having a conversation that might give him away as a wedding crasher. A woman about forty approached him. He smiled.

"Nice wedding, huh?" she said.

"Very nice."

"It's great to see someone their age and so in love."

"Yeah."

"How do you know Alice and Lynn?"

"Uh…the church. From church," JP said. "Will you please excuse me?" He walked away, feeling rude and uncomfortable. He spotted an exit on the side of the hall, walked toward it, opened the door, and looked around outside. It appeared safe to leave. No one appeared to be on the sidewalk. All he had to do was cross the street to the parking lot where his car was parked. The street in front of the parking lot was lined with trees and shadows from the one street light on the corner.

JP crossed the street, breathing a little easier, thinking he was probably safe when an arm reached out from behind a tree and grabbed him.

A bolt of raw adrenaline shot through JP's veins. He clenched his hand and plunged forward with his right arm when a fist hit him on the side of his face. He fell backward, groaning as he fell. One of the men caught him before he hit the ground; the other hit him again. JP brought his knee up and stretched his leg out, giving "The Terminator" a cowboy boot to the groin that sent him to the ground. Mr. Clean pulled JP's arms backward, giving his friend time to stand up. When he did, he punched JP in the stomach and face. He punched again. And again.

JP's anger boiled up. He could feel the blood trickle down his face. Pain shot through his body like someone was tying his intestine in knots.

Mr. Clean grabbed him by the chin. "Who you following, Asshole?"

"No one."

The man hit him in the stomach again. "Sorry, I didn't hear you. I thought you said 'no one.'"

"So you're dumb and deaf," JP responded tasting blood.

Mr. Clean repeatedly slugged his fists into JP's abdomen while "The Terminator" held him. "Stupid wise ass." Another punch to the face. "Who you after?"

"All right, all right." JP took a breath. He saw a couple walking up the sidewalk. They crossed the street. The man hit him again. "Ok. Her name is Linda Romano."

"What do you want with her?" The man stood nose to nose with JP. His breath smelled of garlic and alcohol.

"I'm a PI. Her husband thinks she's cheating on him." JP could taste the blood in his mouth.

"Did you see her?"

"Only for a minute. She came in and sat down at the bar alone. I went to the restroom, and when I came back she was leaving. I started to follow her and you two showed up."

"Mr. Clean" slapped JP on the face. "Stay out of Pececo's, you hear?"

"No more Pececo's," JP said. "The Terminator" punched him in the stomach. When JP doubled up, he hit him on the back of the head. JP fell to the ground unconscious.

28

Leonard Cohen blared out of Sabre's cell phone. "Bob," Sabre said into the phone before he could say anything. "Are home pregnancy tests always accurate?"

"How would I know? Why are you asking me?"

"You're the closest thing I know to a doctor."

"But I'm not a doctor."

"Well, your dad is."

"That doesn't mean I know anything. Besides, he's a urologist. It's a little different field," Bob said.

"Same general area on the body. Anyway, you know stuff. Just tell me. Are they accurate?"

"I've heard they're generally correct. So, was it positive?"

"No, thank God! But now I'm worried it may be wrong."

"Then make an appointment and get yourself checked."

"But you think it's correct, right?"

"Sobs, you're acting crazy."

"I know. But I'm scared. I don't want to be pregnant."

"You're not pregnant."

"But I've been feeling sick."

"You've also been under a lot of stress with Betty's case and the Kemp case. That's probably what's making you sick. I just called to see how you were doing. Get some rest. Bye."

"Wait. Have you heard from JP?"

"No. You haven't either, I take it."

"No, and he's starting to tick me off. He promised me he'd check in every day. He's always so diligent about time and such. I've been trying to call him, but I'm not getting an answer. He didn't call me last night, and when he's investigating he usually checks in with me at the end of the day."

"When did you talk to him last?"

"The night before last, but he didn't say much."

"I'm sure he'll call you today," Bob reassured her, but Sabre thought she heard concern in Bob's voice. She knew this was unusual behavior for JP.

"Why do you suppose he doesn't answer?"

"Uh...because he's busy...."

"You don't suppose there's something wrong, do you?"

"What could be wrong? There you go getting yourself worked up."

Sabre shook it off. "You're right. There's nothing wrong. Later."

She took a long shower, washed her hair, and put on some Red cologne. It was Luke's favorite. She was relieved the pregnancy test was negative and had almost convinced herself it was accurate. She put on her favorite jeans and a top that showed a little cleavage and drove to the airport.

Sabre circled the airport three times before she spotted Luke. He waved and smiled when he saw her. After he put his suitcase inside the trunk, he opened the car door and leaned in for a long kiss. "Hmmm....You smell good. You taste good, too," he said.

Sabre felt that wonderful feeling of love or lust or whatever it was. It was warm and wonderful and scary. "I'm so glad you're home."

"Me, too." He reached for her hand, brought it up to his lips, and then kissed it gently.

"How was your trip?"

"Good. Uneventful, but productive."

She caressed his leg. "What did you do? What's a typical work trip like for you?"

"I'm sure it would bore you."

"No, I want to know what it is you do." She bent her head down, tilted it, and opened her eyes wide, looking up at him like a puppy dog. "I'm really interested."

He smiled down at her. "Okay, but you need to try to stay awake when I tell you. This time I had to work on a software program for a large corporation. It's a program that sorts and inventories their parts in the warehouse."

"How do you know that stuff?"

"I'm familiar with this program because I've been working on it for several years now. But even if I didn't know it, there are certain basic things that can go wrong. Eventually, if you're going to work on programs like that you have to get to know them. Otherwise, you're limited as to what you can do."

Sabre turned to look at Luke and felt a pain in her ribcage. "Oh," she squeaked.

"See, it's painful."

Sabre laughed and then grabbed her chest, deflecting the pain. "No, it's not you. There was a little incident at court today." Before Luke would go on about his trip, he made Sabre tell him what happened. She didn't want to dwell on it and turned the conversation back to Luke. "So, how many of these different programs do you work on?"

He shook his head, but answered. "I have contracts with six major corporations. That keeps me busy." He placed her hand on his knee. "What's this sudden interest in my work?"

"It's not sudden. I've always been interested. I just know so little about computers, other than the things I need to know to do my legal briefs; I don't really know what questions to ask." Sabre squeezed his knee. "Besides, if we're going to be living together, I ought to at least know what you do for a living."

Luke put his hand on Sabre's shoulder, rubbing gently down her arm. He reached up and touched her hair and the nape of her neck. Chills ran down her body. She turned and smiled at him. They drove in silence for a few miles, but he never took his hands off her.

"Anything new with Betty?"

"No, we're just waiting. JP's investigating, but so far he hasn't come up with anything new. Something needs to break for her soon, though. Her trial will be here before we know it."

Luke leaned in toward Sabre and kissed her on the ear and whispered, "Do you have any plans this weekend?"

"I hope so."

Luke sat up straight. "Let's get away," he said, not whispering any longer.

"Where to?"

"Let me take care of that. I have a great idea. You just pack a few things and we'll get away from the phones and the outside world. It'll be just you and me."

"Sounds heavenly," Sabre said, drawing out the words.

"Any chance you could leave tomorrow early?"

"Maybe." Sabre thought for a second, hoping. "I have a light calendar and a quick visit to Betty scheduled. I should be able to leave after that."

"Great. It's a date." Luke said, not taking his eyes off her.

Sabre looked from side to side. "What?"

Luke smiled and said, "I was thinking how much my mother would love you."

JP woke up with the worst headache he could ever remember. He felt the hard concrete floor on his cheek. A spider, about four inches from his face, walked rapidly across the cement. JP struggled to stand up. Every muscle in his body hurt. He staggered forward and sat down on the hard bench in the ten-by-ten cell. The stench of urine emanated from the cell next to him. He remained seated for a moment, trying to figure out what had happened and how he was taken to jail. The last thing he remembered was the thugs from Paceco's beating him up.

The loud voices and the banging on the bars by other inmates hurt his head. JP walked to the front of the cell and peered out the best he could. He spotted a policeman down the hallway.

"Excuse me, Officer."

No one responded.

He yelled louder. "Excuse me." And louder. "Sir." The policeman turned around and walked back to JP's cell.

"What do you want?" The officer sounded irritated.

"I'd like to know why I'm in here for starters."

"Like you don't know?"

JP raised his right hand, palm up, gesturing confusion. "I don't know. Someone beat me up and I'm in jail. I don't get it."

"That someone who beat you up was protecting the old woman you mugged."

"What old woman? I didn't mug anyone."

The cop tapped his stick on the bar. "Well, the old woman and the guy who stopped you say differently."

"That's crazy. I'd like to make a phone call."

"Yeah, when it's your turn." The officer's voice filled with indifference as he walked away.

Several hours passed before anyone else came to his cell. JP asked for a phone call and the officer told him he'd check on it. He never returned.

JP lay down on the bench, tossing and turning as he wondered how he'd clear up this mess and anxious to talk with Sabre before Luke did. He finally fell asleep. When he woke up, his head wasn't pounding quite as badly, but his body still ached. He commenced yelling for someone to release him or give him his phone call.

"It won't do you any good," the man in the cell across from him said. "They'll do it on their time."

Just then a short, overweight officer with a mustache and a badge that read "Skully" came to JP's cell, unlocked the door, and stepped inside. "Please turn around and put your hands behind your back."

JP did as he was told, but asked, "Why?"

"You're being moved to another facility."

"May I make my phone call first?"

"You can do it when you get there." He slapped the handcuffs on JP's wrists and pulled lightly on his arm to move him along. His big belly bumped up against JP's back as he walked.

JP hesitated. The officer pulled harder. "Come on, John Doe. Let's move it."

"I have a name. It's J...."

"I don't give a damn. You're John Doe to me. The next place can do the paperwork."

It was almost dark when JP was placed in the police car. Skully sat in the driver's seat and another uniformed policeman took the passenger side. "Hey, George, thanks for your help this morning."

"No problem, Skull."

George reached up and closed the glass between the front and back seats. JP couldn't hear what they said after that.

They'd driven for about an hour when JP realized he had seen the same building at least twice. He tried to ask what was going on, but with the glass between them, they either couldn't hear or just chose to not respond. JP grew more anxious.

It was dark by the time they stopped the car in front of a small restaurant. Both men stepped out of the car and went inside. JP could see them through the window. A young couple, who had been sitting in the booth by the window, stood up and the two officers sat down. They ordered a meal and coffee, and ate it while JP waited in the backseat of the police car, handcuffed, hungry, and in pain. The longer he sat there, the more his anxiety turned to anger.

Over an hour later, the officers came out and got back in the car. JP yelled to get their attention. They didn't respond. After several attempts, he kicked at the back of the seat until George opened the glass window between them. The officer just raised his eyebrows without saying anything.

"What the hell is going on? Why don't you take me to the station so I can make my phone call?"

"They keep changing our orders. Everything is full. Guess you'll just have to wait." Skully laughed. George started to close the window.

"Wait," JP said. "Look, I didn't do anything and I just want to make my phone call."

"Right, and I'm Mel Gibson. Listen, you piece of crap, we don't like assholes who mug old ladies, and we don't care much for private dicks, either." He slammed the window before JP could respond.

They continued to drive around until late into the night when they finally took JP to another jail. The clock on the wall read 12:25.

29

As Sabre was finishing her morning calendar, she shifted through her notes and saw Betty had been moved back to Las Colinas. They'd house her in a special area until she was fully recovered. Sabre drove to the jail, but rather than being taken to a regular interview room, she was escorted to a jail cell to meet with Betty behind bars.

"I'm sorry I haven't been by to visit you in a few days. I haven't been feeling that great," Sabre said.

"What's wrong?"

"Just a touch of the flu. I'm fine now." Sabre touched Betty's fingers through the bars. "How are you holding up?"

"Okay, I guess. Sorry we have to meet like this. They wouldn't put me into a regular interview room because of the recent problems they've had."

"What problems?"

"They've discovered a new source of drugs in here and they're trying to put the kibosh on it. It just means tighter security for us. Less day room time, stuff like that." Betty cleared her throat. "Anything new on my case?"

"I'm sorry, Betty. I wish I had some good news for you, but I don't. JP is still investigating, but so far nothing." Sabre, frustrated with Betty's reluctance to help, decided to take a more direct approach. "We really need your help with this. What is it you're holding back?"

"Nothing," Betty snapped.

"I know differently," Sabre said sternly. "Betty, I'm trying to save your life here. I need to know what's going on."

"I have nothing to tell you that'll help the situation."

"Let me be the judge of that. Sometimes the smallest thing can turn a whole case," she pleaded.

"I can't."

"Well, tell me this. When you lived in Charleston, did you

know anyone with the last name of Kemp?"

Betty shook her head. "No. Why?"

"It's not important."

Betty became quiet for a second. "Sabre, I know you're angry at me, but I need you to do me a favor. I have no one else I can ask."

Sabre looked at Betty's aging face, so filled with despair, and thought Betty had seen her last day of happiness. "Sure. What is it?"

Betty's face showed the pain and her eyes pleaded for help, but she hesitated. Then finally she said, "I need you to check an email for me. I have a friend who has been ill, and I have no way to communicate with her."

"Of course. That's no problem. Just give me the information and I'll check it as soon as I leave here."

Betty paused. Sabre could see she was reluctant to give her the information. "Is everything okay?"

"I'm just worried." She gave Sabre the email address and the password. As Sabre wrote it down she saw what she thought was fear in Betty's eyes. They looked hollow. She didn't blink and was staring into space, her shoulders raised almost up to her ears.

Sabre didn't want to add to Betty's despair, choosing not to tell her about the fun weekend she had planned with Luke—that she was free to go somewhere and Betty couldn't. Instead she merely said, "I'll be tied up for the weekend, but I'll come see you on Monday. If you need anything, call Bob Clark. He'll be available, and he'll be able to reach me if he needs to."

Sabre drove back to the office, prepared the files for court on Monday, answered her mail, and then went online to check Betty's messages. When she opened her email, Sabre was surprised at how it differed from her own. Sabre's email was filled with messages and had twenty or more folders with saved messages. Betty's had only one message. The subject line read, "Urgent." Sabre opened it immediately. It simply read, "Neil is dying. You should come." Sabre gasped. *Was that the sick friend Betty had talked about? No, that had been a woman.* Betty said "her." So, who's Neil?

Sabre was eager to return home to Luke. He'd be there waiting for her to start their long weekend together, but she felt she had to give this information to Betty. She printed the email and headed back to Las Colinas. She still hadn't heard from JP, so she called him again, but her call went straight to voice mail. This was the third day with no word from him, and her anger was turning to concern. She really needed a break from all this. Her trip with Luke was becoming more and more important to her, hoping the distraction would be enough for her to leave her concern for JP and Betty in Bob's capable hands. She called Bob and left a message for him to follow up with JP.

Sabre walked into the jail and requested another visit with her client. Then she sat down and waited for the guard to bring her to a cell or interview room. It was nearing four o'clock and Sabre saw guards coming in and going out. She'd have to wait until the shift changed. Ten minutes later, she stood up and paced around the small waiting area. She sat down and watched the clock. She read reports. Twenty more minutes passed. She stood up again. She checked with the desk. The shift change was not complete. She tried to be patient but became more and more anxious as she waited. She was already uncomfortable having to bear the bad news. Forty-five minutes later, Sabre was finally permitted to see her client.

When Betty was finally brought to a room, Sabre's wrinkled brow must've given away her concern.

"What's the matter, Sabre?" Betty asked before Sabre could speak.

"I checked your email. You only had one message." Betty's eyes widened. Sabre held up the email for Betty to read.

"I don't have my readers." Betty's chest heaved. "What does it say?"

"It says, 'Neil is dying. You should come.'"

Betty gasped for breath, choking back the tears. She tried to take deep breaths, but continued to heave and gasp.

"Betty, who is Neil?"

Betty breathed in deeply, finally containing herself. "J…Just a fr…friend." Deep breath. "My friend's son."

Sabre, taken aback by her reaction, asked, "Betty, are you all right? Should we call for a doctor?"

"I'm fine. I just didn't expect this." Her voice choked with tears. "This place is awful. My friend needs me, and I can't leave and go to her. I'm just….It's just everything."

"Oh, God. I wish I could get you out of here." Tears rolled down Betty's cheeks. Sabre looked Betty directly in the eyes. "Betty, help me help you. Tell me what's happening. Maybe it'll help me get you released."

Betty looked around; little expression remained on her face. Her eyes found Sabre's. "There's nothing."

Sabre sighed and shrugged. Whatever it was must not be of any value to the case, or it was more important to Betty than her own life. Sabre let it go. "Was Neil ill?"

"No." Betty swallowed, containing the tears. "I don't know what happened."

"Do you want me to reply to the email? Maybe ask some que….?"

"No. No. Don't," she said abruptly.

Sabre was confused about Betty's decision to not follow up. "Are you sure?"

"Yes. I'm sure. Please don't respond. I can't do anything anyway. I'll talk to her when things get better here." Betty stood up and turned in a half circle, then back. Tears wet her eyes. "Thanks, Sabre, but I need to go back now."

"Sure. I'll see you Monday. If you decide you want Bob to do anything, just let him know."

Sabre called for the guard and watched as Betty walked away. Her body made the jerky movements of someone crying profusely, but trying to keep it quiet. *Neil must be very important to her.*

The warm, early summer air blew Sabre's hair around her face as

Luke's convertible barreled north on I-15 toward Barstow. Luke looked perfectly placed behind the wheel of his silver BMW Z4 Roadster. His handsome facial features were illuminated by the full moon. The slight stubble that was a constant battle for Luke gave him a rugged, manly look. Sabre was smitten. At that very moment the ghosts of mistrust vanished from her mind. She spoke with confidence and utter belief in her own words when she said, "I love you, Lucas Rahm."

Luke's smile brightened his entire face. "I love you, too, Sabre Brown." He leaned part way over the console, put his arm around her shoulder, and pulled her body closer to him until her head rested on his shoulder. He kissed her on the top of her head. Sabre felt relieved. She had felt the devotion for a long time, and now she'd finally said it. He deserved to know how much she cared about him. He'd been so good to her and so patient, especially with all the craziness occurring with Betty and John. Yeah, she loved him very much, and it felt good to express it.

"So if we aren't going to Vegas, where are we going? And if we are going to Vegas, why did I need to bring my hiking boots?" Sabre asked.

"You'll see."

"We must be going to Vegas. There's nothing else out here." Luke made a right turn and drove east on I-40. "Okay. So we're not going to Vegas. Laughlin?"

"You just can't wait and see, can you?"

"Nope. I'm lousy with surprises. Most of the time I figure out what they are, even when I don't want to."

"You don't have this one all figured out, but we are staying in Laughlin for tonight. I booked us a suite at the Golden Nugget with a river view. I hope that's all right."

"I love it when you take charge."

They approached the small town of Laughlin with its casinos strategically placed along the riverfront, lights sparkling on the water. It was nearly midnight by the time Luke and Sabre reached their room. They stood on the balcony and looked out at the river and the Laughlin lights. The clear night allowed the moon and the stars to further romanticize the evening. People strolled on the boardwalk below, laughing, talking, and celebrating. Sabre wondered if they could possibly be as happy as she was at this very moment. She was happy just being here with Luke. She had left so much behind—her concern for JP, Betty's issues, the Kemp children. She let it all float out the window. This was her time, time for herself, time with the man she loved. Nothing was going to spoil it.

30

Breakfast for JP that morning was scrambled eggs and dry toast in his cell. A tall, thin guard delivered it without comment. He opened the cell door and reached out the tray to hand it to JP.

"I need to make a phone call. Please take me to a phone."

"I can't."

"What do you mean, you can't? I'm entitled to call my lawyer."

"Just delivering your food." He stood in the doorway and moved the tray closer to JP.

"I want my lawyer."

"You want the food or not?" He started to pull the tray back. JP reached for it. His stomach felt the need for nourishment even if his head didn't. The man closed the cell door, locked it, and walked away without another word.

JP sat down and ate. It was gone quickly. He hadn't realized just how hungry he was until he started to eat. His head and most other parts of his body still hurt from the beating the thugs had given him. He lay down, trying to get comfortable, but it hurt no matter how he sat or lay.

He stayed there for about an hour watching inmates and guards come in and go out. A guard passed his cell with a man in a suit carrying a briefcase. He let him into the cell adjoining his. He heard the suit say, "I'm Marco Quiñones. I'm with the Public Defender's Office." The suit reached out his hand to shake the inmate's. They walked to the back of the cell and sat down on the bench. JP couldn't hear what else was said.

JP waited and watched until the suit stood up and started to walk toward the front of the cell and then he said, "Excuse me, sir."

At first Quiñones didn't appear to hear him or chose not to respond.

"Please, I really need your help."

Quiñones turned to him and looked him over from head to

toe. "Did the cops do that to you?"

"No, but I need you to call my lawyer."

"They'll let you do that."

"No, they won't. They keep moving me from one jail to another."

Quiñones stepped closer to JP's cell. "How long have you been in?"

"I was brought in the night before last."

"And you haven't been able to call your attorney?"

"Look, I'm a private investigator for some lawyers in San Diego. I got beat up by some thugs and somehow ended up in here. I just need you to contact one of the attorneys and let them know where I am."

Quiñones hesitated, shaking his head. "I don't know."

"Please. Just a phone call. I'm not asking you to do anything inappropriate."

Quiñones took out a pen and pad. "What's your name?"

"It's JP Torn, but they won't even take my name. They have me here under John Doe."

Quiñones wrote it down. "Who do you want me to call?"

"Robert Clark or Sabre Brown in San Diego."

"Do you have any phone numbers?"

"I'm sorry, but I can't remember the other numbers. I have them in my cell phone. I never commit numbers to memory anymore, but the office numbers will be listed under their individual law offices."

Quiñones looked at JP's face again. "Do you need medical help?"

"No, I think I'm okay. Just a little sore." JP extended his hand through the bars. "I really appreciate your help. Thanks."

Quiñones shook his hand. "Sure." He then walked to the cell door. "Guard." An officer came, unlocked the cell, and let him out.

JP paced back and forth in the cell, feeling too restless to sit, and as long as he didn't make any sudden moves, it hurt less than sitting. He could only hope Quiñones would call, and do it soon.

Finally, JP lay back down, his mind racing. He knew Sabre and

Bob would be worried about him by now. And Bob would know he was in trouble since he hadn't called, but how would they ever find him while he's listed as a John Doe and constantly moving around?

Startled, JP sat up as an officer opened his cell door. It couldn't have been more than ten minutes since the public defender had left. Could it really have happened that fast? Or were they moving him again?

"Let's go," the officer said.

JP stood up, put his hands behind his back, palms facing each other, pushing out slightly with his wrists, hoping the cop would cuff him without paying attention to the placement of his hands. The officer cuffed him without comment and they walked out down a long hallway, turned right, walked down another, and exited out the door toward a police car where Skully and George were waiting for him.

"Thanks, Philip," Skully said.

"No problem. He's all yours."

George opened the back door for JP to get in. He resisted. "Come on, guys. This is insane." The officer pushed him into the car and closed the door.

JP watched the buildings go past him as they drove through the city and on to the freeway. This time they continued to drive out of Chicago. JP tried to watch the signs to see where they were going, not sure it would matter. A few minutes later, they pulled off the freeway and into a parking lot. The car stopped and the officers stepped out; one stood on each side of the car. They opened the back doors. For the first time, JP felt frightened.

"What are you doing?" JP asked.

"Relax, just putting a blindfold on you," George said.

"Why?" George reached in from JP's right side. JP moved to the left. Skully pushed him back and Skully hit his head against George's head.

"Damn!" George backhanded JP across the face. Skully grabbed JP by the arm and pulled him up in the seat. The handcuffs cut into his arms as he was yanked up. "Sit still and let me do this or you're going to have worms for brains."

JP sat still and George put the blindfold on him. The policemen got back in the car and JP heard someone crack open the glass between them. He could still not make out what they were saying most of the time, but he could hear mumbling.

The car moved along at speeds that felt like freeway driving. They drove for a couple of hours before they finally stopped. JP could tell by the odors they were at or near a restaurant. He heard the passenger car door open and close. And when George returned, JP could smell the hamburgers and fries. It made him hungrier. He hadn't eaten since breakfast and not at all yesterday.

They drove for another few hours, stopping at an occasional traffic light or stop sign. JP heard the glass window close. The car was moving more slowly now with some twists and turns in the road. They made a sharp right turn and the ride suddenly felt like they were driving over baseballs, further aggravating JP's sore bones and muscles.

After about ten minutes of bumpy road, the vehicle came to a stop. The back car doors both opened. JP was pulled out of the backseat of the car on the passenger side.

"Let's go," George said.

"Could you take my blindfold off so I can see where I'm stepping?"

"Just stand up."

JP turned his body toward the door and reached his feet to the ground one at a time. Stabilizing his footing, he scooted forward in the seat. George took his arm and helped pull him up and directed him a couple of steps away from the car door.

"What are....?" JP felt a fist hit his stomach. He doubled over from the force, and another blow was planted on the side of his face. He fell backwards onto the ground, his head bouncing on the hard surface. The car doors slammed and the car drove away, scattering dirt on his body.

31

By eight o'clock on Saturday morning Sabre and Luke were driving east on Highway 40. The morning desert air was already warm, the convertible top was down, and Sabre had guessed their destination—the Grand Canyon. She liked the idea. She loved to hike and she liked that Luke came up with the plan. She sat back in her seat, her head against the headrest, and soaked up the sun through her heavily applied sunscreen.

They drove for miles in the desert, sometimes talking, sometimes not. Sabre knew their relationship had reached that point where they didn't have to be talking to be comfortable. The silence didn't feel like an elephant in the room, instead it was rather peaceful and right. Their presence in each other's company was enough.

"Where are we staying when we get there?"

"At the local lodge. We have a reservation."

"I thought you had to reserve months in advance for lodging there. How did you pull that off?"

"I have a connection."

"You have a connection to someone at the Grand Canyon?" Sabre sounded skeptical.

"Yes. You don't know the half of it, honey." Luke smiled when Sabre tilted her head and wrinkled her forehead. "All right, it's not all that mysterious. One of the guys I contract with has some connections. He said I could use his name anytime and they'd take care of me. So I did, and voila. We have a room."

"You're amazing." Luke leaned over and kissed her lightly on the cheek.

Both of them were famished by the time they reached the canyon. They stopped at the Bright Angel Restaurant for lunch where they sat side by side in a booth and ate tasty cheeseburgers with outstanding onion rings. Luke leaned into Sabre and licked a bit of sauce off the side of her lip with the tip of his tongue.

They finished their meal and walked hand in hand to the canyon rim where Sabre first viewed the stupendous gouge in the earth's surface. It hit her with such force she leaned back into Luke. He wrapped his arms around her and held her as she gazed into the vast, overwhelming spectacle before her.

"It's really magnificent, isn't it?" she said.

"One of the most beautiful places on earth." They held hands and walked alongside the rim for a few minutes. "Let's put our hiking boots on and go down. Are you up to it?"

Sabre knew she wouldn't—and shouldn't—be satisfied with looking. She needed to feel the power of the two-billion-year-old rock under her feet and fingertips. She needed to interact with the landscape to achieve the full effect. "Sure. It's all about the adventure. Right?"

They packed their backpacks with four large bottles of water, put on their hiking boots, and started down the canyon. Luke led the way down the rocky trail. It was the hottest part of the day, and the bright sun had Sabre's sunscreen already melting away. But then they'd go around a curve on the trail and the shade would be cool, almost too cool. The views were breathtaking; the sun shone on the rocks, giving them a bright yellow-orange color. The sharp edges carved by the water millions of years before couldn't have been more striking if they were planned—layers and layers of artistic masterpiece and unending color spread before her.

Other hikers were plentiful as they started the trek down. A family of four followed them to the trail. A gray-haired couple ventured ahead of them. They soon passed the couple and lost track of the family. Other hikers were just ascending out of the canyon as they were entering it. Each one politely said hello or commented on the beauty they had just experienced.

For the first two miles the hike zigzagged at an unrelenting pitch, but the surrounding beauty kept Sabre going downward, ignoring the strain on her body. Not until she descended into the canyon did she gain a real sense of its true proportions. The adventure and the beauty kept her walking, although her legs were beginning to tire. They stopped occasionally and took a drink of water, careful not to overdo or use up their supply.

Sabre absorbed the beauty of the jagged-edged cliffs, the steep slopes, and the stepped-pyramid appearance of the canyon walls. In addition to the bright yellow and orange colors which Luke had explained came from the iron in the soil and rock, she was overwhelmed by all the other stunning colors. Sabre thought about the many times her brother, Ron, had been here. He'd tell her tales of his adventures to this "heaven on earth," as he called it. He had explained how the canyon resembled an oil painting. The varied hues of red, black, pink, brown, blue, and lavender were even more incredible than he had described. Saffron prevailed in some lights; in others, vermilion was prevalent; but somewhere in the canyon, every color of the palette was displayed. No wonder it was one of Ron's favorite hiking spots. Sabre wondered where Ron was now, and if he was able to enjoy this beauty.

They continued down the winding trail for approximately two miles and reached a comparatively gentle slope. Sabre looked up and saw the huge towers that bordered the rim. The towers had shrunk to pigmies.

The sun beat down. Sabre wiped the perspiration from her forehead and blew her nose to clear the dust away. The adrenaline from the journey pumped her up like a caffeine high and prevented her from feeling tired. The spectacular views, the excitement, and her love for Luke drove her into the canyon. Luke, although leading the way, looked back watchfully every ten or twenty yards.

Luke stopped and waited for Sabre to catch up. He gave her a kiss on the lips. "How are you doing, baby?"

"Great. This is fabulous. I'm loving it."

"You okay to keep going?"

"I'm feeling good, but we're going to have to climb back up. Do you think we should turn around before it gets too late?"

"I've made arrangements to ride the mules back up. We'll be okay, as long as you're all right."

"I couldn't be better."

Luke took her in his arms and kissed her deeply and passionately. Then he swatted her on the butt. "Good, then on we go."

They continued the hike, passing the occasional pine tree or juniper bush and some dry, low growing bushes; in the midst of the sparse vegetation, Sabre spotted a bright red flower on a hedgehog cactus. They met fewer and fewer hikers as the day wore on. Not everyone went all the way down. Many went just far enough to obtain a taste of the canyon. But Sabre wanted the full experience, and she trusted Luke to keep her safe. She skipped along the level parts of the trail feeling exhilarated.

Enveloped in nature's grandeur, they continued to descend the multicolored rock walls, craggy cliffs, and sandy slopes. Sabre stood still, leaned against the canyon wall, and was dazzled by the panorama before her. She looked out at the labyrinth of structures, endlessly varied in design and color in pure harmonious tones, and thought about the millions of years it took to form and the many creatures that had passed through.

Sabre took a deep breath and moved on down the path, only to step on a loose rock. Her feet came out from under her. She grabbed for the wall, but couldn't hold on. She stumbled forward, trying to stay away from the edge of the cliff, and yelled out, "Ahhh...." She felt herself falling forward. She leaned sideways toward the wall, grabbed a juniper bush, and felt her knee hit the ground. She rolled over against the wall and stopped.

Luke ran back to her. He knelt beside her, grabbing her by the arm. "Are you okay?"

Sabre sat up, breathing heavily, said, "Yeah. Yeah. I'm okay." She took a deep breath. Feeling pain in her knee, she looked down. The scrape on her knee was filled with dirt, and the blood ran down her leg.

"Here, stand up; see if you can walk." Luke helped her to her feet. Sabre took a couple of steps. "Okay. Let's get you cleaned up. There's a little area right down there where we can sit more comfortably."

"Thanks." Sabre's face reddened, feeling clumsy for stumbling.

She made light of the fall, walking as normally as she could even though she felt some pain. They sat down a few yards later. Luke took the first-aid kit out of his backpack, cleaned up her knee, and put a bandage on the scrape.

"Are you all right to walk?"

"Yeah. It's just a little scrape. I'm fine."

"We could turn around, but we're almost to the bottom where we can get the mule ride back up. If we turn around and go back, we need to walk all the way."

"I'm fine. Let's keep going."

"Want me to kiss it and make it better?"

Sabre pointed to her lips. "How about right here instead."

He kissed her and then started the lead. "I'm going to walk a little slower and I want you to stay closer to me."

"Yes, sir!"

"You joke, but I'm serious. I don't want anything to happen to you."

They continued down the canyon until they reached the bottom of the trail. A little cove ahead invited them in. The rocks on the floor of the cove were flat and well worn. Several rocks formed steps leading to a shelf that made a prime place to sit. In the middle of the cove, a waterfall flowed over a huge rock about ten feet above their heads into a small pond in the rocks below. Sabre and Luke were hot and dirty and the water was inviting. Two young couples, appearing to be college age, splashed in the pond and washed their topless bodies in the flowing water.

"Should we join them? I'd love to wash off," Luke suggested.

"Maybe without the 'topless' part. But let's rest a little bit first. If they leave soon, we can have it all to ourselves."

They sat down on the rock shelf and leaned back against the wall. They sat together, drinking their water, and taking in the romantic essence of the cove. "I love you," Sabre said, testing this new phrase. It felt right.

"I love you, too." His response validated her.

32

The cool water splashed across Luke's half-naked body. Sabre felt sprinkles as she stood just outside the full force of the waterfall. Luke, wearing only his boxer shorts, leaned into her. "Sure you don't want to strip?" he whispered in her ear.

She smiled and nibbled his ear. "I'm just fi…."

Luke pulled her into his arms and under the gushing water. She laughed and screamed, "It's cold!"

He held her out in front of him at arm's length looking at her wet tee-shirt clinging to her body, her flat, wet hair dripping on her face. "You're so beautiful."

Sabre hadn't felt so wanted and so loved in a very long time. She melted into his body as he pulled her back to him and kissed her longingly. Then he swept her up in his arms, walked out from under the waterfall, and carried her to a flat rock in the sun. Only a few minutes had passed as they lay there drying off when Sabre looked up the pathway and saw the mules trekking up the canyon. She sat up and pointed.

"Luke, look. The mules have left." She jumped up. "Let's go. Maybe we can catch them."

He took her hand and pulled her back. "Relax, there are more mules. That's not the last group to go up."

"Are you sure?"

"Yes, I'm sure." He kissed her hand and then her arm. "Just a few more minutes to get dry and then we'll go."

Sabre lay back down, spreading out to feel what was left of the sun's warmth. She closed her eyes, content, relaxed, and confident Luke would take care of her.

She opened her eyes to a scuffing noise to see Luke being yanked off the rock next to her by two men. One of them stood about six feet tall with broad shoulders, a full head of hair, and dark brown eyes with thick eyebrows. The other man was several inches shorter, but he was just as muscular and had a flat top and mustache. The tall man spun Luke around, and dragged him behind some rocks. Luke was kicking and struggling, but he was unable to break loose.

"No. Stop," Luke yelled. "Don't hurt her!" The tall man covered Luke's mouth and continued to drag him off.

Sabre stepped back, her bare feet unstable on the slick rocks, and she slipped and fell just as the shorter man reached for her. He missed her arm. She reached for a rock, picked it up, and as he leaned down toward her, she hit him on the side of the head as hard as she could with it. He fell backward onto another rock and then rolled to the ground. She jumped up and looked around for Luke, but couldn't see him. Still holding the rock, Sabre skulked along the canyon wall, following in their path until she reached a turn. She peeked around but couldn't see anything. As she continued along the wall she reached another area with a slight turn. Voices emanated from behind the rocks, but she couldn't decipher the words. Moving closer, she inched her way along the wall, hoping her breathing wouldn't be heard. It sounded so loud to her. She stood still, holding her breath as she heard Luke's voice. Sabre peaked around the corner and saw the man behind Luke holding a gun.

Sabre felt a knot in the pit of her stomach. She was no match for the man. Her only hope was to find someone to help. Terrible confusion clouded her brain. She froze for a moment, her limbs unable to move. She took a breath and stealthily moved back around the corner the way she had come. When she reached the waterfall, she looked for her backpack. It was gone. It was there when they showered in the waterfall, but she couldn't remember seeing it after that. She walked around the man who had assaulted her, afraid to stop to see if he was breathing. She began running around trying to find help. She heard the loud blast of a gunshot ring out, echoing through the base of the canyon. She ran to the path and started upward.

Even though she was already tired from the hike down and drained from the sun, she ran as fast as she could up the canyon, her bare feet cutting into sharp rocks. The sun was starting to go down and there was no one near. Far up the canyon, she could see tiny clusters of people. She kept going, looking back every few steps to see if she was followed. So far, she didn't see anyone.

Pure adrenaline kept her going for a while, but finally she couldn't run any longer. She stopped for a second, caught her breath, and then started hiking toward the crest. She had such a long way to go and she knew that, once Luke's captor discovered his buddy, he would come after her. It wasn't as if she could take an alternative route. There was only one way out, and that was up. She only hoped he took some time to search for her at the bottom before he started after her. Her mind raced between going back for Luke, or going forward to find help. She knew she was no match for anyone, especially someone with a gun. She plodded on, praying she had made the right choice.

As the sun started to drop, the air cooled. Sabre's clothes were still damp, and the slight sunburn from the walk down mixed with the cool air provoked chills. Her sore feet made it difficult to hike. She sat down for a second to check them. The pain was excruciating. She picked up her right foot and rested it across her knee. She had blisters on her toes and her foot bled in several places. She removed her t-shirt, and using a sharp rock to make a hole, she tore off a piece of her shirt. It was difficult to tear, but the rock helped her to break the threads and peel off the piece of fabric. She wrapped it around her right foot, tying it off at the top around her ankle like a sandal.

Then she tore off a second piece of her shirt and did the same thing for her left foot. She put the top back on; it barely covered her shoulders. She knew she was going to be cold no matter what, but her feet had to keep moving or she'd die in the canyon.

She trudged on. The "shoes" softened the blow to her sore feet. They were thin, however, and still uncomfortable, but at least she didn't feel the unbearable pain she had previously suffered. She shivered in the shaded spots on the trail and warmed up in the sunny areas. She climbed as fast as she could. Her dry mouth acted as a barometer for her body's serious need for water, and her stomach pains indicated dehydration.

She felt herself getting weaker and dizzy. She moved closer to the wall, using it for support, all the time moving forward and checking her back. Nausea set in and she stopped for a second, leaning against the wall. The cramps in her stomach were becoming intolerable. She looked up toward the top and then toward the bottom. She appeared to be less than halfway there. So far to go. She took a deep breath and tried to conjure up pleasant thoughts, picturing herself on an island, lying in a hammock, and sipping a cool, summer drink. She couldn't maintain the image. She just had to keep going. She needed to get help for Luke.

Sabre could feel the cramps forming in her legs with each step she took. She lifted her foot, only to catch it on the tip of a rock, and her feet flew out from under her. Down she went, grabbing at the air for a hold. She fell face down into the dirt and rocks, digging her hands into the dirt, sliding just far enough to rip apart her already skinned knee and her bare belly. She lay there for a second, not wanting to get up. It felt good to not use any energy. If she just lay there, eventually someone would find her and carry her up the mountain. Her body gave into the pull, but her mind would not. She would not give up. She would get up and keep going.

She pushed up with both hands until she was on her knees, and then one leg at a time, she stood up. Weak, dirty, and bleeding she started back up the trail, telling herself to put one foot in front of the other, talking her way through each step.

The sun had almost set. Sabre shivered as she climbed, never passing a single hiker. She had vomited twice and her head was pounding, but she could see the ridge of the canyon and it kept her going. She could see the figure of a man in the darkness standing near the top. He seemed to be watching her. He was an older gentleman. When she became closer, he called, "Are you okay?"

She tried to respond, but her words were not audible. She shook her head back and forth, but she wasn't certain he could see it. *One more step. One more step.* She was going to make it. A feeling of emotional and physical security passed through her body. That feeling of safety lifted the weights from her legs and made the next few steps much easier. Just as she made the last step out of the canyon, she heard someone walking behind her. She stepped out, turned around, and the tall man from below grabbed her and picked her up. Her body trembled. The weakness returned. Utter terror took over where hope had dwelled for those last few seconds of her climb.

"Go get help," he instructed the old gentleman.

"No." Sabre tried to say more, but the gentleman was moving swiftly across the grass away from them. And she was in the arms of her captor, moving toward the parking lot, too weak to fight or call for help.

33

The cold wind whistled through the trees, shaking the leaves and rattling branches. JP scooted himself along the ground in an attempt to find something to help him tear the mask off his face. Unable to see, he feared falling over a cliff or wall. He came upon a stick, lifted his body up enough to lay his shoulder on the end, turned his head to the side, and leaned back trying to catch the blindfold on the stick. He felt it tug. He scooted down as far as he could while still holding the stick in place. The blindfold caught on his forehead. He twisted and turned his head until it finally came off his eyes. He shook his head until it fell to the ground.

Trees surrounded a grassy cul de sac about one-hundred-fifty-feet wide and about six-hundred feet deep. All he could tell in the moonlight was he'd been dumped at the end furthest from the opening with no visible roads or buildings.

JP stepped into the clearing and leaned forward as far as he could, stretching his arms behind him in an attempt to pull the handcuffs over his behind. The cuffs cut into his wrists. Pulling harder helped move his hands slightly lower on his buttocks, but as he did the cuff caught on his jeans. He raised his hands just enough to break loose and then tried again. The cuffs dug deeper into his wrists as he inched his hands down, pulling his body backward. Just a little farther and they'd be at the bottom of his derriere. He stretched. He pulled. He tucked into a ball and rolled backwards slipping the cuffs under his butt. There he lay like a turtle on his back, hands under his knees. He took a deep breath. He was almost there.

Moving his knees as close as he could to his chin, JP leaned to one side, stretched his left leg straight up in the air, turned his right leg at an angle, and stretched it back as far as he could toward his head until he could get his foot tucked under his right wrist. He pushed and pulled, catching the cuffs on his pant leg. He pulled his knee back in an attempt to get his foot higher on his arm, avoiding the cuffs catching on the bottom of his pants. His wrists hurt. The ground felt hard on his back, but he continued rocking his body back and forth until he finally maneuvered his right leg through. The left leg was easier; he had more room to work with. Pointing his knee out to the left, he pulled his hands up, and slipped his leg through. He rolled over, pushed himself up with the palms of his hands, and stood up. Although his wrists would be bruised and sore for awhile and he could see in the moonlight that he was bleeding, his arms and shoulders felt better, and he had a better chance of getting out of the cuffs.

JP walked a little way into the woods to avoid the wind, unzipped his pants and took a whiz. *Second best feeling in the world*, he thought.

His next plan was to get out of the cuffs. He knew if he couldn't squeeze through the locked cuffs, he wasn't getting out without a key or some tool and assistance. Help wasn't likely to happen. If anyone saw him with cuffs, they'd surely turn him into the cops and he'd be right back where he started. He'd done everything he could when they placed the cuffs on him to ensure possible escape. He'd faced his palms inward and he pushed his wrists out.

JP stretched his left hand out straight and then touched his thumb to his pinkie, scrunching his hand together and making it as small as he could. With his right hand he grabbed his left hand; his thumb and index finger squeezed hard. He caught his other three fingers on the handcuff and pulled them forward, continuing to squeeze as he pulled the handcuff off. He had one hand free. He then tried the same thing with the other hand. The cuff was either on tighter or his right hand was just a little larger. Whatever the case, it took longer and hurt more to pull the cuff off. At last, JP tossed the cuffs into the woods, shook his hands, stretched his arms, and then lay down and huddled up against a tree to wait for the morning sunlight.

The first light of dawn bid good morning to JP. The smell of cow dung and raw milk filled his nostrils. It could only mean there was life nearby. He followed the odors and started through the trees. Within about sixty feet he found himself in another clearing. Steam filled the air and the smells grew stronger. His nostrils led him forward until he came upon a dirt road. Following it to the end of the clearing, it turned left and he could see buildings ahead.

He walked for a good quarter of a mile, the smells more pungent as he went. Farm buildings sat on his right, and he could see a paved road ahead with cars occasionally passing by. He thought about walking to the road and hitching a ride, but where would he go with no money, no ID, and no phone? As he neared the road, he could see a large dairy already in action for the morning. He walked up to one of the buildings and looked around. As he started to walk around the building he heard someone say, "May I help you?"

JP turned around. A man about five foot eight with a rather round belly stood behind him holding a crowbar in his right hand. His face said mid-twenties, but his thinning hair made him look much older. His white uniformed shirt read *Chuck* just above his left pocket. JP glanced at the crowbar and then at the man. His face was soft and non-threatening. JP reached out his right hand to shake his. "Hi, I'm JP."

The man switched the crowbar to his left hand, extended his right, and said, "Chuck."

"Nice to meet you, Chuck." JP smiled. "I know I must look awful, but I've had a bit of bad luck. My car broke down last night, and before I could get help, these punks came by, robbed me, beat me up, and left me back there tied to a tree." JP pointed in the direction he had walked in from.

"Those creeps. This used to be such a nice place to live but the last few years it's gotten bad even here. The city is moving too close to us. Dang druggies and gangs. I got me a shotgun. They better not ever come near my home 'cuz I'll show them a thing or two."

"It's bad everywhere."

"It's just awful in the city, but it shouldn't be like that here. This is God's country. It was always so peaceful out here."

JP was starting to regret his story. He apparently had hit a nerve. "Do you have a cell phone I could use to make a phone call and get some help?"

"No, I don't have a cell phone and I better not let you use the dairy phone. That's just for business and we're not supposed to use it for personal calls, but I was just headed into town. Why don't you ride with me? It's less than a mile and I have a friend there who'll let you make your call."

"Thanks. I appreciate that."

Chuck led JP to his pickup, threw the crowbar in the back, and slid into the driver's seat. As JP opened the passenger side, Chuck was gathering up the fast food bag and empty wrappers. He shoved the wrappers and an empty cup inside the bag and tossed it out the window. He looked at JP and, as if to explain the inappropriate deed, said, "I'll pick it up when I get back."

JP nodded.

Chuck began asking questions even before they'd pulled out of the driveway. "You from around here?"

"No. I'm from San Diego."

"You drove from San Diego?"

"No, I rented a car in Chicago."

"Eww, Chicago. That's an awful place. I've been there a few times. Don't care to go back. But San Diego, I hear that's a real nice city. If you like cities, that is. I'm not much for city living. Give me the country any day. Too much crime and nonsense in the city. That's probably where those punks who attacked you are from."

"What city is that?"

Chuck glanced at JP with a quizzical look. "Lansing, of course. Didn't you pass through it on your way here?"

"Oh yeah. I just wasn't sure if there was another big city nearby. I don't know my way around Michigan." JP looked around. He could see the tall water tower with letters spelling Elsie across the side.

"Flint isn't too far away. Saginaw is close, too. They're all too close for me." Chuck stopped at a stoplight. "Well, here we are, the big town of Elsie."

They drove up the main drag into town, where all the businesses appeared to be on one main block. Chuck parked on Main Street in front of a big red brick building with white trim and a shingled awning. The left portion of the building housed the hardware store. Hand painted in green letters on the door to the right were the words, "Corner Space For Rent." On the corner, near the streetlamp, stood a white milk can with black spots. It resembled cowhide and was being used as a flower pot, housing magenta petunias.

JP stepped out of the car into the small town atmosphere. It had been a while since he'd been to a town without the hustle and bustle of traffic. Still early, only a few people were on the streets. His nostalgic feeling transported him to his childhood in Garfield, Texas, a small town where everyone knew everyone. They nosed their way into each other's business, but they also took care of one another when they needed help. Some of the old buildings in Elsie even resembled those from his home town—wooden structures, always in need of paint. Even the old man watching the sunrise from a bench between the pizza parlor and the bakery was a sight likely to be seen in Texas. The only difference between Elsie and Garfield, or Elsie and any other small town he'd ever been to, was the statue of a Holstein cow reaching about eight feet tall near the bank.

The unlit neon "Open" sign hung on the door of the hardware store. Chuck knocked and yelled, "Hey, Roger, open up." The lights were out with no sign of life inside. Chuck knocked harder. "Hey, Roger." Inside, the lights came on and a disheveled man about forty limped towards the front of the store, unlocked the door, and flipped a switch; the "Open" sign lit up.

Roger rubbed his eyes, "Is it ei..eight o'clock already?"

"No, I'm early, but we need your help," Chuck said as he stepped inside.

"Sure, what c..can I do?" Roger stuttered.

"This here's JP." Chuck nodded his head toward JP. "He's had a bit of trouble, as you can see. Some punks beat him up and stole his wallet and everything from him. He don't have any money or anything, 'cuz those gang members from the city took everything. I hate what they do. They need to stay in the city where they belong. They better not mess with me. That's all I've got to say."

"Come in." Roger walked to the back of the store.

"He needs to use your phone." Chuck turned to JP. "And make sure you call the cops and report this. If they can't do anything, we'll keep them out of here ourselves."

"I will, Chuck. Don't worry," JP said, continuing with his charade.

"Over he...here." Roger directed him to a phone on the desk. "The old m...man won't m...mind."

JP picked up the phone to dial and realized he didn't know many phone numbers, one of the drawbacks to cell phones and automatic dial. The time difference was two or three hours earlier in California; he wasn't sure which. Bob would be home. He racked his brain for the number, thinking he should know it by heart since it hadn't changed in ten years. Looking at the keypad, he punched in the area code and the prefix and, let his fingers dial the number without giving it any more thought.

"Hello," Bob said sleepily, then cleared his throat.

"Bob, it's JP."

"JP." Bob's voice grew louder. "Where the hell are you?" Before JP could answer, Bob said, "Some attorney named Quiñones called last night and said you were in jail in Chicago, but I couldn't find you."

"I was, but now I'm in Michigan and I need your help. But first, how's Sabre?"

"Sabre's fine. She's gone for the weekend with Luke."

"Luke's back?"

"Yeah, he returned Thursday, and they left on Friday."

"Damn it."

"Why? What?"

"I don't know for sure, but Luke lied to Sabre about where he was going and there's a link between him and Betty."

"What do you mean, a link?"

"Luke was in Chicago, not Dallas. And he's now living in the house where Betty lived as a teenager."

"This isn't making any sense. Do you think that's a coincidence?"

"I don't know. I don't have all the pieces yet, but it doesn't take a genius to spot a goat in a flock of sheep." JP heard Bob chuckle. "You just keep an eye on Sabre. She may be in danger."

"I can't reach her. Her phone seems to be shut off."

"Well look, I've lost my money, my phone, and my credit cards, and I need you to wire me some money so I can get out of here."

"Done." Bob paused. "Where do I send it?"

JP pulled the phone down under his chin. "Chuck, is there a Western Union in this town?"

"No, sorry, man. There may be one in Saginaw, but I know for sure there's one in Bay City."

"How far is that?" JP asked.

"Too far to walk. I'd take you, but I've got to get back to the dairy."

"Is there a bus or taxi? Never mind, I don't have any money. I'll hitchhike," JP said.

"I...I need to go into town as soon as the old man gets h...here. Y...you c...can ride with m...me."

"Thanks, Roger." JP spoke into the phone again. "Wire the money to the Western Union in Bay City. If there's more than one, send it to the one with the street name earliest in the alphabet. Once I leave Elsie, I may not be able to call you again until I get the money."

"Got it. What else?"

"I need you to get me a flight out of Bay City, Michigan. If you make it for mid-afternoon I should be able to get everything done and make the flight."

"But you don't have any ID. How are you going to fly?"

"I'll figure that out. Just make the reservation."

"I'll take care of it right away." Bob cleared his throat. "So, JP, what happened? Does it have anything to do with Luke or Betty?"

"I'm not sure yet," he said, slapping his hand on the desk, "but I'm sure as hell going to find out."

"What else do you need?" Bob asked.

"I need you to reach Sabre. Luke's cheating on her or up to something else, but at the very least he's lying to her. Just protect her until I get there."

34

Roger didn't talk much on the ride into Bay City, a refreshing break from the ride with Chuck. They passed fields, mostly green, that had either been harvested already or weren't yet planted, JP didn't know for sure. Many appeared to have once been corn. Beautiful two-story homes and old buildings needing paint dotted the landscape amid the green woods and fields. So many shades of green, a virtual green sea in such contrast to the southern California brown hills JP was accustomed to. Each town they passed through, no matter how small, had its own water tower proudly displaying its name. The rain dropped lightly on the windshield, providing an even homier feel to the landscape as it passed by.

Bay City offered freshly built bridges spanning beautiful rivers and many new buildings without the hustle and bustle of big cities. JP observed that the economy had affected much of Michigan, as evidenced by the empty businesses they saw along the way, but the changes weren't as obvious in Bay City.

JP had looked up the Western Union and called it from Elsie, so they found the place without too much difficulty. The small, old wooden building with its flat shingled roof and a brick façade front looked like a convenience store, not exactly what JP had expected. On one side of the entrance sat a propane cubicle. On the other side, an ice dispenser stood next to a yellow and black wall sign that read "Western Union." Signs selling lottery tickets, cigarettes, worms, and ice cream dotted the windows. JP walked to the back of the store where he filled out some paperwork, used the phone provided, and obtained his money while Roger waited in the car.

The local Target was different. It sat at one end of a large, relatively new, inside mall. As Roger stopped the car in the parking lot to let JP out, he asked, "Y..you going to be okay?"

"Yes, thank you so much for all your help." JP handed Roger a fifty-dollar bill.

"No n…need f…for that." He tried to hand it back.

"Please. You probably saved me a whole day. It'll pay for your gas and you can take Chuck out for a drink or something."

"I…I d…don't dr…dr..drink anymore."

"Then take him out for lunch. Thanks again." JP walked away.

He went into Target, bought a complete change of clothes, a razor, a trial-sized deodorant and toothpaste, a toothbrush, and a comb. Then he walked to the AT&T store they had passed earlier. After a good twenty minutes of cajoling, answering password questions, and speaking with different managers, he was able to buy a phone. He walked out of the store and immediately called Bob.

"Any word on Sabre?" JP asked.

"No, I still can't reach her."

"Dang." JP pulled at the neck of his t-shirt as if to loosen it. "And the airline ticket?"

"You fly out of Bay City at three-forty this afternoon and you get into San Diego at nine o'clock. I'll be there to pick you up. But, JP, I don't think you can get on an airline without ID."

"Don't worry, I'll figure out a way. Give me Sabre's number. I'll try to call her too, but please let me know if you hear from her. I'd feel a lot better if she weren't with Luke."

"Do you think she's in danger?"

"I don't really know enough to guess what's going on. I need to get home and regroup."

The rain had stopped by the time JP hailed a cab. "Is there a Holiday Inn Express near here?"

"Just up the street a few miles." The cab driver popped the trunk open and moved toward the back door to open it for JP, but his passenger had already opened it for himself. "Do you want to put your bag in the trunk?" The driver looked at JP's one plastic Target bag.

"No, thanks."

"Are you vacationing?" the cabbie asked, as they pulled away from the curb.

"Yeah." JP didn't feel like making idle chit chat.

"How long are you here for?"

"Not long."

Two miles later, the cab pulled over to the curb in front of the Holiday Inn Express. JP handed him his fare plus a five-dollar tip. "Sorry, man. I didn't mean to be rude. I'm just tired."

"No problem." He looked at the tip and smiled. "Thanks."

JP walked into the hotel. It looked like every other Holiday Inn Express, not fancy but clean and fresh. He checked in, took a cup of coffee off the counter, and went to his room. He immediately shed his clothes and took a long shower, brushing his teeth before he got out. He slipped into his new boxer shorts and made a phone call to his reclusive friend, Billy, in Idaho. He knew Billy from community college at Mount San Jacinto, where they had shared police courses together. They became roommates and best friends for several years, raising hell together in their young adult lives. Billy hailed from a long line of cops and his father encouraged him to follow in their footsteps. Billy attended the police courses, along with philosophy and constitutional law classes in which he excelled. He never made it to the Academy, though. Instead he became a student of the law and used his knowledge to fight the system. JP and Billy had remained friends for all these years, bonded by their past while separated not by just a half a country but also their basic approach to life.

"JP! What's up, brother?"

"I need to know how to get on a flight without any ID. I remember you saying something about flying without showing them your ID and it worked for you, right?"

"Yeah, but do you want to refuse to show them, or you don't have any with you?"

"I'm in Michigan and I lost my wallet. I need to get back to San Diego, stat."

"The best way is to just tell them you lost your wallet and you need to fly as a selectee. It used to be you could just refuse to show ID and they had to let you on as long as you submitted to a secondary search. But they changed that a year or so ago. Now TSA has a policy that if you "willfully refuse" they don't have to let you on the plane. We're contesting that, of course. They have no right to require Americans to carry ID to travel. It violates our constitutional rights. I'm working on a…hey, you don't need to hear all that right now. Just tell them what happened. Not any more than you have to, since it's not really any of their business, but talk nice to those yahoos and they should let you on."

"Thanks, Billy. You've been a big help."

"Peace, brother."

The clock read ten-forty-eight. JP set the alarm on the clock in the room and on his phone for twelve-forty-five p.m., double checking the alarms. If he slept for two hours he could arrive at the airport with a couple of hours for check-in. He slumped down on the bed, then sat back up and called the desk for a wake-up call. He was determined to not miss his flight.

When the radio blared a rendition of *Pretty Woman*, JP sat upright in the bed and reached for the button to shut it off. His phone alarm sounded, and before he could silence either of them, the phone rang with his wake-up call. Assuming it was automated, he picked up the receiver and set it back down without answering. He finally found the button to shut off the radio and opened his phone to stop the beep. He was groggy and his head hurt from not enough sleep, but he didn't waste any time. He called the desk for a cab and went into the bathroom to brush his teeth again.

His few belongings left behind, he went to the office to check out. The cab was waiting. The cabbie drove him the twenty minutes to the airport with almost no conversation. JP wondered if he spoke English, but was pleased he didn't have to talk. He picked up his phone and dialed Sabre. No answer.

At the airport, JP went directly to the kiosk and printed his boarding pass; he then took a deep breath and entered the first line through security. He was greeted by a young man who was no more than twenty and looked more like twelve; the man's nose and eyebrow rings were removed, as evidenced by the holes. "ID, please." He said nonchalantly.

"I don't have an ID. I lost it."

"Sorry, you can't fly without ID," he said, with more authority in his voice.

"I need to get home. I lost my ID. I need to fly as a selectee."

"A what?" The left side of the guard's lip turned up, exposing another hole where jewelry had once been.

"A selectee," JP said. "It's what you do when you lose your ID."

A blond man, who was about six-three, weighed two-hundred-fifty pounds, and stood about three passengers behind JP, said, "Come on, man. Let's go."

The TSA novice stood up taller and attempted to sound knowledgeable. "You can't fly without ID. That's the law."

JP spoke softly. "People fly everyday without ID when they lose it. They'll just put me through an extra search."

"Sorry, no can do."

The big man behind JP moved forward around the other passengers. "Does he look like a damn terrorist? Let the man on and let's go."

"Sir, you need to stay in line."

JP was wishing the big guy wouldn't try to help. He didn't want to call any more attention to himself than he needed to. Billy had told him to keep it low key.

The big man walked past security and started up the escalator.

"Hey," the TSA novice yelled. "Come back here."

Seven security guards appeared before the big guy was half way up. Two more guards were standing at the top. The big guy fought to keep their hands off of him, flailing his arms with such force he knocked one guard down the steps. More guards seemed to appear out of nowhere.

"Leave me alone. I just want to get on the damn plane." He reached the top of the escalator and the two guards each grabbed one arm. Another guard behind him pushed forward, and they threw him to the ground and handcuffed him. The man was still yelling obscenities as they stood him up and took him away.

So much for low key. JP turned to the TSA novice. "Look, I'm sorry this has caused so much commotion, but I was robbed and I've been through hell the past couple of days. I know there's a procedure for this. Please help me out here."

A TSA supervisor walked up just as JP was trying to explain. "Come with me, sir," the supervisor said.

They walked into a cubicle with just a desk and two chairs. Another security guard walked in with them. They had JP empty his pockets and remove his shoes, and they ran the portable scanner over his body. Gesturing for JP to be seated, the supervisor took a seat across from JP while the second man stood behind him. "My name is David," the supervisor said, without extending his hand. "What's your name?"

"John Phillip Torn. I go by JP."

"Tell me what went down here, John."

JP explained he had to catch a flight but didn't have an ID because he'd been robbed and beaten, pulling back his shirt to show his bruises.

"What's your friend's name?"

"What friend?" But JP knew who they were referring to. "You mean that big, crazy guy?"

"Yeah, your friend who caused the commotion so you could get on the plane."

35

Sabre's body hung from the man's arms. She wanted to fight, but little strength remained; besides, it felt good to be carried. She scanned the area looking for help, but it was too dark to see much and everyone had left the edge of the canyon. As they entered the parking lot, a security guard stepped out from behind a nearby tree. For an instant, Sabre could see his face and attempted to scream. The word "help" barely came from her mouth, but it was enough to draw attention.

"Is she okay?" he asked, looking at Sabre.

Her captor had turned her feet toward the guard so Sabre could no longer see his face.

"She's fine. Too much to drink and too much sun. I'm taking her home."

The guard took a step closer, leaning in toward Sabre. In the loudest voice she could muster, she cried out, "Help!"

Suddenly her feet hit the ground as her captor dropped one arm to draw his gun. A shot rang out, and the guard fell against the man, clutching his shirt in his hands. Seizing the moment, Sabre bit down hard on her captor's other arm. He pulled back in pain, pushing the guard off of him at the same time. Sabre and the guard both fell to the ground in a heap.

There was a van parked next to them. Struggling, Sabre tried to gain enough momentum to roll under it, but she didn't have the strength to move fast enough. She was part way under when the tall man reached down and grabbed her leg and yanked her out. "Stop," a second guard yelled from the walkway. Sabre heard the loud bang of a gun and the sound of a bullet on metal, hitting a car. She saw her captor duck, and felt her leg drop. He ran off, the guard chasing him, bullets flying in both directions. The relief she felt from being out of his clutches was diminished by a greater fear of the flying bullets. She could no longer see her captor when she saw the guard fall. Sabre could hear the footsteps of people running towards them and the tires of a car screeching as it sped away.

She tried to stand. "Just lie still. The paramedics are on their way." There was a gentle touch on her arm and a woman's voice. "I'm Aloma. I work for the lodge." Sabre looked into the concerned face of a woman in her early fifties; her short chestnut hair was just starting to gray and lay tightly against her head, accentuating her olive skin. The woman put something under Sabre's head to cushion it from the pavement.

"Luke..." Sabre's voice was quiet. Her throat parched. Her tongue felt too big for her mouth. The woman leaned in closer to her. "Boyfriend Luke...at bottom of canyon...may be shot." Sabre licked her lips and tried to go on. "Help him."

"Your boyfriend was shot?"

"Yes. Help him." Sabre could hear sirens in the distance. The crowd had grown larger. There were people standing all around her. She saw a man trying to move people away.

"Over here," Aloma yelled. A man in a brown suit walked up. "This woman says her boyfriend was shot at the bottom of the canyon."

"I'll take care of it," the man said and hurried off.

"Water. I need water," Sabre said between parched lips.

Aloma stood up. "I'll be right back. You lie still."

Sabre lay there watching the commotion around her, seeing heads peeking around the cars trying to get a glimpse of what was going on. The sound of the sirens grew louder. Sabre pushed her body over a few inches to her right in an attempt to sit up. It took too much effort, and she suddenly realized the pain. She hurt everywhere. She lowered herself back down just as Aloma returned with a bottle of water.

Aloma knelt on the pavement; placed her hand under Sabre's head, tilting it slightly upwards; and put the bottle to her lips. "Just a sip at a time," she said as she gave her the water in small doses.

"Luke?" Sabre asked.

"Someone is taking care of it. They're sending a helicopter down."

The sirens were suddenly very loud and then stopped. Sabre could see the red lights blinking. When two paramedics approached, Aloma stepped back; they loaded Sabre on a stretcher and then carried her to the ambulance.

One hour and thirty-five minutes of interrogation later, after many questions with the same answers and a few phone calls verifying his information, JP was escorted to the plane. He wondered as he boarded if the big, blond guy had made his flight. He expected he was probably in lockup; tact didn't seem to be his strong point.

The flight itself was uneventful, and Bob was at the airport when he arrived.

"How was your flight?"

"Fine, except getting on was a bitch. Have you talked to Sabre?"

"No. Just what do you think is going on?"

"Frankly, I don't know. I know Lucas lied to Sabre about where he was going. He certainly seemed at home in the environment he was in. He was with another woman, but I don't know if they were 'together' together. He was in the same house where I think Betty lived as a child, but I don't know for certain. And then I was beaten up, which may or may not have anything to do with Betty or Lucas. There are just too many unanswered questions."

"So what do we do now?"

"Since we can't reach Sabre anyway, I'm going to go home and get a good night's sleep. Then in the morning, I'm going to get up, go buy a new cowboy hat, and figure this out."

Five hundred ninety-six dollars and fifty-one cents later, JP walked out of Wild Bill's Western Emporium in El Cajon wearing a new black Stetson Silverton 6X and a pair of Tony Lama's Full Quill Ostrich boots. The boots were on sale.

JP was rested, dressed, and eager to find out what was going on with Betty and Luke and whether or not they were connected.

He called Bob and asked him to meet up at Jitter's Coffee Shop in La Mesa.

JP bought coffee for both of them, took a seat outside, and waited for Bob who arrived within a few minutes.

"So, what did you need to show me?" Bob asked.

JP took out a folder and handed him a drawing he received in his email. "Look at this."

"Looks like a drawing of a house, a very nice house. Whose is it?" Bob asked.

"This is the house Luke was staying at in Chicago."

"So?"

"So I got the drawing from a woman named Mary Lou in Bristol, Wisconsin. I had her email it to me this morning. The picture was drawn by a young girl about thirty-five years ago named Edith Underdahl. She was Mary Lou's best friend and she moved with her mother to Chicago when she was seventeen. Her mother was a maid in this house."

"And you think Edith is Betty?"

"It's just too coincidental to not be. Think about it. I follow a lead on Betty and it takes me to where Lucas is staying in Chicago when he's supposed to be in Dallas. What do you think?"

Bob sipped his coffee. "How do we find out if Betty and Edith are the same person? Can you check her fingerprints? And haven't the cops already done that?"

"That may not work because they weren't taking fingerprints of babies when she was born, and if she never had a driver's license under that name it wouldn't be in the system, unless she was arrested for something."

"So, what do we do? Ask Betty?"

"That's what I'm thinking. It's time to confront her, but since I can't reach Sabre I wanted to run it by you."

"JP, if you're right about this, then Luke is somehow involved."

"And Sabre might be in danger."

Bob tipped his head and raised his eyebrows. "Do you think Luke killed John?"

"I don't know, but he lied about being in Chicago. Why would he do that? Even if he was having an affair, what difference would it make what city it was in?"

"And he spotted you and had you beat up?"

"Possibly. Some pretty tough guys hang out at Paceco's—that's the restaurant I followed Luke to—so it could've been just paranoia from someone else who didn't want their business known. I'm just not sure." JP shrugged. "So should I question Betty?"

"Absolutely." Bob finished his coffee, stood up, and laid a tip on the table. "Did you watch the news this morning?"

JP sat his empty cup down. "No, why?"

"They arrested my client, Kurt K. Kemp, this morning for the murder of that young gay man who was killed in Perris a few weeks ago. They charged both of the Kemps with first degree murder."

"Sabre believed they were involved in that murder because of something the kids had said. She got the investigation started. I guess that takes care of your trial."

"They're so crazy they'll probably still want to fight it." They walked toward their cars. "Hey, do you think I should bill for watching the news this morning?"

Sabre woke to the smell of disinfectant, her arm connected to an IV. Her muscles ached, but her body was rested. She glanced around. The bare eggshell walls in the private room stared back at her. The only color came from the bouquet of flowers on the stand next to her bed.

"Are you awake?" Luke said, as he walked in the room.

"Luke!" Sabre's face brightened with the sight of him. "You're okay. Are you okay? You look okay."

"I'm okay," he said, leaning over and kissing her eager lips. "How do you feel this morning?"

"Much better. I think I just needed some liquid." She stroked his face. "What happened down in the canyon?"

Luke squeezed her hand and then explained. "That guy held a gun to my head for a while, but then he went to tie me up and I was able to get a punch in. That really ticked him off, so he hit me with the gun and knocked me out. When I woke up I was tied to his dead buddy and couldn't move."

"The other guy was dead? Did I kill him?" Sabre's voice choked up.

Luke shook his head and squeezing her hand said, "No. He'd been shot."

"I heard the shot. I was sure it was you. All I could think of was going for help. I started up the mountain hoping I could meet up with someone along the way, but everyone was gone. I barely made it to the top and that big guy grabbed me. If it hadn't been for that security guard I'd probably be dead now."

Luke gently kissed her forehead, her cheeks, her chin. "Thank God."

"How is the guard? There were two of them. Do you know if they're all right?"

"One of them was hit in the right shoulder, but he's going to be okay. I'm sorry, Sabre, but the other one didn't make it. Apparently, he was dead before he reached the hospital."

Although Sabre fought the tears, they still wet her cheeks. "He was trying to save me. He did save me. It just isn't fair."

The tall, blond doctor walking up to her bedside reminded Sabre of her brother she so badly missed. "How's my patient this morning?"

Luke stepped back while the doctor examined her.

"You tell me. May I go home?"

"Probably." The doctor examined her eyes, listened to her heart, and had her squeeze his hand. "How do you feel?"

"Just peachy. May I go?"

"Have you been up this morning?"

"Not yet."

"Let's see how you do. Stand up." He took her arm as she stepped out of bed. "Do you feel weak?"

"Not so much."

"Take a few steps."

Sabre walked to the end of the room, turned around and walked back, and smiled. "Well, Doc?"

He looked at his chart again and then at her. "I'll sign you out, but be careful the next few days, and drink lots of liquids."

By ten o'clock Luke and Sabre were heading west toward San Diego. Sabre, eager to get home asked, "Do we need to stop or can we make this in one day?"

Luke patted her knee. "Whatever you feel up to, honey. I'm fine with driving the distance if you can make the ride."

"I feel pretty good." Sabre picked up her cell phone. "Dang."

"What's the matter?"

"My phone is dead. I should call Bob and let him know I'm okay. He's probably worried."

Luke looked at her and smiled. "Bob is just fine. He knows you're with me, and he doesn't know anything about the incident last night, so he has no need to worry."

"That's true." Sabre stared ahead.

"But you're welcome to use my phone if you feel the need to talk to him. Just don't stay on it long because I don't have a lot of juice, either, and you never know if we might need it in an emergency."

Sabre reached for the phone, then stopped. "You're right. It can wait. I'll call him later."

"Whatever you think. Why don't you put your seat back and sleep. We'll be home before you know it."

As he drove down the open highway, Luke brought number six up on the CD display and punched it in. Michael Bolton blasted the first line of "How Am I Supposed to Live Without You," waking Sabre. She sat up, startled, looked quickly at Luke, and then smiled. "You may as well shoot me as scare me to death."

Luke clenched his jaw, shrugged his shoulders, and winked. "Sorry," he said, as he turned the volume down.

Jails all smell the same, like urine and disinfectant, JP thought, as he sat waiting for the guard to bring Betty to the interview room. Although his work had taken him into many jails and prisons, he had only spent one night in a jail prior to this trip to Chicago. Young and foolish and on leave from the Marine Corp, he tried to take on four sailors in a bar; after all, he was a marine. A fat lip, a bloody nose, and one free night in the Graybar Motel later, he'd learned his lesson. It takes two marines.

Betty entered. She looked older. "Hi Betty. Are you doing okay?"

"Yeah." She looked at JP's face. "What happened to you?"

"Wrong place, wrong time." JP reached into his file and took out Edith's drawing. He held it up for Betty to see, watching her facial expressions as he raised the paper. "Pretty nice drawing, wouldn't you say?"

Betty's eyes closed for just a second. Her neck stiffened. "Very nice."

Her reaction was minimal. JP surmised her many years of deception had taught her to not react. She was good. "It was drawn by a woman named Edith Underdahl."

Betty looked down. Then just as quickly she looked JP straight in the eye. "She's quite the artist."

JP needed to know how good she was at this game. How far was she willing to go with her lies? Would she sacrifice Sabre? Or maybe she wasn't Edith and he had hit another dead end. He asked, "Do you know who killed John?"

"No."

"Was it you?"

Her head jerked up. "Of course not. I loved him."

"Are you Edith?"

"Me? Edith?" JP did not respond. After a few seconds, Betty continued. "No. I've given you my information and who John really is. And what does all this have to do with whoever killed John?" Betty seemed a little irritated. "Why aren't you looking for his killer instead of showing me drawings of castles?"

"You're right. I just keep hitting dead ends with John, er, Jim. Did he have anything in his past that might lead to this? After all, he did change his name and fake his death."

"I told you, that was to avoid the IRS."

"The IRS doesn't usually kill people who don't pay their taxes. They have a hard time collecting if they do."

"I know. I'm just saying there was no one else."

JP stood up. "If you think of anything, no matter how insignificant you may think it is, please let me know."

"Sure, and will you tell Sabre to come see me?"

"Of course." JP saw Betty's mouth turn down, her shoulders slump, and sadness fill her eyes.

JP called Sabre on his way back to his house. It went straight to voice mail. "Sabre, please call me as soon as you get this. I have some information about Betty's case I need to run by you." Just as he hung up, he received a phone call from Bob. "Have you heard from Sabre?" JP asked.

"Yes. She just called. They're on their way home from the Grand Canyon."

"The Grand Canyon? But she's okay?"

"Yeah, she's fine. We didn't talk long because she was using Luke's phone and it needed to be charged. Sabre's phone was dead, and they wanted to make sure they had a phone if they needed one."

"Did she say how long they'd be?"

"Two or three hours. I think they were almost to Barstow."

"Good, that gives me enough time."

"Time for what?"

"I'll tell you later. I'd let you help me, but I may need you to represent me."

"I don't like the sound of that. JP, don't do anything stupid."

"I never do. Well, almost never. I'll call you later."

JP drove home, took a small toolkit from a drawer and a small leather case out of his closet, and drove to Luke's apartment.

He walked up to the front door. Two young women in bathing suits came out of the apartment next door. JP rang the doorbell. When they had passed by, he took a long thin tool out of the toolkit and attempted to unlock the door. He couldn't get past the deadbolt. JP walked around the corner unit apartment looking for open windows, but found none. He considered breaking one, but decided against that. Remembering the barbecue at Bob's, he walked back to his car and called Bob.

"Did you keep your bottles from the barbecue?"

"What the hell are you talking about?"

"From the barbecue last Sunday. Did you keep your bottles? Don't you recycle?"

"No, but Marilee does. I'm basically an inconsiderate slob who doesn't care about the planet. Why? What do you need?"

"I need those bottles of 'Goose Island Oatmeal Stout' Luke was drinking. What a dork. Who drinks that stuff anyway? I need the bottles to see if I can lift some fingerprints from them. By the way, I looked it up; those beers are from a Chicago brewery."

"Come on over. I'll get the trash out, but you get to be the trash digger."

Three bottles later, JP drove to meet a friend from the police department. He gave him a bag with the bottles and then went home to check birth records in Chicago. Within a few hours JP had the information he needed. He drove to Sabre's condo. She needed to know what he found out, and it couldn't wait until morning. JP saw Luke's car in front of her garage as he drove up. He passed by, turned around, and parked where he could see her front door.

Luke unloaded Sabre's things from his car and carried them inside. He took Sabre in his arms and pressed his lips on hers, a light soft kiss. "Are you sure you'll be okay?" he asked.

"I'll be fine. I'm going to take a nice hot bath, have a cup of warm milk, and go to sleep. Go."

"I'll call you in the morning." Luke said, as he walked out the door.

JP watched Luke leave Sabre's house. He waited until about five minutes after Luke left, making sure he didn't return. Then he exited his car and walked up the driveway to her condo. Before he could ring the doorbell, he heard something in the bushes to his right. He turned just as he felt a rock hit his head.

36

Sabre woke up in her own bed before daylight. Familiar surroundings and thoughts of her love for Luke spawned a feeling of euphoria. She and Luke had survived the ordeal in the canyon. Life was back to normal. She remembered the look on Luke's face when he had seen her in the hospital. It had been a long time since she'd had someone love her the way Luke did.

Her muscles ached as she moved to get up. Her legs felt weak as she stepped onto the carpet. Taking baby steps, she walked to the bathroom. She loosened up with each step. By the time she had showered and brushed her teeth, most of the stiffness was gone and only tired muscles and sore feet remained.

Sabre picked up her phone and called Bob. "You okay?" he asked.

"Yeah, I'm fine, now."

"What do you mean, now? Where's Luke?"

"Luke's at home and he's fine, too."

"What happened?"

"It's a long story. I'll tell you when I see you in the cafeteria at eight-fifteen. Hey, have you talked to JP?" Sabre asked.

"Yes, he's back. I saw him yesterday. He has some information to share with you before the hearing starts. He left me a message last night saying he'd learned a lot more and it should really help Betty's case, but I didn't speak to him, so I don't know what that's all about."

"Good, see you in a few."

Sabre dialed JP's phone, but as it went to voice mail another call came in. Sabre smiled when she saw it was Luke, and switched over to his call.

"Good morning, darlin'. How do you feel today?" he asked.

"Sore, but I'm okay. I need to get to court for Betty's preliminary hearing. I'm meeting Bob a little early so we can go over a few things before court."

"Is Bob all right?"

"As far as I know. Why? He asked about you, too. Is there something I should know?"

"No, I just thought he'd be upset when you told him what happened."

"I haven't told him yet. I'll tell him when I see him."

"But he asked if I was okay?"

"Yeah." Sabre hesitated. "What's going on?"

"Nothing, I guess he just likes me. I need to get ready for court."

"What time does the DA want you there?"

"The subpoena says eight-thirty, but he said I didn't need to be there until ten."

"Ok, I'll see you then."

Sabre arrived at the courthouse in El Cajon about eight-fifteen. She called Bob but it went to voicemail. While she waited for him in the cafeteria, she called JP, leaving him a message.

At eight-twenty-five neither Bob nor JP had arrived. She went upstairs to the courtroom and checked in with the court clerk. She handed the clerk her card. "Sabre Brown for the defendant, Betty Smith/Taylor. Is the bus here from Las Colinas yet?"

"Let me check," the clerk said. She picked up the phone and called the sheriff's desk in the back. She hung up and said, "They don't expect the bus until nine. I'll let you know when it arrives."

"Thanks." Sabre went out in the hallway to wait for Bob and JP. The court couldn't hear the case until her client arrived, so she had plenty of time.

She sat on a bench in the hallway and looked through her case file, eager to hear what JP had to help her case. It was looking pretty hopeless from what she saw. Sabre checked her phone for the time. It was eight-forty-six and there was still no sign of Bob or JP. It wasn't like either of them to be late. She called each cell phone, getting voicemail on both. She waited. She called again at eight-fifty-four, and again at nine-ten. She really wanted the information before she spoke with Betty.

Just as Sabre was about to go in the courtroom, the bailiff came out. "The bus is here from Las Colinas. You may see her now."

"Thanks."

Sabre walked down the hallway toward the "in custodies," past small holding cells with prisoners who were appearing on charges from drug use to murder. When she saw Betty in the cell, she thought how much Betty had aged in such a short time. Her gray roots were becoming more prominent and her face ashen from lack of sunlight. Her bright smile was non-existent, and the worry lines grew deeper with each day of incarceration. Sabre prayed JP had what she needed to get Betty out of here. Where was he? And where was Bob? Sabre faked a smile as she approached.

In an attempt to keep Betty's hopes up, Sabre said, "JP has information that's going to help us with your case."

"What is it?"

Sabre shrugged. "Actually, I don't know exactly, but he told Bob it was big, and he knows you're innocent."

"What do you think it is?" Betty squeaked, then cleared her throat. Sabre wanted to think it was excitement she heard in her voice, but it sounded more like fear.

Sabre forced a smile. "We'll soon find out." Sabre stood up. "I'll see you in court in a little bit." She left, hoping JP's findings would be enough to persuade the court.

Sabre went outside the courtroom and attempted to call Bob and JP again. Still no answer. She was starting to get concerned, wondering if they were riding together and had an accident. She went back inside and shared her concerns with the DA.

He responded, "The court's ready for us, and I'd like to put the coroner on and Lucas. I won't call you until your co-counselor is here, and you may cross-exam my witnesses later. Would that work for you?"

"Sure, we can do that."

The sheriff brought Betty in and seated her next to Sabre at the table closest to the bailiff. The court clerk stood up. "May the court come to order." Not used to the formality, Sabre took a second before she realized everyone was standing up. The judge walked in, stepped up to the bench, and stood until the clerk spoke. He was one of the few remaining judges who still held to the formal introduction. "The Honorable O'Neil Thomas presiding in the case of the State vs. Betty Smith aka Betty Taylor," the clerk continued.

"Please be seated," Judge Thomas said.

The DA began, "Dillon Lewis on behalf of the State of California." He looked at his folder for a second and then said, "Your Honor, counselor for the defense was expecting her co-counsel here this morning and has some concern that he hasn't arrived. She has, however, agreed to proceed with two of my witnesses and save her cross for later so that we may get started, if that pleases the court."

"Fine. Call your first witness," the judge responded, obviously used to delays and continuances.

"The State calls Dr. Edward Settle to the stand." A tall, handsome gentleman with a mustache and in his late forties walked up to the witness chair and remained standing.

The clerk spoke. "Please raise your right hand." The doctor did so. "Do you swear to tell the truth, the whole truth, and nothing but the truth, so help you God?"

"I swear."

"Please state your name and spell your last name for the record."

"Dr. Edward Charles Settle. S-E-T-T-L-E."

The doctor sat down and the DA began his questioning. "Where are you employed, Dr. Settle?"

This part of the testimony bored Sabre and her mind began to wander. Whenever Sabre heard someone sworn in, she remembered what an attorney from Cambodia had once told her. He said the oath "to tell the truth" was also required in the Cambodian legal system, but it was typically sworn to Buddha, the spirits of the courtroom, or the ghosts of Khmer warriors. The wording threatened dire punishments if the witness lied. They swore, "If I am home, let fire destroy my house for eight hundred reincarnations; if I am in a boat, let it sink for eight hundred reincarnations; when I become a ghost, let me eat bloody pus, or swim in boiling chili oil for eight hundred reincarnations." Sabre shuddered at the thought, and began listening to the DA questioning the doctor about his credentials. She knew enough about the doctor and his stellar reputation to know it wasn't necessary to continue with this line of questioning. At the first opportunity, she interrupted, "If it pleases the court, the defense is willing to accept a curriculum vitae in lieu of this testimony."

The DA agreed and continued with the specifics of the case. The medical examiner's testimony established the cause of death as stab wounds to the heart, explaining John only lived a few minutes after the attack. Sabre looked at Betty, tears running down her cheeks. The doctor established the time of death to be between nine and eleven p.m. Sabre needed Bob for cross-examination. He had prepared for it and was better at it than she was. She knew the case well, as she always did, and she could do it if she had to, but Bob charmed the witnesses; when it came to cross, they were putty in his hands.

The state called their next witness. Sabre watched her handsome, clean-cut boyfriend walk into the courtroom, so confident and professional looking, unlike most of the witnesses she dealt with. He took the stand. The clerk said, "Please raise your right hand." Luke raised his right hand. "Do you swear to tell the truth, the whole truth, and nothing but the truth, so help you God?"

"I do," Luke said confidently.

"Please state your name for the record, and spell your last name."

"Lucas Rahm. R-A-H-M."

"Thank you. You may be seated." Luke sat down, looking directly at the district attorney." Sabre was glad. She didn't want to be smiling at the prosecution's witness.

The DA stood up. "Are you acquainted with the defendant, Betty Taylor?"

"Yes, she's a friend of mine."

"And her husband John, he was a friend as well?"

"Yes, sir." Sabre was proud of how well Luke handled himself on the stand. He didn't appear to be frightened as most witnesses were. He sat up straight, looked the prosecutor in the eye, and answered without hesitation. She thought about a time when she had to testify and she was nervous, stammering over the answers. It was easier being on her side of the table.

"On the evening of the murder, where were you?"

"Objection, vague as to time," Sabre said, an automatic response.

"Where were you around five o'clock?"

"I went to Viejas Casino with my girlfriend."

The DA looked over at Sabre. "That would be the defense attorney, Sabre Brown, correct?"

Sabre shot the DA a dirty look, but she knew he was making a record for appeal. She should've made the full disclosure statement before the preliminary hearing started, but Bob was supposed to take care of that and she simply forgot. *Where is Bob, anyway? Something must be wrong.* "Your Honor, for the record, the court is already aware of my involvement as a witness in this case, and my client has filed a waiver for any conflict."

"Duly noted, Ms. Brown, and the State will be afforded every opportunity to cross examine you or call you as a hostile witness if that's necessary." The judge looked at the DA. "Please proceed, Mr. Lewis."

"Thank you, Your Honor." He looked at his notes. "Who went with you to Viejas?"

"Sabre Brown rode with me. We met Betty there for dinner and then we gambled some."

"When you say 'Betty', you mean the defendant Betty Taylor, correct?"

"Correct."

"What time did you leave there?"

"About ten-thirty."

"Did the defendant leave with you?"

"No, she said she...."

"Objection, hearsay." Sabre responded automatically to the

tone of the question, although she was more nervous today than she had been at her first trial. She had to get this one right. *Maybe she shouldn't be doing this case. Maybe Betty would be better with a public defender. Where is Bob? And where is JP?*

"Withdraw the question. Was the defendant with you the entire time you were at Viejas?"

"I wasn't with her every minute."

The DA kept up the pace. "What do you mean, not 'every minute'?"

"We were gambling at different places in the casino." Sabre could see Luke wasn't giving the information willingly and thought how hard this must be for him to have to testify against his friend.

The DA raised his voice a little in frustration. "Was there any period of time— say more than an hour—that you weren't with the defendant?"

"Yes."

"When was that?"

"After dinner, Betty and Sabre went to play bingo while I was playing blackjack."

"How much time lapsed before you saw the defendant again?"

Luke paused for a second, slowing down the DA's questioning. Sabre wondered if he did it on purpose. "About an hour and a half." Then he added before the DA spoke, "We were still at the casino."

"After you left the casino, when did you see the defendant next?"

"Around four-thirty the next morning, at her home."

"Where was the defendant?"

"She greeted us at the door."

"Who is 'us'?"

"Sabre and me."

"What did she look like?"

"Objection, vague." Sabre wasn't giving the DA an inch. Besides, she wanted this to go on as long as she could to give Bob and JP time to get there.

"Sustained," the judge responded in a monotone voice.

"Was there anything unusual about the defendant's appearance?" Lewis continued.

"She had blood on her pajamas."

"A little blood or a lot?"

"Objection, vague."

"Overruled," the judge turned to Luke, "you may answer the question."

Luke looked at Sabre. She gave him no response, no nod, no change of expression. She was well trained in not giving signals to witnesses. Nothing frustrated her more than to see an attorney encourage a witness by their body language.

"A lot," Luke answered.

"What did you do next?"

"I went into the bedroom."

"And what did you see?" the DA asked.

Luke hesitated. "I saw John lying on the bed covered in blood."

"What did you do?"

"I checked to see if he was alive."

"And was he?"

"No."

"How did you know that?"

"He wasn't breathing. He had no heartbeat."

"Anything else?"

"He felt cold and a little stiff." Betty shifted in her chair. She took a tissue from a box in front of her and wiped the tears from her cheeks. Sabre patted her hand.

"Did it appear there had been any kind of struggle?"

"No. Nothing was really out of place."

"Did you see a knife?"

"No." Luke shook his head. "No knife."

"Was there any indication the victim had a weapon of any sort?"

Luke thought for a second. "No, there was nothing around. He just had a rosary in his left hand."

Sabre's head shot up. *Oh my God.* Sabre swallowed. She looked at Luke to see if there was any change in his expression. She saw none. She reached over and squeezed Betty's hand.

The DA continued. "What did you do then?"

"We called the police."

"No further questions," the DA stated.

Sabre stood up. Her voice shaky, she said, "Your Honor, I'd like to continue this case until tomorrow morning. I'm very concerned about my colleague, Mr. Clark, as well as my detective. It's extremely unusual for either of them to not be here."

"Very well. The witness is ordered to return. We'll see you all tomorrow morning at nine o'clock. And, Ms. Brown, please tell Mr. Clark he'd better have a good reason for not appearing in my court."

"Thank you. I will, Your Honor."

Luke walked out of the arena, past the railing, into the gallery, and out of the courtroom. The bailiff came to take Betty. Sabre touched her on the shoulder. "Betty, don't worry. It's going to be okay. It's all going to be okay." Sabre tried to speak without her voice trembling, but she wasn't very effective.

"What's wrong?" Betty asked.

"Nothing. Go. I'll see you real soon and I'll explain everything."

Sabre took a deep breath, trying to calm herself and her voice. She had to sound normal for Luke. She gathered up her things, slowly breathing in and out, calming herself. She walked out. Luke was waiting for her just outside the courtroom.

"Want to get some breakfast or an early lunch?" Luke brushed Sabre's cheek with the palm of his hand.

Sabre stepped back. "No, I need to get back to the office. I have too much to do."

Luke looked at her and frowned. "You okay? You look a little pale."

"I'm just tired. The hike out of the canyon was quite an ordeal on top of the bruised ribs from the courtroom. My body's still recovering."

"Baby," Luke said, taking his hand in hers. "Maybe you should go home and get some rest."

She raised her briefcase. "I will, after I get a few things done at the office."

Luke leaned in to kiss Sabre. She flinched. The word "rosary" echoed in her brain like the steady beeping of an annoying car alarm. If Luke noticed her reaction, he passed it off perhaps as a result of her injured ribs. "Will I see you tonight?"

"I'll call you. Let me see how I'm feeling."

"I'll walk you to your car."

"Actually, I need to go talk to the DA for a minute. You go ahead. I'll call you this afternoon."

Sabre was relieved when Luke finally left. She had to figure out what was going on and she needed to find Bob and JP. She called Bob's office. They hadn't seen him. She tried both Bob's and JP's cell phones. The calls went straight to voice mail. Sabre walked into the clerk's office and asked to see Betty. They led her to the back, where Betty sat in a small cell with another inmate. Betty came forward and they spoke through the bars.

"Betty, I need to ask you a few questions, and I want you to think very carefully."

"Go ahead."

"The night of the murder I saw you holding a rosary. Where did you get it?"

"John had it in his hand. It was dangling there just like Luke said." Betty looked up, eyes wide. "But how would he know?"

"Did you tell anyone John was holding the rosary when you found him?"

Betty shook her head. "No, I don't think so."

"Think." Sabre said, holding on to a bar with her right hand. "It's real important. Did you tell the police? Anyone?"

"No. I'm pretty sure I didn't. I'd forgotten about it until it came up today." Betty's brow wrinkled quizzically. "So, how did Luke know?"

"I don't know. I know I didn't tell him. I need to know if anyone else told him."

"Who do you think told him?" Betty looked confused as she took hold of the bars with both hands and leaned her face into them.

"No one else knew as far as I can tell." Sabre spoke softly. "I didn't tell anyone, so if you didn't tell—."

"Oh my God." Betty's eyes widened. "You think Luke killed John? That's not possible. Sabre, what are you thinking? That's crazy."

"I know," Sabre said, shaking her head. "There must be some other explanation, but how else would he know?" Sabre's mouth was dry. She swallowed.

"Well, someone must've told him. Maybe Bob?"

Sabre shook her head aggressively. "Bob didn't know either. I never told him." Sabre willed herself to breathe. She held Betty's gaze. "Now is the time for the truth, the whole truth. Let's start with how you met Luke."

Betty didn't seem to have the strength to look away. "John met him first." The words came unwillingly as she continued. "Luke had a flat tire, and John helped him fix it."

Sabre gazed at her old friend. Betty looked every moment of her age. "Where were they?"

"Just outside the trailer park where we live, er, lived. Luke walked into the park and talked to John, who was outside piddling around."

"And you had never seen him before?"

"No."

"When did you see him next?"

"He came back the next day and brought John a six-pack of beer for helping him with the tire. They drank the beer and visited. After that he started coming around occasionally. He didn't know anyone else in San Diego, so John kind of took him in."

"And you're sure John didn't know him before? In his past?"

"No." Betty shuddered. "Sabre, you're talking lunacy. This is

Luke you're talking about. You know him. In fact, you know him better than anyone. Do you really think he could kill John?"

Sabre shook her head. "No, but not only did he know about the rosary, he said he saw it dangling from his hand. Why would he say he had seen it if he hadn't? It's not like he saw it in a photo or something and it stuck in his mind." Sabre breathed in deeply and blew it out in an exaggerated breath. "And now Bob and JP are missing."

37

Sabre drove back to the office and enlisted the help of Elaine, her receptionist, and Jack, the other attorney in the office. She had spoken to Bob's wife on the way, and Marilee had no idea where he was. All Sabre had managed to do was worry her.

"I'll call the hospitals," Elaine volunteered.

Jack said, "I'll call the sheriff and highway patrol. You call the city police departments.

Sabre called San Diego Police Department and spoke with a very nice young lady, who checked the records and informed her there was no accident that involved anyone meeting the description of Bob or JP. There had been no fatal accidents for six days and no recent accidents wherein anyone was transported to the hospital. She was also informed that they couldn't really do anything until a person had been missing twenty-four hours.

Sabre hung up the phone and dialed the El Cajon police department. She was starting to panic. Sabre knew there had to be something terribly wrong or she would've heard from one or both of them by now.

The day was nearly gone, the sun starting to set, and still no word from either of them. According to Jack's friends in the sheriff's department, no accidents of any consequence had been reported.

Sabre walked into the lobby, heard the tail end of Elaine's conversation, and asked, "Did you find something?"

"No, sorry. The hospitals have had no one admitted matching their descriptions, either together or separately. One man who was taken to Kaiser had gray hair, was wearing a suit, and was about Bob's height. But his age was off by a good ten years, and the man knew full well who he was and had ID to prove it."

Sabre had just about reached her limit. She was tired and sore and more worried and confused than she could ever remember being. Her two best friends were missing and she couldn't turn to the one person she wanted to turn to—Luke.

Sabre's stomach ached from the anxiety she felt. Her hands trembled as she drove her car towards Luke's apartment. She kept telling herself to breathe, but it wasn't helping. Her left foot twitched and her throat constricted. She had to know. The last thing she wanted to believe was that Luke was involved, but after his testimony she had to know for sure. She drove past Luke's apartment and saw his car parked on the street in front of his door. Her heart pounded faster. Her throat felt dry. She wanted to go inside and confront him, have him explain how he knew about the rosary. There had to be a good explanation. She would feel better once she was convinced he wasn't involved. She slowed down, looking for a parking spot. She didn't see one and circled the block. This time she saw an empty spot a few car lengths from Luke's apartment. She started to pull in and then changed her mind. *What if he's the killer?* She drove around the block again.

The third time she returned, Luke's car was gone. She saw it ahead of her at the stop sign. She slowed down to get more distance between his car and hers. Then she followed him out of the complex and to the street. She breathed in and out slowly, her hands trembling. She stayed back far enough where he wouldn't see her. Luke entered I-8 heading east. Sabre kept a few cars between them, but Luke was picking up speed and it was getting too dark to distinguish one car from another. She thought she saw him take the Waring Street off ramp.

He must be going to his storage unit.

Sabre's phone rang in her ear, startling her. The Caller ID read "Luke." She hesitated, not sure if she wanted to answer it. She inhaled, composed herself, and said, "Hello, this is Sabre."

"Hi, baby."

"Oh, hi," she said, in a "glad it's you" voice as if she didn't know at first who was calling. "Where are you? I hear street noise." Sabre took the Waring Street exit. She could see some taillights ahead but couldn't make out if it was Luke's car.

"I just went to the ATM and now I'm going to the market to

pick up a few things for dinner. Why don't you come over. I know you've had a rough day. Let me make you a nice meal, and we can just relax and watch a movie or something."

Sabre felt her whole body tremble. Her chest ached where her bruise was; her wounds throbbed as he lied to her. She knew then she had to find out. She had to know for sure. But why would he kill John, and why would he lie about his storage unit? Sabre had a hunch.

She breathed deeply to make her voice sound normal. She couldn't let him think she was upset. She heard a siren in the distance, afraid he would hear it too and know she was nearby. She muted the phone until the siren died away, and then said, "I'm not sure I can. I had a minor client institutionalized tonight at Alvarado. I only have four hours to get in to see him. That's where I'm going right now." The act of lying to someone she loved made her dizzy. She grasped the steering wheel tighter to finish the lie. "If it's not too late I'll call you when I leave Alvarado." The gate on the storage place closed just as Sabre arrived. Someone had just gone in and she was pretty certain it was Luke. Sabre drove down the street, turned around, and parked where she could see the entrance.

"You have to eat. Why don't you just come by afterwards. I'll make you a plate. I don't care how late it is."

"We'll see." Sabre, again overcome by how well he took care of her, told herself there had to be an explanation. "Sometimes these visits take hours, depending on the client. I'll call you."

"Ok. I love you, babe."

Sabre heard herself whisper, however unwillingly. "Love you, too."

Ten minutes passed before Sabre saw Luke's car pull out of the driveway from the storage place. *What was he doing in there? And why would he lie about it?* Sabre didn't have the answers but she was going to find out. There was no use in trying to get into his storage unit without a key, so she pulled out behind him, keeping her distance. She followed him on to I-8 west, then the fifteen north, and the Friar's Road off ramp. She dropped back. He was going home. *How could she not know this man who had seen her naked and professed his love to her? And whose love she had returned. This man who treated her like a princess and made her feel so safe? There was no way he could be a cold, calculating killer. She would prove it to herself.*

Sabre drove to the Coffee Bean in Mission Valley, ordered a cup of decaf coffee, and waited about fifteen minutes before she called Luke. She had a plan.

"You done already?" Luke asked.

"Yes, I got in right away, spoke with the young man, and left. I couldn't get much out of him but enough to know he needs to be there." Sabre's lies were getting easier. "So, is dinner ready?"

"It will be shortly. I'm just throwing on a quick stir-fry. Come on over. It'll be ready by the time you get here."

Sabre sat and sipped her coffee, letting enough time pass to account for the drive from the hospital. She had to face Luke, and she had to get the key to his storage unit. She kept telling herself to breathe; she needed to be calm when she arrived at Luke's. But in the midst of the warm evening air, Sabre felt a chill as she stepped into her car.

Luke greeted her with the same tenderness he always did. He pulled her close, wrapped his strong arms around her, and kissed her gently, lingering on her lips. She felt the sweet taste of love. She compelled her body to relax, her mind struggling with the truth. He felt so good. How could she question his intentions? She wanted to believe in him, to trust him, but her skeptical mind did not allow it. Right now she had to convince Luke there was nothing wrong with her, but what she really wanted was for him to convince her he was genuine. She kissed him back, maybe a little more passionately than she should have. He responded in kind. "Hmm…," he said as he kissed her lightly on the forehead.

Sabre wondered if she would be able to get past all this if he were innocent. But if he weren't, she was in as much danger as everyone else. *If he killed John, did he also kill Bob and JP?* The thought made her shudder just as their embrace ended. She tried to relax, but not in time. "Are you cold?"

"I got a chill outside, and it's very warm. I hope I'm not getting sick."

"It's probably from all the trauma to your body," Luke said, as he led her into the living room. "Sit down, relax; dinner's almost ready."

When Luke left the room, Sabre glanced at the shelf near the television where he sometimes left his keys. They weren't there. Nor were they hanging on the hook by the kitchen door. Her first thought was that he knew why she was there and was hiding them. Then she realized that was crazy. How could he possibly know she wanted his keys? She continued to look around. No keys.

"Oo…!" She jumped when Luke came up behind her and touched her shoulder.

"I'm sorry. I didn't mean to startle you. You sure are jumpy. Is everything okay?"

Sabre turned and leaned on Luke. He embraced her and she let herself melt into him. "I just need your arms around me. It's been a rough day. I'm afraid I'm not going to be able to help Betty, and my client in Alvarado tried to kill himself today. And I still feel weak and gun shy from the canyon debacle."

Luke held her until she let go. "Come on. Let's get some food in you and get you to bed." They walked into the kitchen. "I'll take care of you."

Sabre felt another chill, and was glad she had already let go of Luke. Just as she sat down to eat, she spotted Luke's keys on the kitchen counter partially hidden by a package of angel hair spaghetti. He must've set them down there when he brought in the groceries.

"Go ahead, sit down. I'll fix your plate."

"Thanks, but not too much. I'm not very hungry."

Sabre picked at her food, trying to eat enough to allay

suspicion. Her stomach growled. Apparently, she was hungrier than she thought. The stir-fry tasted good, but her stomach was in knots and she had a difficult time swallowing. She tried to breathe normally as she pondered how to get her hands on the keys.

Sabre stood up as Luke did and picked up her half empty plate from the table. Luke said, "Just sit. I can do this."

"No, I'll help. I'd like to help."

Luke cleaned off the plates and put them in the dishwasher. Sabre retrieved a container from the cupboard above the keys for the extra stir-fry. Maybe she could slip them in her pocket. She looked at Luke. He smiled at her. She walked to the stove, filled the container, put it in the refrigerator, and brought the pan to the sink. Luke took the pan, washed it, and set it on the counter to dry.

Sabre picked up the package of spaghetti, intentionally catching Luke's keys on her pinkie. She carried them to the pantry to put the package away.

"Wait," Luke said.

Startled, Sabre turned around and the keys hit the tile floor. The sound they created could just as well have been a fire alarm. Sabre jumped. Blood flooded to her face. She looked at Luke to see his reaction, but he was smiling. A few hours earlier she would've interpreted that smile as empathizing with her embarrassment, but now she wondered if he knew what she was up to.

"I'll never be able to find my keys if you put them in the cupboard," he said. She wondered if he was teasing.

"I'm sorry. I didn't realize I had hold of them. They must have caught on the spaghetti package."

Luke picked up the keys and took the package of spaghetti from Sabre's hand. "No problem, but the spaghetti goes over here," he said, as he placed the package in a drawer. "Come on; let's go sit." Luke put his arm around Sabre's shoulder and guided her into the other room. He stopped just inside the doorway to hang his keys on the hook. Sabre could see the key to the storage unit. It had a round black rubber disc that slipped over the end of the key, making it easy to identify. She recognized it from when she went with Luke a few weeks earlier.

Luke sat down on the sofa, taking Sabre's hand and gently pulling her down to him. Sabre leaned back. Luke reached his arm around her and pulled her close to him, her head falling onto his shoulder. She made her body relax. Luke picked up the remote, turned on the television, and found a movie channel with Katherine Hepburn and Spencer Tracey starring in *Adam's Rib*. Sabre looked up at him quizzically. Luke smiled at her and said, "I know you're a fan. You told me when we first met."

Sabre felt weak. She forced a smile. How could he be perfect in so many ways? She had to be wrong about him. There must be some explanation. She considered confronting him, but she knew if she was wrong there was no turning back, and if she was right she may be putting Bob and JP at risk.

"You're very sweet, you know," Sabre said.

"I try," he said, gently squeezing her tighter.

Sabre sat there, calculating how to get her hands on the key. Luke didn't seem to be going anywhere as long as she was there. Sabre had just about given up when Luke untangled himself from her and stood up. "Excuse me for a moment." He walked toward the bathroom.

It was now or never, she thought. As soon as she heard the bathroom door close, she stood up and walked over to the hook with the keys. She took them down and started to turn the storage key around the key ring to remove it. The tight key ring made it difficult to get the large rubber end through it. Sabre shook as she struggled with it. Just as she got it started, it slipped and the keys fell to the floor. That loud jingle on the tile floor sounded even louder than the first time she dropped them. She looked up as she reached down to pick them up. Luke was still in the other room. The key dislodged from inside the ring and she had to start over. Fumbling, she tried again. Her face felt hot and she shook. She told herself to breathe. When the key was about halfway around the circle, she heard the toilet flush. Sabre peeked around the corner as she continued to maneuver the key around the circle. She heard the water in the sink run.

Good boy, Luke. He never neglects to wash his hands.

The key was off. She stuck the key in her pocket and placed the key ring back on the hook as Luke walked in. "What are you doing?" he asked.

"Just getting some water."

He stepped closer to her, felt her head, and took her hand in his. "Your face is red and you're shaking."

"I…I don't feel very well. I think I'll go home."

"Do you want to see a doctor?"

"No, I'll be fine. It must be the flu or something. I'm just going home." Sabre picked up her bag and walked to the door. Luke followed her out and walked her to her car. When his lips approached hers to kiss her goodbye, Sabre turned her head.

"Don't," she said. "I don't want to get you sick."

Luke put one hand on either side of her head, turned it down, and kissed her on the forehead. "Call me when you get home."

"Sure."

Sabre was still shaking when she tried to put her key inside the ignition. After finally starting the car, she drove off wondering if Luke saw her put the keys back, if he suspected anything, and when he would discover the key was missing.

Approximately three blocks from Luke's apartment, Sabre pulled into a Shell gas station. She took a drink of water, some deep breaths, and wondered if she had just made the biggest mistake of her life. If Luke were innocent, how would he ever forgive her for that kind of mistrust? She wanted to return and lose herself in his arms, but it was too late. What she had to do was prove he didn't do anything and pray he'd forgive her.

Within ten minutes she pulled up to the storage facility. The gates were closed, and without the combination she would have to wait for someone else to open them so she could follow their car inside. She parked across the street and waited. It was nearly eight-thirty and there was no activity in or out of the facility. Every few minutes a car would drive by and Sabre would tense up, hoping it was someone who'd open the gate but concerned it might be Luke. About eight-forty a car pulled into the driveway. The gate opened. Sabre started her car and tried to follow, but cars approached from both directions and by the time she crossed the street the gate was closed.

Sabre drove around the block until she found a parking spot on the north side of the street so she wouldn't have to cross traffic. Though farther from the driveway, she figured she still had time to make it before the gate closed. Every headlight coming from the east increased her anxiety, for fear it may be Luke.

A little after ten, just as Sabre was thinking she may be there all night, a red Ford truck pulling a boat appeared. The gate opened and Sabre was able to drive in behind it. Once on the grounds, Sabre tried to remember where the storage unit was. The truck went straight past the rows and rows of identical cubicles. Sabre tried to remember which way they'd gone when she was there with Luke. She remembered they had turned right just as they entered. She turned and drove all the way to the end of the units and made a left. That much she knew was correct. She knew it wasn't an end unit on an end row, but she thought it wasn't far from the end, perhaps five or six cubicles. That left a lot of ground to cover.

Sabre stopped her car in the dimly lit lot, took a flashlight from the trunk, and started her search. She started with the second row, the second unit, and worked her way down the row for about ten units with no success. She went back to her car, drove to the third row and started again. It was awkward holding her flashlight and testing the key, and since there was enough light, she left the flashlight in the car. At the sixth unit, she stopped when she saw lights from a vehicle coming up the back side of the facility. She started walking quickly back to her car. Before she reached it, the red Ford truck passed through the alleyway; it was no longer pulling the boat.

Sabre finished her lock checks on that row and moved to the fourth row, and then the fifth. Still nothing. On the sixth row she saw car lights at the other end. The car pulled in and stopped, but the driver left it running with its headlights on. She couldn't see much, but she was able to see someone exit the car, open the unit, and within in a minute or two climb back in the car and drive away. Sabre continued down the row until she reached the fourth unit. The key fit. The lock opened. She removed the lock, set it down, and tried to open the roll-up door. It was heavy or stuck and would not budge. She yanked on it for a bit before she discovered that the lever where the lock was attached had to be shifted to the left. She still couldn't get a good grip on the door to get it open. She reached all the way to the bottom of the door and saw a metal piece protruding. She stepped on it and pulled up from the handle. The door rolled up. It was too dark to see beyond a foot or so inside. She ran back to her car and retrieved her flashlight.

Amongst the neatly stacked boxes, tied to the metal beams running up the middle of the unit on either side sat JP and Bob. Each had his hands tied behind him, his feet tied together, and duct tape over his mouth. Neither was able to move or even struggle enough to make any noise.

"Oh my God," she gasped.

JP turned his head toward her "mm…mm…"

"Hold on." Sabre grabbed a hold of the tape and yanked it off his mouth

"Damn…that hurt."

"Sorry."

Sabre glanced around for something she could use to cut him loose. "Just a second," she said, as she ran outside to her car. She opened her trunk and removed a pair of scissors from her briefcase, then ran back inside.

"What happened?" Sabre asked, as she leaned behind JP to sever the rope holding his hands.

"Luke..."

"Damn it, Sabre!" Luke's voice cut through the air behind her sending a chill through her body. "Stand up and back up."

Sabre didn't have time to try and cut the rope, but quickly wedged the open scissors between the ropes on JP's hands and placed the handle in his palm. She stood up, turned around, and faced the gun pointing directly at her.

38

"Sabre, Luke killed John," JP yelled. "And he…."

Luke stepped around Sabre, placing himself between her and JP. Keeping the gun on Sabre, he kicked his foot backwards. JP jerked his head to the left, but caught the hard sole of a Ferragamo loafer on the side of his head just behind his ear.

"He's not who you think he is," JP continued, as he tried to cut through the rope. Luke swung around, his usual calmness gone, and slammed the butt of the gun into JP's temple. The scissors fell from JP's grip as he passed out.

Sabre darted out of the storage unit, running as fast as she could with her sore feet to the end of the row. As Luke chased after her, she skidded around the corner and dodged behind his car. She could hear his footsteps pounding on the blacktop, getting closer and closer to her. She had to run to her car. There was nowhere to hide, just locked storage units one after another. Unfortunately, there was enough light from the distant lamp poles that Sabre could be seen. Running anyway, she reached her car, her keys in her hand ready to start the engine. She looked up. Luke had just turned the corner, gun in hand. He was just a few feet away. She jerked open the car door so hard, the pain surged in her chest. In the moment she took to catch her breath, Luke slammed the door into her sore rib, thrusting her against the car.

"O-w-w-w…," Sabre yelled out in pain.

Luke shoved the gun in his waist band. He put one hand on each of her shoulders and turned her around. "Come on, Sabre." He shook her. "Listen." She struggled to get loose, but he held her tightly. "Please, you need to hear me out."

"What's to hear?" Sabre tried to break loose, but his tight hold remained. "You have my two best friends tied up and locked in a storage unit. And you killed John."

"I love you, Sabre." He shook her desperately.

"You love me?" The absurdity of what he said nearly knocked

her off her feet. Her face wrinkled in disgust; her head shook in disbelief. "You love me?" Her voice escalated. "You just had a gun pointed at my head! That's not love."

"Please." He stroked the side of her face. Sabre jerked her head away. He put one hand on each side of her head, pulling so tightly he pulled her hair. She tried to bury her fear, but even in the dim light Sabre could see the anguish mixed with anger in his eyes. "I really do love you," Luke told her. "Come away with me. We'll go far away from here, to the Amalfi Coast in Italy. I own a villa there. It's the most beautiful place on earth with white houses set in the cliffs. My villa overlooks the most amazing deep, blue water, and you'll have servants and luxuries like you've never known. No one will know where we are and your friends can go free." He released her arm with one hand and stroked her face. "You'll see. We'll be so happy."

Sabre felt his tender touch and for a moment almost felt sorry for him. She thought about how good things had been between them, how perfect everything was just days ago. She stared into his eyes. He leaned in to kiss her, holding her gaze. She waited until his lips almost touched on hers. Then she raised her knee and kicked him as hard as she could in the crotch. Her mother would be proud. He doubled up, loosening his grip, and his hands reached for his groin. She shoved him as hard as she could and ran back toward the open storage unit. She went in and grabbed a broom she had seen near Bob. She had to step over him to get it. She accidentally stepped on his foot, and tripped, catching herself before she hit the ground. Bob groaned. She grabbed the broom and by the time she was at the door of the unit, Luke was there, with his gun in his hand once again. Sabre swung the broom at him. He dodged it. She swung again. She had been held captive once before, and she swore she'd never let that happen again. Luke smiled at her, escalating Sabre's anger. She charged at him with the broom, screaming like a mad woman, tears rolling down her cheeks. Luke grabbed the broom and whipped it out of her hands. It fell to the ground. Sabre lunged at him, her face red with anger, fists in the air ready to pound. She could taste the salty teardrops on the side of her mouth. He grabbed her by the waist and threw her down to the floor, her legs and arms flailing in the air. She fell on top of JP, sprawled across him face up. She tried to push herself up, but Luke pulled his gun from his waist, knelt, and pointed the gun at JP's head.

"Another move and I'll kill him."

Sabre raised her hands slowly, palms open, fingers spread apart. "Ok. I'll stop. Don't hurt him." She rolled off JP and scooted herself up to where she could lean against a box next to him. JP didn't move. "Is he alive?"

With the gun still held to JP's head, Luke felt his chest with his other hand. "His heart's beating." Sabre just looked at him. "Feel for yourself."

Sabre reached over slowly and felt JP's chest. She could feel the beat. She sighed.

"If you want him to stay alive, you're going to do what I say."

Sabre nodded her head.

"Go over there, and bring me that duct tape and rope on top of those boxes." He gestured with his head toward some boxes behind Bob.

Sabre stood up, took three steps, and retrieved the items for Luke.

"Now, tape his mouth."

Sabre did as she was told. "How could you do this? And how could you kill John?"

"You have no idea what that man did to me."

She tried to make her voice sound sympathetic. "So tell me."

Luke took the rope. "Come here. I'm going to lay the gun down and tie your hands. If you try to run, I'll pick up the gun and shoot both your friends and then come after you."

"Okay. Okay. I won't run." Sabre stood still while he tied her hands in front of her. At least he was kind enough to not put them behind her.

"Now, sit down," he commanded. She sat down next to JP and

leaned against the boxes, trying to make herself as comfortable as possible. She shook with the fear of being in captivity again, but she feared more for the lives of her friends. Luke tied her feet together.

"Please, Luke. I need to know why," Sabre pleaded.

Luke took a deep breath, blowing it out with an exaggerated sound. "He took everything from me...my father, my mother, my brother."

"You mean he killed them?"

"No, but he betrayed my father and broke my grandfather's heart."

"How did he do that?"

Luke's eyes looked almost tearful. "John worked for my grandfather from the time he was about fourteen years old. My grandfather took him in and raised him with his own son. When John was subpoenaed to testify against my father and grandfather, he sneaked off in the night like a common thief with his girlfriend and her precious baby boy." He snarled when he said "precious."

Sabre was confused. "Wasn't that a good thing if he left without testifying against them?"

"It would've been if he hadn't squealed like a pig first, giving the prosecutor plenty of information to put my grandfather in prison for life and my father for the first five years of my life."

"But, Luke, that was such a long time ago."

"The Pacecos don't forget a betrayal."

"Who are the Pacecos?" Silence. Sabre looked him in the eyes. "That's you? That's your name? Luke Paceco?"

"No, it's Tony Paceco."

"Talk about betrayal. You betrayed me. I didn't even know your name. Everything about you is a lie," she spat.

Still kneeling in front of Sabre, Luke reached up and cupped her face in his hand. "No, not everything. I really love you," he said softly.

Sabre yanked her head away. "You make me want to vomit."

Luke pulled back. "I'm sorry you and your friends are involved, but the rest is as it should be. John is dead. Betty will pay for it."

"Why should Betty pay? She was nothing but good to you." For a second, Sabre thought Luke looked sad. Maybe it was guilt. Then the look was gone.

He shook his head and said, "Right."

Luke picked up the duct tape from the floor, tore off a piece, and leaned down to Sabre. "It didn't have to be this way," he said, as he stretched the tape across her mouth. Sabre struggled, flipping her head from side to side. Luke pushed her head against the box, holding it with one hand, and smoothed the tape down across her mouth with the other. He picked up the flashlight and walked out.

"Someone will be here shortly to take care of you. I have to go find an alibi."

The door slammed shut. The lock clicked.

39

In the total darkness, Sabre scooted over to JP and tapped him with her tied hands. He made a grunting sound through the tape on his mouth. She rolled over him and positioned herself behind him. JP rolled to his left, exposing his tied hands. Sabre felt around for the scissors. She picked them up, placing three fingers of her right hand in one hole and her thumb in the other, and slid down where she had a better angle at the rope. With the scissors slightly open, she tried to wedge it between the knot on JP's hands. She poked his wrist with the point. JP jerked. "Mmm…," she tried to apologize.

"Mmm…, mmm…," JP responded. Sabre assumed he meant it was okay. It didn't matter; she had to do this. She could apologize later. While JP held his hands steady, Sabre tried again. She pushed until she had the scissors lodged into the knot, but when she tried to cut it, the rope was too thick. Using her left hand to push against her right, she pushed the scissors off the knot. Then, Sabre opened and closed the scissors repeatedly, gnawing at the rope. The scissor was dull, the rope thick, and her bound hands were weak, but she continued to apply pressure; finally, she felt the rope start to give way.

Her hands needed to rest. Her fingers cramped, and her thumb was sore from the pressure. Stopping, Sabre pulled her fingers out and stretched out her hand, keeping the tip of her thumb in the hole so she wouldn't drop the scissors. When she resumed, she could only move the scissors about a quarter of an inch at a time. Open, close. Open, close. Finally, after what seemed like an hour, she felt the rope break through. She dropped the scissors, and helped JP get the rope off his wrists. As soon as she freed his hands, he pulled the tape off his own mouth and then reached out in the dark to find Sabre's face. Holding her head with one hand, he pulled off the tape with the other.

"Ach…," Sabre squeaked.

"Sorry, there's no easy way to do that."

"We have to get out of here. Luke said he was sending someone 'to take care' of us," Sabre said.

"I know. I heard him. Where are the scissors?"

Sabre patted the floor until she found them and picked them up. "Here," she said, handing them to JP.

"Ok. I'm going to cut your wrists free." He held her hands steady, careful not to hurt her when he slid the scissors under the rope and cut her loose.

"Thanks, JP."

JP cut through the rope on his feet, and then groped around in the dark to find Sabre's so he could cut hers. Then he helped her to her feet. "We need to get Bob loose," JP said. He put his arm around Sabre and they walked slowly across the floor, JP running his hand along the boxes to guide him.

Sabre dropped to her knees, feeling in the dark until she reached Bob's face. He wiggled when Sabre touched him. "Hmm…," he said. Sabre yanked the tape off.

"Damn," Bob bellowed. "I won't have to shave there for a week."

"You goofball." She reached her arms around him and gave him a quick hug. JP cut his wrists and feet loose.

"Now, we just need to get out of here," Bob said. But JP was already looking for a way. He stepped toward the door counting the steps until he smashed into it. The metal door clattered in the silent dark room. "What the hell?" Bob asked, reaching for Sabre.

"I found the door," JP said.

"No kidding. You moron. Did you think it had moved?" Bob said. "You scared the crap out of us."

"It's three running steps. We can ram it and get an opening."

"What?"

"These doors are set between two metal pieces. The door rolls down a slot between them and it isn't very deep. I think if we ram the door it will pull away from the edge and we can get out," JP explained, as he walked back to Bob and Sabre, taking small steps with his arms out in front of him.

"Ok," Bob said. "I'm game. How do we do this? Do we do it together?"

"I'll help," Sabre said.

"No," JP said quickly, "you just stand back. Bob and I'll do it, but we need to go one at a time until we get a little light coming in. Otherwise we'll be crashing into each other. I'll go first." Before Bob could object, JP ran full force toward the door, turning his body slightly to the left just before he reached the door.

Crash! His body against the metal rang out in the quiet night. The door pulled away from the edge, creating an opening about six inches in length and illuminating their cage enough to see where they were stepping.

"Wow, that was great." Bob tapped JP on the shoulder. "You're a real cowboy, you know it?"

"Hmpf...." JP flinched to avoid the tap and the compliment. He hadn't yet recovered from the beating in Chicago and now he was tender from the whack against the door. He shrugged it off, picked up the broom Sabre had used to attack Luke, and started hitting at the opening on the door. He tried working his way down the door, but it wasn't making the hole any bigger.

"My turn," Bob said, as he prepared to run at the door.

JP stepped back and let him go at it. Another crash. This time it separated the door farther from the edge, exposing about two feet. JP stuck the broom in the edge of the opening and pushed it to the right, trying to pry it open. The opening grew a little wider and longer. Continuing to pry, he created an opening about three feet long that was a couple of feet from the floor.

"Ok, Sabre, you can fit through here." JP took a hold of her arm. "I think it's best if you back out. Just be careful you don't cut yourself on the metal. Some of it may be sharp."

Sabre lifted her leg back behind her, stepped through the hole onto the ground, and then started to pull herself through, guarding her face with her hand.

"Watch your arm," Bob yelled.

"Ow! Dang." Sabre tucked her arm in but she had already

scraped it on the metal protruding from the wall. Her body was outside. She pulled her other leg out. "I'll go get the car," she yelled, as she ran off.

Bob rummaged through a pile of wood alongside the wall opposite the opening and found a three-foot-long two–by-four. "Here, use this." He handed it to JP who dropped the broom and used the board as leverage to pry the metal apart. It opened enough for any grown man to pass through. Bob stepped out, followed by JP, just as a black Chrysler Sebring turned the corner at the west end of the lot. It was heading toward them. Bob glanced to his left. "Sabre's down there." He pointed toward her. "Run!"

As JP and Bob ran to the end of the units, the Chrysler picked up speed, its tires screeching on the pavement. JP was in front but Bob was close on his heels. When they reached Sabre's car, they were both breathing heavily. JP opened the front passenger door and jumped in. Bob grabbed the back door and flung it open. The Chrysler, just a few yards away, came straight at them. "Drive," he yelled at Sabre. She shot forward, hoping Bob had made it inside. Bob had one foot in the car, his right hand on the inside top of the door. JP grabbed his left hand just as the Chrysler hit the tail end of Sabre's car.

"Faster," JP yelled as he pulled Bob inside. Sabre hit the accelerator and made a sharp turn to her right. Bob's door slammed shut. The Chrysler veered around the corner behind them. Sabre pushed down as far as she could on the gas pedal. They gained ground. Turning left at the end of the storage rows, she prayed the gate was still open. They all looked up to see about six or seven feet left of open gate.

JP looked back at the car behind them and saw the passenger reach outside the window; the light on the lamppost near the exit showed shining metal in the man's hand. "Get down!" They all ducked as a bullet shot through the back window and out the front. With her head bent but still seeing the road, Sabre accelerated through the gate, knocking her side mirror off. The gate closed behind them. The Chrysler was still going forward at full speed.

Sabre drove out into the street in front of a yellow Mustang coming from her left. The Mustang screeched and swerved, horn honking, and the driver yelled obscenities. Sabre kept moving, making a right turn to avoid the fence across the street.

She remembered her cell phone, reached down, picked it up, and tossed it in the back seat to Bob. "Call 9–1–1."

As she approached the red light on Waring Road, she could see in her rearview mirror a car speeding towards them and the Mustang between them. "Oh no!" She let out a deep breath.

JP turned back and looked. "Damn it! They're through the gate."

A shot rang out. Sabre's window was open, and the wind whipped her hair across her face for a second, covering her eyes. She almost missed seeing the Mustang as it zipped past her and ran the red light. It moved faster than her Toyota Camry could ever go. Sabre's foot reached for the brake.

"You have to go through the light," JP yelled.

"I…I know, but then I have to turn left. I need to slow down."

You'll be fine." JP raised his voice even louder. "Just speed up when you make your turn. The momentum will carry you through. Go! You can make it." Sabre sped through the red light and turned left. "Faster," JP yelled.

Sabre gunned it, her back end screeching as it fishtailed. She fought to control the car, but as she straightened out she overcompensated and hit the gravel on the opposite of the road. With the car sliding sideways, JP fell against her. He braced himself on the console, reached for the steering wheel, and guided the car back on to the street.

"The cops are on the way," Bob yelled from the floor of the back seat where he had fallen when JP had yanked the wheel.

"They better hurry," Sabre said under her breath as she turned right on to the freeway ramp.

"We just entered I-8 heading west off Waring Road." Sabre

heard Bob screaming information to the dispatcher. "Where should we go?" He listened for directions and then responded, "We can't stop, you idiot. They're shooting at us."

Sabre heard another shot in the hollow evening air as it pinged off the rear of the car. Her hands held the wheel so tightly her fingers turned white.

"Damn it!" Bob yelled as he ducked, but the bullet had burned across the side of his head. It cut through his hair, leaving a path of smelly, burned flesh about four inches long. The phone tumbled to the floor in the front seat as the bullet lodged in the dashboard. Bob ducked down as far as he could, blood running down the whole left side of his face. "I've been shot," he said, but not loud enough to be heard in the front seat.

JP reached down and picked up the phone. The end of it was completely missing, seared right off. He looked at Bob. Bob nodded.

Sabre drove faster, swerving in and out of cars, driving mainly in the far left lane. The Chrysler followed her from one lane to the other. Almost to I-805, she cut across five lanes to take the upcoming off-ramp headed north. She saw lights from a police vehicle in her rearview mirror and could hear sirens coming from all directions. "I see cops behind us," Sabre said.

"And over there." JP pointed to two cop cars going north. "And there." He pointed to the police cars going east on the 8.

"And look," Sabre said, pointing toward the 805 South.

The Chrysler continued going west on the 8. Several cop cars with lights and sirens blaring followed it. Three others followed Sabre on to the ramp to the freeway. Sabre slowed down and pulled over as soon as she saw a place large enough to park.

The police vehicles surrounded the car, guns drawn. "Step out of the car with hands up."

Sabre's legs shook as she stepped out of the car, barely able to hold herself up. She looked back and saw Bob covered in blood. "He's been shot. We need an ambulance," she yelled.

"I need a cigarette," Bob murmured from the back seat.

40

S abre shivered from the air conditioner in the waiting room outside Detective Nelson's office. JP walked up with two cups of coffee. He handed her one. "Decaf with extra milk," he said.

"Thanks. Where did you get this?"

"I still have some friends here."

"Bob's going to be okay, isn't he?"

"I believe so," JP said. "The paramedic didn't think the bullet went too deep, and Bob was conscious when they took him."

Sabre ran her fingers up and down her coffee cup. "How did you know Luke killed John?"

"When I went to Chicago, Luke was on my plane. He didn't go to Dallas; instead, he was going home. He didn't see me, so I followed him to a restaurant called Paceco's...."

"That's his last name. His real name is Tony Paceco. He told me that when we were in the storage unit, but I think you were still passed out. I guess he thought I was going to die and it wouldn't matter if I knew." Sabre shrugged her shoulders. "Sorry, I didn't mean to interrupt."

"So from there he went to this mansion, which I found out later was called 'Villa Paceco,' so now I'm assuming that was his home." JP paused. "And Sabre, h...."

Detective Nelson walked in. "Come on in, you two." He led them to his stark office with its beige walls and worn carpet. His desk was cluttered with files except for one corner that held a five-by-seven photo of his wife and two kids. "Have a seat." He nodded his head toward the chairs. "By the way, I just checked on your friend, Bob. He seems to be doing all right. You'll be able to see him shortly."

"Thanks, Greg," they responded in unison.

"Now, will one of you tell me what happened tonight?"

Sabre described the nightmare in detail. Nelson looked up from his pad where he was taking notes and turned to JP. "So, how did you get there?"

"I was at Sabre's door last night, Sunday night, to tell her what I had learned about Luke when he knocked me out. The next thing I knew I was tied up and in the storage unit. This morning he brought Bob in. I couldn't talk to Bob because he had our mouths taped, so I don't know what happened to him."

"And what did you learn about Luke that you had to tell Sabre?"

"I learned he isn't who he said he is. We now know his name is Tony Paceco and he lives in Chicago." Nelson wrote a note on his pad. Then he picked up the phone, dialed a couple of numbers, and said, "See what you can find out about a Tony Paceco from Chicago."

Nelson looked at Sabre. "And you say Luke…Tony…confessed he killed John?"

"Yes."

"Did he admit that to you as well?" he asked JP.

"No."

Nelson turned back to Sabre, "Did he say why?"

"Just that John took his father, mother, and brother from him. He said John ran off instead of testifying against them, but that he told enough to the cops that they were able to send his grandfather to prison for life and his father for five years. He said his grandfather raised John and that he worked for him for years. He kept talking about how John 'betrayed' them."

"Did he say anything else about the mother and brother?"

"No. I assume he meant they were devastated by it all." Sabre thought about what else he said. "Oh yeah, and he said, 'Things are as they should be. John is dead and Betty will pay for it.'"

"So, you think he framed Betty?"

"Yes, although I don't know why." Sabre squinted at JP and then at Nelson.

The detective pulled at his shirt collar. "I'm afraid Luke's confession to Sabre won't hold up in court." He looked at Sabre. "You're the attorney. What do you think?"

"It will, because there's more. This morning in court, Luke said that when he found John he was holding a rosary in his left hand."

The detective shuffled through the file looking at the photos. He picked up a photo and turned it so Sabre and JP could see it. "There's no rosary in his hand."

"I know," Sabre nodded. "Betty was holding it when we arrived at her place that night. She said it was John's from his childhood. I didn't realize at the time she had taken it out of his hand."

"And you're sure you saw Betty with the rosary before Luke saw the body?"

"Yes, she was holding it when we walked in. Luke went to the bedroom, and I spoke with Betty about the rosary. He couldn't have heard that conversation."

"So the only way Luke would know about the rosary is if he saw the body before he went there with you," JP chimed in.

"That's correct," Nelson said. The phone rang. He picked up. "What did you find out?" He listened for a minute. "Ok, thanks. And add his name to the APB." He hung up the phone. "Well it seems Tony Paceco and Luke Rahm are one and the same. He does live in Chicago at the Villa Paceco family home. He was named after his grandfather, Antonio Paceco, well-known mobster in his day. Antonio's son, Vicentio—Luke's, or should I say Tony's, father—wasn't as well respected as grandpa. He couldn't seem to keep himself out of jail. He spent several prison terms but they never nailed him for anything really big. He has a reputation for not being the brightest light in the stadium."

"So where are pops and dad Paceco now?"

"Granddaddy died in prison about ten years ago and Vicentio is apparently dying of cancer. Rumor has it young Tony Paceco may be taking a leadership role. He inherited a lot of the family money from his grandfather. The Paceco restaurants all belong to Tony. That's about all I know so far."

Sabre stood up. "Well, Greg, if you don't need anything else, I'd like to get over to the hospital to see Bob."

"Sure, I'll call…." The phone rang, and Nelson picked up the receiver. When he hung up, he said, "They caught the guys who shot at you. They're bringing them in as we speak."

Sabre walked toward the door. JP extended his hand to the detective. "Thanks, Greg. Let me know if you get anything out of those thugs."

As soon as they could no longer be heard by the detective, Sabre asked, "What else did you find out that you weren't telling in there?"

JP cleared his throat. "Betty isn't who she says she is, either. I think her name is Edith Underdahl, and she worked as a maid in the Paceco Villa when she was about seventeen. She was pregnant, and her mother had moved her away from Bristol, the small town where she was raised. They landed in the Paceco Villa, and they both worked there. Edith gave birth to a boy who apparently was raised by his father back in Bristol. The child's name was Neil."

"Neil? You're sure it was Neil?"

"Yeah, I'm sure. Why?"

"Betty received word from a dear friend of hers who had a son named Neil who was dying. She was visibly upset by it." Sabre almost shouted. "Oh my God. Neil must be Betty's son. That poor woman. She should be with him, not in jail." Sabre took a deep breath and blew it out. "Go on, what else did you find out?"

"According to Edith's childhood friend, Mary Lou, Edith fell in love with someone in the 'castle,' someone she shouldn't have. She gave her son to his father to rear, and she disappeared. Father and son stayed in Bristol until the boy was about ten, and then they moved somewhere, which may or may not have been Texas."

"So where did John fit in?"

"I'm not sure, but my guess is he was the one she fell in love with in the Villa Paceco."

"So, why wouldn't she tell us all of this? What was she afraid of?"

"Afraid for her own life, for her son's life, maybe. I don't know. I guess you need to ask her."

"I will when I see her tomorrow. There isn't anything we can do for her tonight. Let's go see Bob."

As they walked to the car, JP said, "Sabre, I don't want you to stay at your condo tonight."

"I don't really want to with Luke still out there."

"Yeah, that's what I'm talking about. He confessed to you about John. You are the only one who can testify about the rosary, except for Betty, but no one is likely to believe her since she has an ulterior motive. He has reason to want you dead."

41

"Hey, honey, what's with the mummy look?" Sabre said as she walked in the door of Bob's hospital room. "Hi, Marilee. How's the patient?"

Bob's wife stood by the side of his bed, doting over him. "He's still ornery. The bullet to his head didn't change his personality at all."

"Geez, I was hoping it would make him nicer."

"Real funny, guys. Here I lie with a hole in my head and you make fun of me."

"Oh, please. Don't even give me an opening like that, Superman. Besides, you don't have a hole in your head. Your head was too hard. It deflected right off," Sabre said. "Is he giving you a hard time, Marilee?"

Bob spoke up. "I just told her she should go home. I'm going to be fine."

"Don't listen to him. If you want to stay, stay." Sabre turned to Bob. "I'm glad you're okay. You were darn lucky. We all were." She reached down and kissed Bob on the forehead. "I'm not staying. I just wanted to come by and make sure you were all right and to let you know they caught the guys who were chasing us."

"Good, and what about Luke?"

"Nothing on him yet, but they'll catch him."

"You be careful."

"I will. In fact, I'm staying at JP's tonight." Sabre squeezed his hand. "I'll see you in the morning. I'll come by right after the Kemp hearing. Wagner will be there appearing for the mom. I'm sure he can cover for you." She started toward the door. "Oh, and JP said he'll see you tomorrow. He's waiting outside for me because they'd only let one of us in." She turned toward Marilee. "Good night, Marilee."

JP and Sabre entered his home. Everything looked the same as it did when she had bunked there six months earlier. The brown leather sofa faced the forty-two-inch plasma screen. She saw the four shelves of videos placed in no particular order, the hand-painted oil of a big oak tree on one wall, two pictures of John Wayne on another, and the bookshelf full of Louis L'Amour, Stephen King, and Joseph Wambaugh novels. Nothing had changed, including the putter that stood against the bookcase. A photo of JP's deceased father in a marine uniform sat atop the bookcase next to a pair of marble cowboy boot bookends holding two very old books. The books apparently had some special meaning to him, although he never shared what it was. Memories of last year flashed through her mind. He had been kind enough to let her stay with him when she was being stalked and when her condo burned down. A shiver went down her spine. That was such a frightful time, but this...this was worse in some ways. Now she was not only afraid, but she ached inside. There was no pain like that of losing someone you loved. So much had occurred in the past few hours, she hadn't had time to grieve her loss; Sabre vacillated between heartbreak and rage.

"May I get you anything?" JP asked. "Are you hungry?"

"No, thanks. I couldn't eat anything, and I know where everything is if I want something later. I'm just going to take a bath and then go to bed." She hugged JP. He hugged back and then gently rubbed his hand up and down her forearm and shoulder. "Oh yeah, there is something. Do you have an iPod I could use? I can't exactly use my iPhone since it's in an evidence locker with the end shot off."

JP walked to a shelf, picked up his iPod, and handed it to her. "And it's filled with good country music." Sabre smiled. She'd grown up hating country music, but her stint with JP had converted her.

Sabre carried a newly purchased toothbrush as she headed for the guest bathroom. In her other hand was a pair of JP's blue boxer shorts and a black tee shirt that read "Just a country boy." As the bath water ran, she looked under the sink for bubble bath and found her favorite; it had been left behind from her last stay. She poured it into the tub, and as she stood up, she caught her image in the mirror. She looked messy, tired, and sad. Her shoulders drooped, her mouth turned down, and her eyes had no life in them. She told herself to breathe. Inhale. Exhale. Time: it would take time, but she would heal. At least that's what she told herself.

She put her hand in the bathwater and adjusted the temperature, making it a little warmer. She picked up her toothbrush and started to brush her teeth. She flossed and then washed her face. The tub nearly full, she shut the water off, undressed, and connected the earpiece on the iPod. She stepped into the blanket of bubbles, sat back in the tub, and sang along with Carrie Underwood as she bellowed out, "Before He Cheats." Feelings of anger and sadness rumbled inside her head. Tears rolled down her cheeks as she thought about how she would like to take a Louisville Slugger to Luke's precious BMW Z4 Roadster. *How could I have been so stupid letting him suck me in?* She closed her eyes and started to sing along with Carrie. Halfway through the first line of the chorus Luke joined in, singing along with her.

Seeing Luke standing over her, she yanked the earphones out and screamed.

"No one can hear you. I took care of JP." Sabre screamed again. "You look beautiful. Get out of the tub." Sabre didn't move. "I said, 'Get out of the tub,'" Luke's voice was louder and more commanding. Then more softly, he said, "Please."

Sabre stood up, covered in bubbles. She reached for her towel and quickly wrapped it around her.

"You are gorgeous," Luke said. Sabre tucked the towel in, tightening it so it wouldn't fall. She hated that he was looking at her naked. She felt violated. *How could it have felt so good yesterday and feel so horrible today?* Luke reached for her hand to help her out of the tub. When his hand touched hers she yanked it back. She shivered. "You're shaking. Are you cold?"

"No, I'm angry, you son-of-a-bitch."

"Hey, I've never heard you talk like that before. Such a potty mouth."

"You'll have to excuse me, but I just found out my lying, cheating, murdering boyfriend isn't exactly who I thought he was." Her voice escalated with each word.

"Okay. Calm down. Let's deal with this."

"Deal with this? We can't just deal with this. It's not like you left the toilet seat up or the toothpaste cap off. Luke, or Tony, or whatever the hell your name is, you killed someone. Someone I loved."

Luke glanced around the bathroom before picking up the black tee shirt sitting on the long counter by the sink. He held it up and read the front. "What a bumpkin," Luke said, as he grabbed the blue boxer shorts and handed them to Sabre. "Get dressed. I'm sure JP will be delighted to have you in his shorts."

"What does that mean?" Sabre scowled.

"You just don't see it, do you?" Luke turned facing her more directly. "Never mind. It's not important now."

As he turned his back to the mirror, Sabre could see his gun tucked in the waistband of his jeans. She struggled to keep her balance as she stepped into the underwear, the towel draped over her body. Then, holding the towel with one arm, she slipped into her bra before she dropped her towel. She had to figure out what to do. She knew he wouldn't believe a sudden turn around in her attitude.

"You're going to kill me, aren't you?" Sabre asked calmly.

"It didn't have to be this way," he said, reaching out and touching her hair and cheek. His fingers felt cold on her skin, and before she could flinch he pulled them back and shoved her away. "But I can't trust you."

"You can't trust me?" Sabre asked, shaking her head from side to side. She struggled to get her feet into JP's boxer shorts and pull them up, Luke watching intently her every move. Was he admiring her body one last time before the kill? She pulled the tee shirt over her head, her arms trembling. Why didn't he just shoot her in the tub? She wondered if he was going to kill her or try to seduce her. Right now, she thought killing would be the better way to go.

"Let's go," Luke said.

"Where?"

He didn't respond. He took her arm and led her out of the bathroom. He walked behind her down the hallway into the living room. Her steps felt heavy and uncertain. The bathroom light and the rear porch light shone into the corner of the living room; otherwise, it was quite dark. The light reflected on the wall in a diagonal pattern, just short of the bookcase. She could barely see where she was walking.

Sabre took another step, starting into the darker area of the room. Luke reached out for her. She jerked away and took another step. He stepped closer, grabbing her arm this time. Sabre reached for the marble boot-shaped bookend. She twirled around and swung the bookend at Luke's face, but missed and planted it in his shoulder. He jolted back, holding on to her arm to keep himself from falling. Sabre swung again. Luke deflected the blow with his left arm. Crack!

"Damn it!" Luke caught his balance, let go of Sabre, and shoved her forward. She fell against the sofa, hitting her head on the sharp edge of the wooden arm and slid to the floor. The pain was intense. As she looked up, she saw Luke pull his gun from his waistband and point it at her. "Get up," he shouted. Sabre stumbled to her feet, pain throbbing from the back of her head. "Walk toward the front door."

"I'm walking." Sabre spit the words at him. She walked a couple steps forward, went around the sofa, and took a couple more steps to the door. Luke was about two feet behind her.

"Open it. Slowly," he commanded. Sabre commenced opening the door.

"Move another step and you'll be openin' up a worm farm," JP said from the doorway of the master bedroom, not six feet away with a shotgun aimed at Luke's chest. Luke looked at JP, then at Sabre, and back at JP again. He sighed and lowered the gun to the floor but lunged forward toward Sabre, trying to swing her around to use as a shield. JP stepped forward, flipped his shotgun around, and butted Luke on the side of the head. Luke moaned as he fell to the ground. "That's the last time you you hit this cowboy in the head."

42

Sabre's few hours of sleep weren't enough to leave her as clear minded as she would've liked to have been. But she was awake enough to watch the Kemps go down. The contempt she had for their actions toward their children was multiplied by their involvement in the hate crime that took the life of the young man in Perris. She wondered how many other crimes they'd committed.

Sabre asked for priority on her case, explaining to the bailiff about her ordeal the night before. She then took a seat inside the courtroom. Betty was waiting to be picked up from Las Colinas and Sabre wanted to arrive downtown in time for Luke's arraignment. And then there was Bob still at the hospital. "Where's Wagner? Anyone seen him this morning?" Sabre asked.

The bailiff walked toward the door into the hallway. "I'll find him and drag him in. We'll get you out of here."

Within minutes Wagner walked in the door, followed by the bailiff who smiled and winked at Sabre. She nodded thanks.

Shortly thereafter the judge took the bench and the parents shuffled into the courtroom. Dressed in orange jumpsuits and with their feet in chains, they were being escorted by sheriff deputies. Both parents were seated at the end of the table; the deputies stood behind them as they always did with the "in-custodies." Sabre sat at Wagner's left, between him and county council, so Wagner could talk to both parents. Robin, the CASA worker, remained in the back of the courtroom.

Wagner stood up and said, "Richard Wagner for the mother, also appearing on behalf of Mr. Clark for the father. Mr. Clark had an emergency this morning. I request a continuance so he can be here for his client."

"Do you anticipate a trial setting at the next hearing, counselor?"

"Most likely, Your Honor."

"Most likely, indeed." The judge said with a smirk. "Why don't we just pick a date right now, then."

"That's fine. The parents enter a denial to the new petition and request a trial date."

They went off the record while they picked a date that worked for all calendars. "Back on the record," the judge said. "The parents are ordered to be produced for the next hearing."

Sabre spoke up, "Your Honor, I'd like concurrence if these children are moved to a relative."

"So ordered. No, on second thought, I want this put on calendar before these children are moved to a relative. Anything else, counsel?" No one responded. "All orders remain in full force and effect."

Robin and Sabre walked out together. "So, we're still going to trial?" Robin asked.

"These parents are going to fight to the end, but it won't matter. They can't do much from their jail cells and the department has a good case against them. I expect the real fight will be for disposition. Hopefully, we can find an appropriate family member for these children to live with," Sabre said.

"I've been talking to some of the relatives, and so has the social worker. I think we found a place for them. There's an aunt on the dad's side." Robin opened her file and rifled through it. "Yeah, here it is. She's dad's sister. And she won't have anything to do with him or her parents because of their beliefs, but she doesn't want her niece and nephew to grow up in foster care. She left home at sixteen and the only contact she's had with the family in recent years is time she spent with the children. There's no reason why that placement shouldn't work. She has to be a strong woman to survive that upbringing. She'll get through to those children."

Betty waltzed down the steps and away from Las Colinas, sucking in the exhaust-polluted air as if she were in a mountain meadow. Sabre stayed close by her side.

They walked in silence until they reached the car. Once inside, Betty said, "How can I ever thank you?"

"You may start by answering a few questions. I think I already know the answer to this, but tell me anyway. Why didn't you come clean with me and tell me what was going on?" Sabre asked as they walked to her car in the parking lot.

"I'm so sorry. I've been hiding and lying so long. And I was too afraid, afraid for myself and for Neil. And then I heard Neil had a car accident, so I thought they'd found him and tried to kill him."

Sabre backed up, drove out of the parking lot, and onto the crowded street. "Before you go on, they're having Luke's arraignment this morning. Do you want to go, or do you want me to take you home?"

"No, I'd like to go with you. I'd like to talk to Luke if that's possible."

Sabre looked at Betty with a puzzled look, but when Betty didn't volunteer an explanation, Sabre let it go. "I don't know if you'll be able to do that. Even if you could, he may not want to see you." Betty's mouth turned down and her eyes pleaded. It was apparently important to her, maybe for closure. "I'll see what I can do." Sabre still had so many questions. "So, let's back up a little. Your real name is Edith?"

"Yeah." Betty shifted in her seat. "I was born in Bristol, Wisconsin. At seventeen, I found myself pregnant, and my mother couldn't stand the disgrace of it all. She'd been raising me alone, and we were already considered white trash. The pregnancy was the final straw. She packed me up and we moved to Chicago. She had a cousin who got her the job at Villa Paceco. We both worked as maids in the house for old man Paceco. Antonio was his name. He had two sons, Salvatore and Vicentio. Salvatore was about twenty-eight at the time and Vicentio a couple of years older. Salvatore's childhood friend was an Irish boy named Shane Behan who had come to live with them when he was about fourteen. He worked in the family business for Paceco, first running numbers and later carrying out more onerous, malicious tasks. He'd be called upon to do most of the dirty work, probably so Paceco's sons wouldn't get their hands as dirty. Shane was so handsome. I fell in love with him almost from the moment I met him. I told him I was pregnant. It wouldn't have been long before he knew anyway, but he didn't care. He loved me, too, and said he'd take care of me and love my child like his own."

Listening intently, Sabre drove on to the freeway. "So, John's real name was Shane Behan?"

"Yes, but not for long. We changed our names when we went on the run. It took a while to break the habit of calling him Shane. But we had to learn to not use our real names, and to not respond when we heard them. Once, I was in a store in Tennessee and someone recognized me. She kept saying my name, and I just ignored her. Finally, she walked right up to me, looked me in the face, and swore she knew me. I denied it, but she wasn't convinced. That was enough to make us move on."

"So, why did you leave Villa Paceco?"

"There was a big shakedown on the Paceco Family. The old man, Vicentio, Salvatore, John, and a whole bunch of others were arrested. The prosecutor offered John a deal and witness protection if he'd testify against the family, but John couldn't bear to betray Paceco or Salvatore. They had given him a home, an education, and even though he hated what he was doing, he was loyal to them. When he was released on bail, we ran. Soon we were running from the law and from the Pacecos."

"Why the Pacecos?"

"Word got out that John had given names and dates and enough information so the cops could get their convictions, and then left town. But he didn't snitch. Someone did, but it wasn't him. John was pretty sure it was Vicentio. He was such a weasel. Vicentio should've gone down for murder, but instead he got five years. He let his pop take the brunt of the fall. The prosecutor was happy because they got rid of the leader. They weren't too worried about Vicentio taking over when he was released because no one respected him, and Salvatore's heart wasn't in the business. But Vicentio turned out to be a little smarter than they gave him credit for, and what he couldn't do, old man Paceco did from his prison cell. They still managed to keep the business going strong."

They pulled into the parking lot at the El Cajon Courthouse. Sabre parked in the parking structure and shut off the car. "We're early. Let's just stay here and finish talking." She took the keys out of the ignition. "So, had you already had your baby by then?"

"I gave birth to fraternal twin boys, Neil and Byron, about three weeks before we left."

"Twins? So, what happened to them?"

"When we left we took Neil with us, but Vicentio raised Byron."

"So, your son was raised with Luke?"

"Yes, and that's why I'd like to talk to Luke, to ask him about Byron. I don't even know if Luke knows that Byron isn't his brother."

"So, why didn't you take Byron when you left?"

"We tried so hard, but we couldn't get him. Here's the thing. One of the twins was very light, the other very dark; they were polar opposites. Their father had dark olive skin, dark brown eyes, and brown hair that appeared almost black. At the time, Vicentio had been married about six years and his wife hadn't gotten pregnant yet. She tried to convince me to give her the boys, telling me I was too young to raise them and they'd have a better life. She even offered me a great deal of money. I wouldn't do it, but the worst part was she never really wanted Neil. She wanted Byron, the dark one, the one who matched her family. She was always holding him and taking care of him. I hardly ever got to hold him. I knew it wouldn't be long before we left and then I'd have them all to myself."

"But you didn't. You didn't have either of them."

"We had to sneak out one night. It was all planned. John took Neil, and when I went to the nursery to get Byron, he wasn't there. He was in the room with Vicentio and his wife. Up until then, both boys had been sleeping in the nursery, but I knew she was becoming more and more attached to Byron. We had to leave. John promised he'd go back and get him. It's the only promise he ever broke, and he never forgave himself. You know, he spent his entire life trying to do good and make up for the horrible things he did when he worked for Paceco. What a shame it ended the way it did. And to think, Paceco got his revenge after all."

"So, John never went back for Byron?"

"Oh, yeah. He went back half a dozen times. He almost got himself killed. He was shot once in the shoulder, but he managed to get away. By then, Byron was about a year old, and Vicentio's wife was pregnant, probably with Luke. They guarded the kids like Fort Knox. We could never get close enough to get Byron."

"But what about Neil?"

"Our life was not exactly 'Leave it to Beaver' material. We had to keep moving from place to place. Just as we would get settled somewhere, they'd find us and we'd have to move on. It was no life for the boys. I couldn't do that to Neil, and I was afraid for his life if they caught up with us. I considered leaving John and raising Neil. John even encouraged me to do it if that was my choice, but it was too risky. I didn't have the knowledge John did to stay on the run and keep my boy safe. The Pacecos knew about me and probably the cops as well. I just couldn't put Neil's life at stake. So I took him to Gary, his father. No one knew who the father was, so I figured he'd at least be safe and loved there. His grandmother was around to help, and she was very excited to have him."

"Did you stay in touch with Neil?"

"Not much. I always had a number for Gary, his father, but he didn't have mine. Gary was married when Neil was about eleven. Nice woman. I saw Neil a few times, but neither he nor his stepmother knew who I was. It was too risky for all of us, especially Neil. He never asked for any of this. A few years ago, Gary and I set up email communication."

"And Gary emailed you about Neil's accident?"

"Yes, and now I need to find out how he's doing."

Sabre handed Betty her cell. "Call him. Find out."

Betty's eyes brightened in appreciation. She made the call, but the look in her eyes changed to sorrow and tears dripped down

ZOVA BOOKS

ZOVA Books is an independent publishing
company serving discriminating readers and
booksellers of quality. We strive to create
dynamic and successful partnerships for our
authors, vendors, and retailers.
ZOVA Books seeks to build the next generation
publishing firm.

Visit us at www.zovabooks.com

ZOVA Books is a proud partner of
International Justice Mission.
International Justice Mission is a human rights
agency that secures justice for victims of slavery,
sexual exploitation, and other forms of
violent oppression. IJM lawyers, investigators and
aftercare professionals work with
local officials to ensure immediate victim rescue
and aftercare, to prosecute perpetrators and to
promote functioning public justice systems.

ZOVA Books donates a percentage of
every book sold to
International Justice Mission.

Visit IJM at www.ijm.org